HOW TO KILL A WITCH

HOW TO KILL A WITCH

THE PATRIARCHY'S GUIDE TO SILENCING WOMEN

ZOE VENDITOZZI & CLAIRE MITCHELL

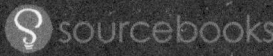

Copyright © 2025 by Claire Mitchell and Zoe Venditozzi
Cover and internal design © 2025 by Sourcebooks
Cover design © Emma Ewbank
Cover image © CSA-Printstock/Getty Images
Case tartan © Witches of Scotland Limited
Internal design by Tara Jaggers/Sourcebooks
Internal images © Science History Images/Alamy, Mariusz Switulski/Alamy, Trinity Mirror/Mirrorpix /Alamy, The Picture Art Collection/Alamy, Chronicle/Alamy, Historic Images/Alamy, Well/BOT/Alamy, Charles Walker Collection/Alamy, Baker, Joseph E., approximately 1837-1914/Library of Congress, Zdenek Sasek/Getty Images, Fotograzia/Getty Images

Sourcebooks and the colophon are registered trademarks of Sourcebooks.

All rights reserved. No part of this book may be reproduced in any form or by any electronic or mechanical means including information storage and retrieval systems—except in the case of brief quotations embodied in critical articles or reviews—without permission in writing from its publisher, Sourcebooks.

No part of this book may be used or reproduced in any manner for the purpose of training artificial intelligence technologies or systems.

This publication is designed to provide accurate and authoritative information in regard to the subject matter covered. It is sold with the understanding that the publisher is not engaged in rendering legal, accounting, or other professional service. If legal advice or other expert assistance is required, the services of a competent professional person should be sought.—*From a Declaration of Principles Jointly Adopted by a Committee of the American Bar Association and a Committee of Publishers and Associations*

References to internet websites (URLs) were accurate at the time of writing. Neither the author nor Sourcebooks is responsible for URLs that may have expired or changed since the manuscript was prepared.

Published by Sourcebooks
1935 Brookdale RD, Naperville, IL 60563-2773
(630) 961-3900
sourcebooks.com

Originally published as *How to Kill a Witch* in 2025 in the United Kingdom by Monoray, an imprint of Hachette UK. This edition issued based on the hardcover edition published in 2025 in the United Kingdom by Monoray, an imprint of Hachette UK.

Cataloging-in-Publication Data is on file with the Library of Congress.

Printed and bound in the United States of America.
MA 10 9 8 7 6 5 4 3 2

This book is dedicated to the people, mostly women, who were accused, tortured, and executed as witches and those who still face those unfounded accusations today.

CONTENTS

Authors' Note ... ix
"In Memoriam" ... xi
Introduction ... xii

Part One: The Law of the Land ... **1**
Chapter 1: How to Believe in Magic ... *3*
Chapter 2: How to Start a Witch Hunt ... *11*
  Portrait of the Accused: **Euphame MacCalzean** ... *27*
Chapter 3: Know Your Enemy, Part 1: *Newes from Scotland* ... *29*
  Portrait of the Accused: **Allison Balfour** ... *47*
Chapter 4: Know Your Enemy, Part 2: *Daemonologie* ... *51*
  Portrait of the Accused: **Janet Wishart** ... *69*
Chapter 5: How to Believe in a Witch ... *71*
  Portrait of the Accused: **Margaret Aitken** ... *89*

Part Two: Building a Case ... **91**
  Portrait of the Accused: **Agnes Finnie** ... *93*
Chapter 6: How to Accuse a Witch ... *95*

Chapter 7: **How to Prick a Witch**	*107*
Portrait of the Accused: **Tituba**	*125*
Chapter 8: **How to Kill a Witch the American Way**	*129*
Chapter 9: **How to Gather Evidence Against a Witch**	*147*
Portrait of the Accused: **The Paisley Witches**	*167*
Chapter 10: **How to Try a Witch**	*171*
Portrait of the Accused: **Janet Horne**	*177*
Chapter 11: **How to Burn a Witch**	*179*
Portrait of the Accused: **Katherine MacKinnon**	*189*
Chapter 12: **How to Bury a Witch**	*191*

Part Three: A Thing of the Past? — **209**

Chapter 13: **How to Lose a Witch**	*211*
Portrait of the Accused: **Helen Duncan**	*223*
Chapter 14: **How to Accuse a Modern-Day Witch, Part 1: The Twentieth Century**	*227*
Chapter 15: **How to Accuse a Modern-Day Witch, Part 2: The Twenty-First Century**	*237*
Portrait of the Accused: **Miss B**	*251*
Afterword: How to Forget a Witch, Then Remember Her	*253*
Acknowledgments	*273*
Reading Group Guide	*277*
About the Witches of Scotland Tartan	*279*
Glossary of Scots Words	*281*
Select Resources	*285*
Image Credits	*293*
About the Authors	*295*

AUTHORS' NOTE

We've used a smattering of Scots, one of the three official languages of Scotland, throughout the book where its vocabulary feels most apt. For non-Scottish readers, there's a glossary of Scots included on page 279.

"IN MEMORIAM"

They tried to tak your spirit, hen,
Destroy that which they couldnae control.
So you spoke and the world didnae listen, hen,
Smoored the smeddum that burned in your soul.
You're deid but never gone, hen,
There's them that still carry your name.
There's them that mind criminals, biding in courts
Heids that should hang heavy wi shame.

Auld Nick didnae ken you from Eve, hen,
You had but yer ain eyes to see.
The wrang wasnae yours,
The guilt was misplaced,
Yer innocence plain as can be.

But they took muckle mair than a life, hen,
A candle snuffed out in its prime.
A state-sanctioned murder ae innocent folks,

A punishment lacking a crime.
Your soul's now at peace wi the earth, hen,
Sleep and be wan wi the sky.
We'll scrieve yer name in books they cannae burn,
Write a legacy never tae die.

But we willnae just beg ae yer pardon, hen,
Those days have lang ceased tae exist.
We noo demand justice fir aw those like you—
Lang gone, but eternally missed.

LEN PENNIE
Scots language poem
commissioned by Witches of Scotland

INTRODUCTION

Allow us to introduce ourselves.

We are Claire Mitchell, a lawyer with an interest in public inquiries, human rights, and crime (and a KC, or King's Counsel, a senior advocate), and Zoe Venditozzi, a novelist and a creative writing/additional support needs teacher. Everybody knows us as the Witches of Scotland, although that is actually the name of the campaign we launched. Having said that, we are very happy to be known as "quarrelsome dames," and yes, we do live in Scotland.

This is how it all started…

In 2019, in the course of her work as a KC, Claire was researching the crime of violating a sepulcher, commonly known as "body snatching"—a crime made famous by the nineteenth-century craze for robbing graves in order to sell the corpses to anatomists. Claire was looking into the 2004 case of two teenagers who broke into an ornate stone mausoleum in Greyfriars Kirkyard (churchyard) in Edinburgh. The boys forced open a coffin, stole a skull, and played football with it until they were caught by a tour guide. It was thought that the head belonged to none other than one of Edinburgh's most famous historical figures—Sir George "Bloody" Mackenzie, who had earned his nickname for imprisoning over a thousand Protestant Covenanters in a field next to the graveyard where he was ultimately buried.[1] As former lord advocate, he was the head of the prosecution system in Scotland for more or less two decades until his death in 1691.

Ultimately, the teen grave robbers were not jailed, but Claire's research on Mackenzie led her down an interesting rabbit hole. She discovered that during his career, he was involved in numerous witch trials, including that of a woman called Maevia, whom he actually defended in 1661. He was reported to have said, "I am not of their opinion, who deny that there are Witches, though I think them not numerous."

And this was where Claire got sidetracked and pulled into the world of witch trials. It was clear that Mackenzie was making an interesting distinction. He didn't entirely take the skeptic's position that witches did not exist, but he did seem to be arguing that accusations were too numerous for them all to be correct. This theory is borne out by the fact that during his time as lord advocate, he endeavored to cut down on the number of cases brought to trial. A sensible middle-ground position at a time of very heightened sensibilities—as we shall see.

Even at this early stage in Claire's reading, though, the human stories exerted a pull across the centuries. As she researched Mackenzie's cases,

---

1   These Covenanters were a group of rebellious Presbyterians who were locked in an ideological (and often literal) battle with the church and state in the seventeenth century. On June 22, 1679, a large uprising was defeated by state forces at the Battle of Bothwell Brig, and up to twelve hundred prisoners were taken to Edinburgh and held in the field. They were denied basic amenities; many were executed, and hundreds more starved to death at the hands of their captors. Mackenzie's cruel treatment of them resulted in the legend of his fearsome ghost, who it is said still haunts the graveyard today. People would look through the doors of the mausoleum and chant the old rhyme: "Bluidy Mackenzie, come oot if ye daur, lift the sneck and draw the bar."

Introduction

Claire came across one poor woman who, during the course of her interrogation, asked her persecutors if it was possible to be a witch and not know it. The desperate situation this woman surely found herself in affected Claire deeply.

At around the same time, Claire read Sara Sheridan's book *Where Are the Women?*[2] In her book, Sheridan reimagines Scotland as a place where all the streets are named after women and there are museums and grand buildings dedicated to the great women of Scotland. This complete reversal of how Scotland was actually constructed brought into sharp focus how much of our civic lives are centered on men's achievements and how neglected Scotland's women are in terms of being a visible part of the geography of our nation.

So it was with this in mind that one day, when she was walking her dogs[3] in Edinburgh's Princes Street Gardens, Claire found herself beside a life-size statue of Wojtek, a Polish bear who became an unofficial mascot for the Allies during the Second World War. Standing there, she realized that there was not one statue of a named woman in Scotland's capital city's main green space. There were plenty of statues of men—artists, authors, soldiers—and even, in this case, a bear. But not a single woman.

And looking above Wojtek's head, she saw the esplanade of Edinburgh Castle, scene of hundreds of executions of innocent women convicted of witchcraft. These few hundred were only a small number of the many thousands of those accused of witchcraft in Scotland

---

2 Sara Sheridan, *Where Are the Women? A Guide to an Imagined Scotland* (Historic Environment Scotland, 2021).

3 Redford and Crombie, as *Witches of Scotland* podcast listeners will be aware.

between the early sixteenth and mid-eighteenth centuries—somewhere between three thousand and five thousand people in total. She thought to herself, *Not only are we not properly recording the brilliant achievements of women in our society in the history books or celebrating their success in public spaces, but we also are not recording when terrible acts have been perpetrated against them.* In fact, on the esplanade at the spot of the executions there was a plaque that merely reinforced the women's—entirely incorrect—status as witches.

There and then, as she stood beside Wojtek, Claire resolved to do something about this. What better way for a human rights lawyer to redress a gross miscarriage of justice in Scottish history than by highlighting the Scottish witch trials, by seeking an apology for the accused and a pardon for those convicted, and by creating a lasting memorial?

At that moment, the Witches of Scotland campaign was born.

A short while before Claire's revelation in Princes Street Gardens, the two of us had met at a mutual friend's wedding, where we bonded over our love of true crime podcasts. Discovering that we both had a ridiculously detailed knowledge of real-life murders, we came up with a theory about why women in particular love true crime. In our view, it was down to a combination of the pragmatism of learning how not to get abducted and murdered (always useful), coupled with an element of bearing witness to all the women who were not so lucky. All the while thinking, there but for the grace of God…

Toasting the happy couple that day,[4] Zoe mentioned she would like to start a podcast but couldn't think of an angle. A few weeks later, Claire got in touch with a simple idea, though one that turned out to

---

4 Mel and Drew.

be surprisingly effective. We would create a podcast about the forgotten witches of Scotland.

From the first recording in 2020, taken on an iPhone propped up on Zoe's washing machine in her basement, the Witches of Scotland campaign and podcast became a worldwide phenomenon.

And then something momentous happened.

On International Women's Day in 2022, the first minister of Scotland, at the request of the Witches of Scotland campaign, issued a formal state apology to all those accused of witchcraft in Scotland—the first time in three hundred years there had been any official recognition of those who were wrongly accused.

It has been an extraordinary journey. The campaign has sparked a worldwide cultural conversation about women's history and women's place in the modern world. Today, the campaign works toward its remaining aims of creating a national memorial and a legislative pardon and is actively working with a number of Witches of Scotland–inspired groups throughout the country to bring these aims to fruition.

How to Kill a Witch is a book that details, step by step, the stages undertaken to identify, try, and ultimately kill a woman as a witch. It is a book that we have researched by studying original documents and by gathering advice and encouragement from some of the best historians and experts in the field. In the course of writing the book, we have followed in the footsteps of those who lived hundreds of years ago, visiting graves, attending memorials, and meeting with experts in history, art, music, writing. Each of these experts has generously given their time to help educate us and our supporters about the history of witch trials in Scotland and around the world. To each and every one of them, we are very grateful. What we learned shocked us, even steeped as we are in the campaign. The truth about the Scottish witch trials is bloody and horrific. We hope that the resulting book is one that underlines the incredible lengths that people—mostly men—have gone to in order to silence women.

How to Kill a Witch also goes beyond what we learned about historical witchcraft trials here and abroad and extrapolates to what we see as the modern-day relevance: when the going gets tough in *any* society, it is the most vulnerable who are accused of causing the damage.

You will soon appreciate that the book is not an academic tome—it is the experience of two women learning about their history and casting a fresh light on their present. As any listener of the podcast will know, we approach our task with reverence for those who were accused of witchcraft and irreverence for everything else.

In fact, we initially started to write the book as a tongue-in-cheek manual for potential patriarchal persecutors out there so they would know just how to kill a witch if they came across one. While the manual idea was dropped as we became more and more involved (and outraged) with what we learned, we still found that starting point to be incredibly useful. Breaking down the persecution of women as witches into its individual stages made us look at the whole process forensically (in the case of chapter 11, we mean that absolutely literally). From identifying a witch to interrogating her, putting her to trial, killing her, burying her, and losing her in history—you will be surprised by how much there is to discover about the subject.

We also examine how other countries such as the United States dealt with their witch problem, using the case study of the most famous witch panic of all, the Salem witch trials, and we end on the question of whether women should still be wary today. We'll tell you about the continued use of violence against women, the rise of women identifying as witches, particularly online, and the increasing number of modern-day witchcraft accusations worldwide.

A word on historical detail (or the lack of it). Shortly after the infamously bloody witch trials of the early 1690s in Salem, Massachusetts, it was accepted that there had been a most grievous miscarriage of justice. The terrible history was commemorated in legal writings and in family campaigns to exonerate the accused, which served to keep the story of the wrongs perpetrated against their kin alive. As a result, the names of those involved and their stories were carefully recorded and subsequently studied by academics, historians, and lawyers.

The circumstances could not have been more different in Scotland. Poor recordkeeping of witchcraft accusations and trials leaves us bereft of much of the detail we would want to know. Sometimes we only know that trials took place because citizen historians have checked parish financial records, which merely recorded the cost of incarcerating the suspects or of hiring a "witch pricker" (of which, more later) or executioner.

The details of the accused and convicted in Scotland were not given the attention of academics and historians at the time. There was no contemporaneous recognition of the fact that thousands of people had been wrongly accused and convicted of witchcraft. Indeed, until International Women's Day 2022, there was no public recognition or apology for the wrongs done at all. With the notable exception of the lawyer and historian Robert Pitcairn, who wrote about the trials a century after they ended,[5] the Scottish legal system all but ignored

---

5   Robert Pitcairn, *Ancient Criminal Trials in Scotland* (1833). We will look at Pitcairn's work in chapter 9.

this brutal history. While many stories were passed down via word of mouth by those who couldn't read or write—no doubt containing a mix of gossip and truth—there were very few contemporaneous *written* works, save for the two we discuss in this book, a pamphlet titled *Newes from Scotland* and a textbook on witch-hunting written by none other than King James VI of Scotland himself,[6] called *Daemonologie* (see chapters 3 and 4).

Why record the history of these terrible witches? the thinking went. Better to convict these women, strangle them, and scatter their ashes to destroy any record of their existence. The view of the state was simple: the witches were dead, and justice had been done. There was no appetite for those victorious in their dealings with the Devil to immortalize the details of his handmaidens.

While modern academics and historians find what scarce detail they can, lack of documentation means that witchcraft trial records are irritatingly incomplete. The best records to date can be found in the Survey of Scottish Witchcraft,[7] an online database of all the known historical information about the trials. We highly recommend this resource, although the researchers note in their introduction that a good deal of evidence is still missing. That said, they have used their great skill to piece together what is available. Incomplete and sometimes vague as the information is at times, this is the reality of working on the history of the Scottish witch trials.

Throughout this book, by pulling together what scant information there is, by speaking to as many experts as possible, and by feasting on every detail that we *can* get our hands on, we hope we have done

---

[6] In 1603, upon the death of his cousin Queen Elizabeth I, he became King James I of England and Ireland. Throughout the book, we'll just refer to him as King James VI.

[7] Julian Goodare, Lauren Martin, Joyce Miller, and Louise Yeoman, *The Survey of Scottish Witchcraft*, https://witches.hca.ed.ac.uk/ (archived January 2023).

Introduction

justice to these women's stories. *How to Kill a Witch* is certainly not a conventional or straightforward narrative, and like its authors, it rushes hither and thither as we plunge deeper and deeper down the rabbit hole of witch persecution. You will find in these pages stories, discoveries, world-renowned expertise, and shameful facts. You will find a sentencing statement for a witch trial, full details of what it takes to dispose of a human body using fire, and portraits of just a few of those many thousands of people accused of witchcraft.

It is our sincere hope that this eclectic, patchwork book that started out as a guide for the patriarchy[8] will in fact provide every woman and marginalized group with the tools to understand how such accusations arise and how to guard against their happening again.

As with our theory about the popularity of true crime, we invite women to use the book as a pragmatic learning tool. To learn about and bear witness to all the women who were—and are—not so lucky while at the same time challenging the damaging patriarchal norms of the society in which we still live.

In sharing what we've learned, we hope to create a worldwide regiment of quarrelsome dames who are fighting for an equal place in the world—in life, in public spaces, and online.

We are nothing if not ambitious.

CLAIRE MITCHELL KC AND ZOE VENDITOZZI

---

[8] We want to be emphatically clear. A patriarchal society is one where men as a group dominate the whole group. When we criticize the patriarchy, that does not equate to criticism of men. Women can be in favor of the patriarchy; men can be against it. Yes, for the most part, patriarchal norms are endorsed by those who have most to gain, and many a time, that is a man, but that isn't always the case. To end the patriarchy, we need both men and women in society to address it.

PART ONE

THE LAW OF THE LAND

1

How to Believe in Magic

When Elspeth Reoch was accused of being a witch in 1616, she confessed that she had been given the power of second sight by two men who had come from the fairy world, whom she had first met at the age of twelve.

Born in Caithness in the Scottish Highlands, Elspeth had been staying with an aunt on an island in Lochaber. The fairy men—one dressed in black, the other in green—had approached her by the loch and told her she was pretty. The one in green told her he could show her how to know anything she wanted. He instructed her to boil an egg every Sunday for three weeks, collect the condensation in her hands, and rub it into her eyes. She did so and developed the power of second sight, after which she earned a small income wandering around her local area, advising folk, discerning pregnancies, and performing healing rituals with herbs.

However, Elspeth's relationship with the man in black, who had come to act as her spirit guide, soon started to sour. Not only were they having sex, but he was also controlling and abusive toward her. He told her that in return for the gifts he'd given her, he would take away her power of speech, whereupon she became largely nonverbal. Elspeth was only fourteen when, unmarried, she had her first child, and later she had another by a different man. Her brother, angry that she refused or was unable to speak, beat her with a bridle, tied a bowstring around her head to torture her, then dragged her to church and prayed for her. Unsurprisingly, these tactics failed to cure her.[1]

Accused of witchcraft (and deception by feigning muteness) in March 1616, Elspeth was brought to trial in Kirkwall in Orkney, where she confessed that she had met with the Devil several times in his guise as a fairy. Found guilty, she was sentenced to death by strangulation and her body burned that afternoon.

Fairies? Witches? The Devil? This tale may seem nonsensical to modern ears. But in order to understand the period between the sixteenth and eighteenth centuries in Scotland, we must embrace a fundamental truth of that epoch: magic was real.

This belief was entirely mainstream. More than mainstream, it was accepted as fact. The sale of magical services was commonplace, and purveyors could be sued if the magic didn't work. Both good and bad magic were believed to exist, and it was an incontrovertible fact that the Devil was real. He could take human form, have carnal connections with his choice of women, and throw wild parties complete with

---

1 Call us suspicious, but the stories she told and her subsequent refusal to speak sound very much like the processing of trauma.

bountiful buffets, drink, and debauchery. He could infiltrate your mind with wicked thoughts, take over your body to do his evil business, and change into whatever animal he pleased. He could use his magic to trick and deceive, to prey on the godly and ungodly alike. Most importantly for us, he could promise foolish women their heart's desire, only to lure them to his dominion as witches.

Woodcut showing witches offering gifts to the devil, from *The history of witches and wizards: giving a true account of all their tryals in England, Scotland, Swedeland, France, and New England; with their confession and condemnation*, 1720

Sometimes such beliefs are written off as the stupidity or ignorance of our forebears. They were nothing of the sort. In an uncertain world, they were a way of making sense of unpredictable events and offering an illusion of control. Folks have been turning to magic and rituals to influence their fate since the dawn of time, and they still do. Clever, modern sophisticates may scoff at these ideas,[2] but they still linger in our culture, superstitious remnants of the prevailing belief system of the early modern period.[3]

Do you avoid walking under ladders? How would you feel if you broke a mirror? What about putting new shoes on a table? People today consult spiritualists to hear from loved ones long dead, consult tarot cards to find their future, pray to specific saints to solve a particular problem, read runes, consult tea leaves, phone a psychic for love advice, pray, manifest, and join cults. This list is far from exhaustive. Ever check your phone's weather app to plan the weekend? In the twentieth century, science-fiction author Arthur C. Clarke wrote that "any sufficiently advanced technology is indistinguishable from magic."[4] In many ways, the only difference between us and our forebears is that now, our technology has (almost) caught up. Our human desire to know what's around the corner—that has not changed.

Until the Enlightenment—which took place throughout Europe in the late seventeenth and eighteenth centuries—there was a widespread belief that the supernatural world was interwoven with the natural, material world and that the powers of the supernatural could both help and hinder the lives of humans. It was common for people to combine

---

2   Claire doesn't. She has a spooky heritage. Her Irish granny Rose told her all about the fairies and Otherworld. She took her to the Poisoned Glen at Dunlewey, Donegal, and showed her fairy rings, magic circles of pebbles. She was also known for reading the cups, a type of fortune-telling. Claire remembers her granny solemnly turning the cup upside down on the saucer, turning it anticlockwise three times, and then turning it rightways up to do her reading. Claire remembers peering in at the tea leaves, expecting them to dance before her eyes, revealing the future. They never did.

3   The early modern period in Scotland covers the years from 1450 to 1750.

4   Arthur C. Clarke, "Hazards of Prophecy: The Failure of Imagination," *Profiles of the Future* (1962).

Christian beliefs and behaviors with magical practices to manage everyday life and its travails. From the mid-eighteenth century onward, religious reformers and newly enlightened thinkers sought to dissuade ordinary folk of their reliance on magic. They were successful to some extent, but the beliefs did not truly go away and remained particularly common in countries that had a strong tradition of acceptance of the "Otherworld."[5]

Celtic mythology tells us that the Otherworld was a place where spirits, demons, fairies, ghosts, and sprites lived. It was a real place but not one known to be frequented by ordinary mortals. Some folk believed fairies had their own world too: Fairyland, a place between heaven and hell, possibly a reflection of the fact that fairies could do good deeds as well as bad. These fairies were not of the Tinker Bell genre. They came in the same sizes and shapes as ordinary humans, sometimes having relationships with them, sexual and otherwise. Some people believed fairies were your dead ancestors who for some reason didn't make it to either heaven or hell. For many, though, fairies were tangible, real creatures, despite sometimes being insubstantial and see-through in their bodily forms. They were once considered independent beings, but as the Reformation[6] spread throughout sixteenth-century Europe, the prevailing Scottish Protestant understanding was that as fairies could not be angels, then surely, they must be of the Devil.

So it was that the Christian theology of God, fallen angels, and the Day of Judgment was woven through with the stories of the Otherworld;

---

5   Ireland, we are looking at you. Despite the pattern of witch trials sweeping across Europe in this period, Ireland remained mostly unaffected, ironically perhaps due to its very strength of belief in magic. People were simply not spooked by the idea of devils and demons.

6   The separation of Christianity across Europe from prevailing Catholic beliefs into two branches: Catholicism, led by the pope in the Vatican, and Protestantism, a new branch founded on the teachings of Martin Luther, which rejected the authority of the pope and espoused a more direct relationship between believers and God.

for many people, the Christian belief system merely slotted on top of the existing supernatural beliefs. Kings, queens, the state, the church, academics, philosophers, civil society, intellectuals, writers, artists, the women in the street—they all believed in magic and its power to do good and bad. We'll say it again: magic was everywhere.

So who was it that conjured up the magic?

Welcome to the (Other)world of service magicians: charmers, cunning folk, and witches.

Service magician is a catchall term for a person who traded in practical magic. The term itself reveals the ordinary way in which people would pay for a piece of magic to be conducted on their behalf. *Charmers*, *chairmers,* or even sometimes *charmerers,* as the name suggests, were those who sold charms; they were literally folk who enchanted. Their work was done with spells, the spoken word, and magical recipes. *Cunning folk,* on the other hand, were people who used ritual or ceremonial magic, for example summoning spirits or performing magical ceremonies. What these two types of magicians have in common is that their magical powers did not emanate from the Devil. In contrast, the power of the third type of practitioner—the witch—was notably different. A witch's magic came to be defined as being wholly dependent on their master, the Devil.[7]

This critical distinction allowed charmers and cunning folk to continue to peddle their wares without harassment. While doubtless the church would have preferred there to be no service magicians at all, they were nevertheless tolerated as they served a useful role in society, providing magical solutions to practical problems, in love, in luck, and

---

7 It didn't start that way, but we'll tell you more later.

in life. A poor crop could mean destitution and starvation for you and your family; a cow failing to produce milk could lead to homelessness; illness could mean imminent death. In such desperate times, is it any wonder people tried every solution available?

The work of cunning folk or charmers was rarely full-time. The roles were a way for people to make a bit of extra money on top of their main day job. So you might consult a farmer who sold husbandry potions or someone more educated, such as a priest.[8]

Hold on now! How could a priest, a man of the cloth, have a spooky side hustle as a cunning person? Well, who better to go to for help than an educated man who has God on his side? It's counterintuitive to us today that priests used magic, but if you think about it, they were already dealing with the supernatural every day.

What if all your linen is lost? A priest might be able to summon an angel or a demon or possibly some divination with a Bible—as long as, of course, the highheidyins did not get to hear about it.[9] That might seem a little bit over the top—troubling an angel to find your lost laundry—but in sixteenth-century Scotland, this was absolutely acceptable. The service magician was someone you could go to for everyday help, however mundane your problem.

But if you can believe in good magic, then it follows you must believe in bad magic. If there is an omnipotent God, able to intervene in the lives of folk at will, there must also be his fallen angel Lucifer Morningstar, the Devil, along with his handmaid witches who

---

[8] We're talking about pre-Reformation Catholic priests here. After the Scottish Reformation of 1560, the Catholic Church was outlawed in Scotland. As we shall see in the next chapter, Protestant ministers tended to take a dimmer view of cunning folk and charmers altogether, though they were just about tolerated so long as the Devil was not involved.

[9] *Highheidyin* is a Scots term that means literally "high head one," i.e., a person in authority.

are ready to cause you harm at a moment's notice. Service magic only becomes a problem when things go south—to hell.

The belief in magic then, real as it was, did not cause the bloody horror of the witchcraft trials. The causes of those? Oh, they were very much man-made.

Let us explain…

2

How to Start a Witch Hunt

It stands to reason that before you kill a witch, you first have to *find* a witch. Despite their devilish powers of deception, once you start looking, they're really not so hard to track down. And once you find one, you find many. Witches rarely work alone.

Throughout history, it appears that witches thrive in times of social unrest. In good times—where people have enough to eat, adequate healthcare, and social harmony—what does the Devil have to bargain with for someone to relinquish their eternal soul? In times of strife, however, when hunger and disease are common, the Devil preys on the weak to relinquish themselves to him and to do his evil bidding with promises of money, food, and good health.

In Scotland between the sixteenth and eighteenth centuries, the Devil had just the right fertile soil in which to plant his seeds. Of course, witches were not purely a Scottish phenomenon—the Devil had bigger plans than that—but we focus on Scotland here to show

how the Devil managed to work his way into the very heart of Scottish society. It was only by the strenuous efforts of godly people that we managed to all but banish ~~quarrelsome women~~—sorry, we mean witches—from our society.

Draw up a chair, grab some paper, and make some notes. You never know when the next witch infiltration will arise.

First, though, a bit of historical background.

By the middle of the sixteenth century, Catholicism was losing its charm for the Scottish folk. Back in 1533 in England, King Henry VIII, still then inconveniently married to his wife Catherine of Aragon, had decided he wanted to wed his (possibly already pregnant) paramour Anne Boleyn.[1] By ending his marriage to Catherine, he initiated a break with Catholicism in England. Admittedly, it might all have been a bit more complicated than that, but the point is this: there was a decline in the Catholic faith in both England and Scotland, and by the late 1550s, Protestantism was very much on the rise.

The Protestant faith was founded by Martin Luther, a German priest who had become disillusioned with the corruption in the Catholic Church. Aside from his view that the Bible was the final word on God's law and not the pope, his main complaint, well founded to the modern eye, was that the Catholic Church's highly profitable trade in indulgences was problematic. The granting of indulgences, which had been taking place since the eleventh century, was the practice of the church granting a reprieve for the amount of time you spent repenting your sins—in heaven or on earth—in exchange for a sum of money. This system proved to be a veritable gold mine for the church

---

1   Anne Boleyn was also described as a witch who bewitched the poor king.

for five centuries. However, Luther, in the famous list of grievances that became known as the *Ninety-five Theses* (1517), concluded that he thought this practice of people paying to cleanse themselves of the punishment of sin was open to abuse by unscrupulous clerics, who were making pots of cash from even more unscrupulous sinning folk.[2]

Enter, in 1559, a Protestant Scottish minister called John Knox (1514–72), whose fiery sermons inflamed such passion that Catholic priests' homes were attacked and Catholic statues toppled. Toppling statues is far from a new thing. In spring of that year, Knox was the driving force behind an armed revolt that ultimately led to the Scottish Reformation. The people of Scotland were whipped up into a religious fervor and, having become disillusioned with the old papist ways, gladly turned to the new religion of Protestantism. The fact that the state was also making it very difficult for Catholics to exist in peace no doubt assisted the conversion of the religiously apathetic. After all, it was the same God and, let's face it, anything for a quiet life.

Problematically, the queen in Scotland remained obstinately Catholic. In 1560, the Catholic dowager Queen Mary of Guise, who had been ruling as queen regent[3], died, leaving her daughter, Mary, Queen of Scots, then eighteen years old, to reign alone.[4] (Mary's first husband, King Francis II of France, also died later that year aged sixteen.) Mary was Catholic, like her mother, but she tolerated the rise of the new religion. The Protestants took full advantage: those in favor of the

---

2   In our view, if anyone should have been annoyed, it should have been the Devil, tempting people to do wrong only for them to buy their way out of it.

3   A regent is a person appointed to temporarily govern a state at times when the official monarch is unable to, either due to being too young (as in the case of King James VI), absent, or mentally or physically incapacitated in some way.

4   Mary, Queen of Scots, was only six days old when her father, King James V, died and she formally inherited the throne.

Reformation quickly convened the new Scottish Parliament and passed two important pieces of legislation (although they were not technically ratified by the new queen). The Confession of Faith Ratification Act of 1560 identified "the trew Kirk" as the religion of Scotland, and the Papal Jurisdiction Act of 1560 removed the authority of the pope in Scotland, citing the fact that in "tymes bipast [it] hes bene verray hurtful and prejudiciall to our soveranis autoritie and commone weill of this realme." These two pieces of legislation solidified the Protestant faith in Scotland. At the same time, six Protestant ministers named John, known somewhat unimaginatively as "the Six Johns," wrote the new rules for the Kirk of Scotland. John Knox was their leader. Oddly, therefore, Scotland had a Catholic queen and a Protestant parliament.

Fast-forward three years, and this new parliament was busy passing legislation to further cement the power of the church in people's lives. It was against this background that the Witchcraft Act of 1563 was conceived.

Usually, an act criminalizing behavior is passed because there is some pressing social need for it. Which begs the question—was Scotland overrun with witches in 1563? It would appear unlikely. The Reformation parliament was, however, very keen to ensure that Scottish folk did not indulge in any extracurricular quasi-religious tomfoolery. God was a man (naturally) who had no truck with charms or spells, Catholic idolatry or indulgences. The new church would be a one-stop shop for all your religious needs, and there was no requirement to seek communion with Himself via anyone but a minister. Also, and perhaps somewhat unfortunately for the evil rich, you could no longer buy your way out of the effects of sinning with indulgences. In these new enlightened times, you had no choice but to follow a religious life, praise God, and be good. Don't, whatever you do, look to any other source for charms or help, consult anyone claiming to have the power to speak to the dead, or carry out acts of witchcraft yourself. The church has you covered.

The challenge for the new church, the state, and, as a subtext, the patriarchy was how exactly does one legislate against Catholics, witches, and the Devil all at once? You do it by passing legislation outlawing acts of witchcraft. There was a precedent for this south of the border—there had already been two Witchcraft Acts in England in 1541 and 1562. Clearly, the Scots legislators needed to keep up. And so it was that the Witchcraft Act was passed and placed on the statute books in Scotland in 1563.

This is a transcript of the original text, to give you a flavor:

June 4, 1563: Anentis Witchcraftis
Forsamekill as the Quenis Majestie and thre Estatis in this present Parliament being informit, that the havy and abominabill superstitioun usit be divers of the liegis of this Realme, be using of Witchcraftis, Sorsarie and Necromancie, and credence gevin thairto in tymes bygane aganis the Law of God: And for avoyding and away putting of all sic vane superstitioun in tymes tocum:

> It is statute and ordanit be the Quenis Majestie, and thre Estatis foirsaidis, that na maner of persoun nor persounis, of quhatsumever estate, degre or conditioun thay be of, tak upone hand in ony tymes heirefter, to use ony maner of Witchcraftis, Sorsarie or Necromancie, nor gif thame selfis furth to have ony sic craft or knawlege thairof, thairthrow abusand the pepill: Nor that na persoun seik ony help, response or cosultatioun at ony sic usaris or abusaris foirsaidis of Witchcraftis, Sorsareis or Necromancie, under the pane of deid, alsweill to be execute aganis the usar, abusar, as the seikar of the response or consultatioun.

Which, translated from old Scots, reads as follows:

June 4, 1563: Against Witchcraft
The Queen and her Estates, in this present parliament having been informed that several types of heavy and abominable superstition are being used by the subjects of this realm, those being witchcraft, sorcery and necromancy, and credence is being given thereto as was in bygone times, against the laws of God. For the avoiding and putting away of all this vain superstition in times to come:

It is put into statute and ordained by her Majesty the Queen and her Estates that no manner of person or persons, of whatever estate, degree or condition they may be of, take upon hand in any times hereinafter to use any manner of witchcraft, sorcery and necromancy, nor to give themselves further to have any craft or have knowledge of it, thereby abusing the people [of the realm]: Nor should anyone seek any help, response or consultation from any users or abusers of the aforesaid witchcraft, sorcery or necromancy, under the pain of death, as much as to be executed against the user and abuser as the seeker of the response or consultation.

So in sum: the practices of witchcraft, sorcery, and necromancy are banned. Anyone who practices or consults those who practice will be executed.

What is especially interesting about the act, at least to us, is that it does not give any guide as to what constitutes the unholy triumvirate of witchcraft, sorcery, and necromancy. One has to understand that, at the time, the descriptions were so commonplace that everybody knew what a witch, sorcerer, and necromancer were. It was plain to anyone that acts of witchcraft were carried out to cause harm to another person or their property (this was known as "maleficium"), sorcery was the act of casting spells, and necromancy was speaking to the dead. Notice too that the crime legislated against is not *being* a witch per se but committing an *act* of witchcraft.

In any case, the overall meaning was clear, and the lawmakers could rest easy, knowing they now had both the law *and* God on their side. The Bible does not have a lot to say about witches, but what it does have is not favorable to them. In Exodus 22:18, the Bible warns, "Thou shalt not suffer a witch to live," a helpful phrase the lawmakers used to make it clear the crime of witchcraft would be committed "under the pain of death."

Let's dig a little deeper into what people considered a witch at the time, as the common understanding shifted over the years. When the act came into force in 1563, a witch was a person who used magical powers to assist people. By the time the act was being enforced with a vengeance in the 1590s, *witch* had a definite meaning: a person who had powers given to them by the Devil. The centrality of the Devil to the definition was something Mary, Queen of Scots' son, King James VI, personally endorsed: a witch was a person who had given themselves to Satan, who had turned from God and had promised their eternal soul to the Devil in exchange for his power. The witches themselves were conduits of Lucifer.

The eagle-eyed reader may have noticed that nowhere in the legislation does it mention that witches were most likely to be women. Indeed, the wording is entirely gender-neutral. How odd then that of the four thousand or so people accused of witchcraft in Scotland between 1563 and 1736 (when the act was repealed), 85 percent of them were women. It's almost as if there was some inherent bias against women in this patriarchal society.

The question of why more women were accused than men is one

contemporary writers were already trying to answer. King James VI, in his book examining the study of witchcraft and other malevolent creatures, *Daemonologie*, posed the question: "What can be the cause that there are twentie women given to that craft, where there is one man?"[5]

A Witch Sailing to Aleppo in a Sieve, Charles Turner, 1807

---

5   Read on to chapter 4 to discover if King James VI came to the same conclusions about women and the patriarchy as we did. (Spoiler alert: He did not.)

For us, the patriarchal answer was clear, if not spelled out. If you were the Devil in those days, who would you go for? The fine upstanding men, morally, intellectually, physically, and spiritually superior? Or the conniving and sinful women?

But this act would put a stop to all the evil corruption. From 1563 onward, it was illegal to commit acts of witchcraft, talk to the dead, or cast spells. But it wasn't until the 1590s, during the reign of King James VI, that the first big witch purge took place north of the border.

The future King James VI was born to Mary, Queen of Scots, and her second husband, Henry Stuart, Lord Darnley, on June 19, 1566, three years after the passing of the Scottish Witchcraft Act. James was the son of the Scottish queen and, on his father's side, a great-great-grandson of Henry VII of England. Such impressive parentage allowed James to claim rights to the Scottish and English thrones and ultimately unite the crowns as King James VI of Scotland and I of England.

James's father, Lord Darnley, was a jealous man, and when Mary fell pregnant with James, Darnley was suspicious that her private secretary, an Italian named David Rizzio, had sired the child. Because of this, it is widely believed that Darnley conspired with a group of Protestant noblemen to accuse Rizzio of adultery and murder him. Whether Darnley was the catalyst or not, the plan was executed on the evening of Saturday, March 9, 1566, when the group of noblemen, led by Lord Ruthven, pounced on Rizzio when he was with Mary and her attendants at supper. Ruthven and the others stabbed him some fifty-seven times with a dagger while Mary, six months pregnant with James, was held at gunpoint.

As so often is the case, one violent act precipitated another. On February 10, 1567, when James was only eight months old, Darnley was staying at Kirk o' Field in Edinburgh when there was a terrible explosion. Darnley was found dead, though it was not the explosion that killed him—he had been smothered. Fingers were immediately pointed at the queen. Outrage—which had not been similarly exhibited for the foreign private secretary's murder—was nursed into outright religious rebellion against the Catholic queen. The queen sealed her fate when, on May 15, 1567, she married the man who was accused of killing Darnley: James Hepburn, the Earl of Bothwell.[6] Her wedded bliss was to last less than a month. In June 1567, rebel Protestant lords arrested Mary and imprisoned her in Lochleven Castle near Kinross. James, by then twelve months old, never saw his mother again.

On July 24, 1567, Mary was forced to abdicate in favor of her infant son,[7] and James was crowned king of Scotland at a mere thirteen

---

6 Although prior to the marriage, Lord Bothwell stood trial for Darnley's murder and was acquitted, he too met a sorry end. After Mary's arrest, he fled Scotland to Norway and eventually found himself in Denmark, where he was imprisoned for the last ten years of his life, tied to a pillar. A mummified body that was said to be his was repatriated to Scotland and shown in the Edinburgh Wax Museum in 1976. Incidentally, this museum, located on the Royal Mile in a former commercial bank, served a dual role in its heyday in the 1970s and '80s: by day, it was a wax museum, and by night, it became the Castle Dracula Theatre, starring its owner, Charles Cameron, the self-styled Godfather of Bizarre Magic, in his Gothic House of Terror. If ever a footnote deserved to be a book in its own right, it is this one. Currently and much more mundanely, it is used as the Faculty of Advocates' consulting rooms, where Claire has conducted many a meeting, although not with mummies, vampires, or bizarre magicians (as much as she would very much like to).

7 Poor Mary's extraordinary story didn't end there. After miscarrying twins, she escaped from imprisonment, raised an army, fled south after being defeated, was taken into custody by her cousin Queen Elizabeth I of England, became embroiled in various plots, and was eventually executed in 1587. Dramatic to the end, the first blow of the axe missed her neck, and when the deed was eventually done, the executioner held her head aloft, and her hair promptly fell off, revealing it to be a wig.

months old. John Knox, the zealous Protestant minister, preached the sermon at James's coronation and continued to remain an influential figure in his young life. With that, the Protestant lords had their young king-to-be under their control, and until he came of age, a total of four subsequent regents were appointed to rule in his stead, with the Earl of Moray chosen as the first.

James grew up as the Protestant king in a time still fraught with religious tensions. He was, by his divine right, God's envoy on earth. As such, he had to be on the lookout for the Devil, whom he understood would very much be plotting his downfall at every turn. It's hard to overstate how much the Protestant faith permeated every part of Scottish culture. The church was the provider of education, moral guidance, enforcement of the law, alms, and protection from the Devil. In much the same way as God was central to the lives of those in Scotland, his opposite number was similarly very much present.

It was widely understood that the Devil could and did take on human form—by compressing air into the shape of a man—to prey on the vulnerable. By all confession accounts, the Devil was a flaneur enjoying wild parties, bountiful buffets, and devilish sex with the women who had given themselves over to him as witches. He was a well-dressed man who occasionally enjoyed a bit of transmutation into the form of a dog, cat, or, when he was trying to seduce honest women, husbands. Alas, many a good woman was undone by having sex with the man she thought was her husband, only to find out it was the Devil in disguise. But more on that later.

Raised in this atmosphere as a young and impressionable orphan, it is not surprising that James grew up hypervigilant against the threats of the Devil. His fears were crystallized in 1589 when he elected to marry a Danish princess (by then, Denmark was a Protestant country like Scotland). Anne of Denmark was fourteen, the older sister of the twelve-year-old King Christian IV. Now considered old enough to marry, she was promised to James, and the couple married by proxy on August 20. James was twenty-three.

Now, the bride needed to actually *meet* the groom. The plan was for Anne to travel to Scotland from Copenhagen in the care of Danish navigator Admiral Peder Munk. But despite Munk's best efforts, the voyage was thwarted by repeated bad weather, and Anne's flotilla of ships was driven back. This setback was extremely embarrassing for Munk, who urgently needed to find someone else to blame. As it happened, Denmark was under the grip of its own witch hunt at the time, so Munk was immediately suspicious that witchcraft was the cause of the problems in getting his precious regal cargo across the waters to Scotland. He certainly couldn't fathom the idea that his seafaring prowess might be to blame.

Rather than return to Copenhagen, Munk and his ships had been forced to dock in Oslo, Norway. From there, they sent word to James of their problems, telling him that they would try again when the seas calmed. James, impatient to meet his young bride, instead marshaled his own ships and sailed to Oslo to meet her in a somewhat grand romantic gesture. They were married again (in person this time) on November 23, 1589. The newlyweds stayed abroad (in both Norway and Denmark) for a number of months, during which period James met Niels Hemmingsen, an influential Danish Protestant theologian who in 1575 wrote a thesis warning against the practice of witchcraft. It is recorded that they had a long discussion on all things theological just before he set sail with his new bride to return home to Scotland.

Hemmingsen had a nuanced stance on witchcraft. He believed it existed, but he was concerned that many of the accusations of witchcraft against "simple folk" could not be fully trusted and may well have been unfounded. Sadly, this more thoughtful position did not seem to be adopted by King James VI.

But it was not only Hemmingsen who had spoken to James on the subject during his Danish trip. Witchcraft was the talk of the Danish court, in particular the witch trials that were currently being held in Trier, an independent Catholic diocese that is now part of Germany. Proving that Catholics were equal to Protestants when it came to witch hunts, the newly appointed archbishop of Trier, Johann von Schönenberg, had immediately set himself the task of ridding the area of witches (along with Protestants and Jewish people). Over twelve years, between 1581 and 1593, witchcraft trials took place with great frequency, and at least 360 people were burned alive as a result. The total number of executions, including those within the diocese who lived outside the main city, might be closer to 1000.

A pamphlet from the trials detailing the accusations and confessions was distributed far and wide. It consisted of six short columns of text beneath a huge etched illustration (of a style resembling Hieronymus Bosch's) depicting witches carrying out acts of witchcraft on their hapless victims. It was no doubt pored over with fear, excitement, and prurient interest and was believed to have directly influenced what was to follow in both Copenhagen and in North Berwick, Scotland.[8]

On May 1, 1590, James and Anne at last returned to Scotland, having once again battled fierce weather on the crossing, and the pair settled into a long, fruitful, and reasonably harmonious marriage (though

---

[8] A copy of the document is still held by the British Library for those who would like to see it.

there was much speculation—even at the time—that James's relationships with his male favorites were sexual).

Meanwhile, back in Denmark, a row was brewing about the royal travel fiasco, and fingers of blame began to be pointed at various players in the whole embarrassing saga. Peder Munk—still suspicious that witchcraft was behind the bad crossing but presumably keen to raise a case against a defender he might get some money out of—launched a legal case against the minister for finance, Christoffer Valkendorff, about the state of the ships, which had, he argued, placed Princess Anne in danger during the crossing. Ironically, Valkendorff then promptly played the witchcraft card in his defense, claiming that the problems experienced by the fleet had nothing to do with anything as straightforward as a lack of proper funding of the admiralty and insufficient investment in the ships. The true cause, he said, was the result of the work of witches, who had sent little demons in barrels to the ship to cause bad weather.

Yes, you read that correctly. Witches and demons traveling in small barrels and sieves was a commonplace witch activity when it came to witchcraft accusations and confessions.[9] But notwithstanding the fantastical nature of these accusations, where on earth was the evidence for this witch-based defense?

As it turned out, someone had confessed to exactly this crime. In May 1590, a Danish woman named Ane Koldings was accused and convicted of witchcraft in relation to matters at the time unrelated to

---

9 So common in fact that when Shakespeare wrote *Macbeth*—a.k.a. the Scottish play—in 1606, he drew on the image to curry favor with the new witch-obsessed king (James had taken the English crown three years earlier). In act 1, scene 3, one of the witches explains how she would intercept a ship at sea, "but in a sieve I'll thither sail." See Charles Turner's *A Witch Sailing to Aleppo in a Sieve* for a great artistic representation of this. The engraving is held in the Metropolitan Museum of Art but is alas not currently on view.

the royal sea crossing. She had become something of a reluctant celebrity in Copenhagen, where she was awaiting sentence in prison and was put on display for visitors to see. Valkendorff, clear in his mind that it was not his fault that the ship transporting Anne had faced peril in the rough crossing, asked the mayor of Copenhagen to interrogate Ane to see if she had anything to do with it. Ane ultimately confessed—under torture—that she, along with several other witches, had met at the home of Karen the Weaver and had cursed the crossing and Anne's ship.[10] They had summoned demons to sail in empty barrels to intercept the royal's ship and cause the bad weather in an effort to sink it.

Ane Koldings was executed for her original crimes in July 1590. A further five trials of women named by Koldings then took place, and each woman was eventually convicted of bewitching the royal crossing. In total, nineteen people, mostly women, were convicted and executed.

Back in Scotland, when he heard of the witches' work, it dawned on James that his return trip had also been bedeviled by bad weather, quite literally it seemed. As the ancient Romans did, James asked himself *cui bono?*—who benefited if James and his new wife were to perish in a watery grave, leaving no progeny? The obvious answer was, of course, the Devil. What better way to disrupt God's plans for Scotland than to leave it without a future king or, failing that, a queen? When the results of the Koldings trials filtered back to him, they proved the Devil had attempted to thwart both the godly king and his new wife on their respective outbound journeys; obviously, the same must've been attempted on the return leg. James knew that the Devil did not usually work directly but instead called in the services of witches to do his

---

10 An early example of the demonizing of women named Karen.

work. So the question remained: *Which* witches had cursed the return royal trip, and how would one go about identifying them?

A lifetime of religious zeal, political paranoia, and influential advice had led James to this point, his recent experiences abroad only reinforcing his deep-seated ideas. Convinced that witches were indeed plaguing his reign, he swept into action.

James became the "complainer"—a term used in Scotland for the person who is the alleged victim of a criminal—in several ensuing witchcraft trials. Often the complainer is a witness with no legal representation, but James far exceeded that role in these trials. He heard evidence; he listened to confessions; he watched the trial process; he consulted his own lawyers. None of this was the normal way to proceed in a trial process, but who was going to challenge the king, as close to God as any man *and* the foremost expert on witchcraft to boot?

And as a result, the first major Scottish witch hunt was underway.

PORTRAIT OF THE ACCUSED

———— ❈–◇–❈ ————

Euphame MacCalzean

NORTH BERWICK, 1590

Euphame MacCalzean was born around 1558 into a privileged family. Her father, Thomas MacCalzean, was a judge in Edinburgh, a senator of the College of Justice, and a provost of the city. Euphame married Patrick Moscrop, and as she came from a family of greater standing, he took her name in order to preserve the MacCalzean line. They had at least five children.

Despite this relatively powerful position in society, in 1590, Euphame was dragged into what became known as the North Berwick witch trials—the first of the major witch trials in Scotland—when a maid named Geillis Duncan accused her and several others of witchcraft.[1] Some of the accusations made specifically against Euphame included having a controlling personality, using witchcraft to domineer

---

1 *Outlander* fans: this is the real woman accused of witchcraft and not the time-traveling Scottish independence fan.

over her husband, murdering her godfather, and bewitching a judge to "bear goodwill" to her daughter. Interestingly, among all this self-serving murderousness, she was further indicted for helping to relieve women of the pain of childbirth.[2] The most shocking allegation leveled against Euphame was that of plotting to murder King James VI.

Along with her co-accused (John Fian, Agnes Sampson, and Barbara Napier), Euphame was alleged to have attended a get-together with the Devil at a beach called Atkynson's (or Acheson's) Haven in East Lothian, where they passed around a picture of the king with the intent of bringing about his destruction. At this meeting, the group of "witches" were said to have engaged the Devil to interfere with the weather in order to impede the king's sea crossing.

Euphame was convicted in 1591 and executed on the hill below Edinburgh Castle on June 25 that year. She was burned alive rather than strangled: the gravity of the crime of attempted regicide meant the most painful death was reserved for her.

The king disposed of her estate, Cliftonhall, to one of his allies, Sir James Sandilands of Slamannan, and her house on the high street in Edinburgh was given to an officer of the royal stables, John Shaw. The patriarchy had once again taken what was rightfully theirs, and the dreadful witch was ash.

---

2   You might be asking why assisting someone in easing their labor pains would be denounced as witchcraft. It seems it was down to the outrageous lack of humility displayed in the attempt to go against God's will: pain was the price of childbirth after all.

3

Know Your Enemy, Part 1: *Newes from Scotland*

North Berwick is a small town on the coast of East Lothian in Scotland, which, at the time of King James VI's return from Denmark, was suffering a major witch outbreak. David Seaton, a local bailiff, noticed that his servant, Geillis Duncan, had what he considered an unnatural ability to heal those who sought her help. What power could this young woman possess other than witchcraft? Seaton was not to know that his observation would spark the biggest witch trial Scotland had ever seen, uncovering a supposed coven of over seventy witches who were said to be intent on killing the king.

To examine these events, we have the best of all teaching tools: an apparently contemporaneous record of events in a twenty-four-page pamphlet titled *Newes from Scotland*, published the year after the trials in 1591. It is believed to have been written by a Protestant minister named James Carmichael, who became a later adviser to King James VI (which may be why the pamphlet is so supportive of the king). Two copies of this short book exist, one in the University of Glasgow, the other in the Bodleian Library at the University of Oxford. To find out how the witch hunt started, we decided to visit the Bodleian and consult the source information in person.

We arrived at the library on a warm, sunny morning. The University of Oxford was established in 1096, centuries before the witchcraft trials, making this great place of learning a witness to those times. After filling out a few forms, we tiptoed through the cold hallways of the first floor to find the book that had been set aside for us to read. Lining the walls was a parade of busts and portraits of various men, silently watching over us. We were ushered into a large library even colder than the halls and were shown to a table where we waited for the 430-year-old document to arrive. Laid before us was a book cushion for the precious pamphlet to rest on, to protect its spine. At last, gloves donned, we received the book from the silent librarian, who left us to our research.

If you want to read *Newes from Scotland* in its original form, it is possible to find it online. However, be warned—you may find this heavy going due to the archaic language it's written in. For the purposes of this book, we've produced an edited précis below in modern-day language. It is an extraordinary document, giving a unique insight into the beliefs and worldview of the time. From the perspective of nearly half a millennium after its publication, it is clear that it is also a nightmarishly extravagant piece of Jamesian propaganda—watch out for the obsequious flattery to the king throughout. Reporting the news, it seems, has never been an impartial business.

Know Your Enemy, Part 1: *Newes from Scotland*

Newes from Scotland[1]

Declaring the damnable life and death of Doctor Fian, a notable sorcerer, who was burned at Edinburgh in January last.

1591.

Which doctor was registered to the Devil, that sundry times preached at North Berwick Kirk to a number of notorious witches.

With the true examinations of the said doctor and witches as they uttered them in the presence of the Scottish king.

Newes from Scotland frontispiece, 1591

Discovering how they pretended to bewitch and drown his Majesty in the sea coming from Denmark, with such other wonderful matters as the like has not been heard of at any time.

Published according to the Scottish copy.

At London

Printed for William Wright.

INTRODUCTION

Here you will find the testimonials of Dr. Fian and the witches as they were uttered in the presence of King James VI. It is the true story of the apprehension of various witches who have been recently arrested in Scotland, some of whom are already executed and some of whom are still imprisoned.

God in His omnipotence has lately overthrown the wicked intentions

---

1 Possibly one of the first examples of "fake news."

of a great number of "ungodly creatures" who had allowed themselves to be enticed by the Devil. These people served the Devil and studied the detestable art of witchcraft, enticing others to join them by means of their sorcery. They all resided in the Lothians, the area in which the king's primary residence was located.[2]

THE ACCUSED

In the town of Trenent in Scotland, there lived a David Seaton. He was a deputy bailiff, and he had a maidservant by the name of Geillis Duncan.

Geillis aroused the suspicion of her employer by leaving home every other night and acquiring the ability to heal the sick and infirm, performing "matters most miraculous."

Seaton began to suspect that these healings had not been conducted in a natural way but rather by "some extraordinary and unlawful means." He became very inquisitive and demanded to know how she was able to achieve these miracles. She gave him no answer.

To find out the truth, Seaton and others tortured Geillis with the use of pilliwinks on her fingers,[3] "a most cruel torment," and also by thrawing—"binding and wrenching her head with a cord or rope." Yet she still did not confess.

At this, Seaton, along with his friends, made a diligent search of the maid's body, and there they found a Devil's mark on her throat.[4] Upon

---

2   Immediately, we can see that the writer draws a link between the coven of witches identified and the fact that they lived in the very area where the king resided. The introduction concludes that God has revealed their terrible intent to harm the king and the country and invites the reader to find out how by reading the tale.

3   Thumbscrews.

4   A Devil's mark (or witch's mark) was a blemish such as a mole, skin tag, wart, scar, or unhealed area on the body. It might not bleed or hurt when the skin is pricked. The mark was said to be physical proof of the Devil's pact with his initiate. You'll see more of this later on in the pamphlet as well as in future chapters of this book.

Know Your Enemy, Part 1: *Newes from Scotland*

this discovery, Geillis confessed that she was indeed a witch and that all her "doings" were achieved by means of witchcraft.

While awaiting trial in prison, Geillis pointed the finger at several other "notorious witches," all of whom were apprehended. This list included the following people:

- Agnes Sampson, the eldest of the witches, living in Haddington
- Agnes Thomson of Edinburgh
- Doctor Fian, alias John Cummingham, schoolmaster at Saltpans in Lothian
- George Mott's wife, dwelling in Saltpans
- Robert Grierson, skipper
- Jennifer Bandilandis
- the porter's wife of Seaton
- the smith at the Bridge Halls
- "innumerable others"[5]

Some of these people have already been already executed, and the rest remain in prison, awaiting His Majesty's pleasure.

Geillis Duncan also named Euphame MacCalzean,[6] saying she conspired and caused the death of her godfather, and she used her art on one of the local judges to cause him to look favorably on her daughter.

In addition, Geillis caused the apprehension of a woman named

---

[5] Academics estimate that after all the accused were interrogated and had given the names of others—who in turn gave the names of more—at least seventy people were accused as witches, possibly as many as one hundred.

[6] Euphame MacCalzean is spelled Euphemia Maclean in the original document. Names and all else were spelled phonetically at the time, and this name in particular lent itself to several artistic interpretations. Other names, such as Agnes Thomson's surname, are similarly spelled various ways within the document. Claire continues to subscribe to this form of spelling.

Barbara Napier for the crime of bewitching to death Archibald, the last Earl of Angus. At the time of his death, it hadn't been suspected that he had been killed by witchcraft; it was just thought he had died of a disease so strange the doctor did not know how to cure it.

Of all the witches mentioned, Euphame MacCalzean and Barbara Napier had previously been thought to be as honest and civil as any women who lived within the city of Edinburgh.[7]

THE ALLEGATIONS

Agnes Sampson, the elder witch, was taken to Holyroodhouse before King James VI and various other noblemen of Scotland, where she was "strictly examined." However, it was to no avail—none of the "persuasions" that the king and noblemen tried worked. She confessed nothing and "stood stiffly in the denial" of all of which she was accused. As a result, she was taken away to jail to be tortured.

It has lately been found that the Devil generally marks his witches with a private mark, as the witches have confessed themselves. The Devil licks them with his tongue in some private place of their body before he receives them as his servants. The mark is commonly given to them under their hair on some part of their body, so it is not easily found when searched; generally, as long as the mark is not discovered, the person who has it will never confess anything.[8]

By special commandment, Agnes Sampson had all her hair shaven off, on every part of her body. Her head was bound with a twisted

---

7   This of course shows the power of the Devil—that even those thought the most virtuous could be turned to his bidding. No one, not even the seemingly godliest women, was above suspicion.

8   Positively fiendish work! The Devil made it difficult for anyone innocent to be believed. The examiners would naturally assume the person had a Devil's mark that hadn't yet been found and that was the reason for the failure to confess.

rope, according to the custom. Yet still she would not admit anything. It wasn't until the Devil's mark was found on her private parts that she immediately confessed all.

Agnes Thomson, another of the accused who had been named by Geillis, was then brought before King James VI and his council and was examined about the witches' meetings and their "detestable dealings." She testified that on the night of All Hallows' Eve, she was with a great many other witches, two hundred in total, and that they all went together to sea in a sieve. They drank from flagons of wine and made merry while they sailed to the kirk of North Berwick in Lothian. After they landed, they joined hands and danced a reel or short dance, singing with one voice:

> *Cummer go ye before, cummer go ye,*[9]
> *Gif ye will not go before, cummer let me.*

Agnes testified that Geillis Duncan went before them, playing a reel or dance upon a small trumpet, until they entered the kirk at North Berwick.

The king was astonished by these confessions and sent for Geillis Duncan, who duly played the trumpet and performed the dance before the king. He took great delight in witnessing these strange testimonies.

Agnes Thomson also confessed that the Devil had come to North Berwick Kirk in the form of a man. The witches had taken too long to arrive, and the Devil said that they had to pay him a penance: they had to kiss his buttocks as a sign of their duty to him. He showed his bare buttocks over the pulpit, and the witches did as they were required.[10]

---

9 *Cummer* is an old Scots word with many meanings, including a trouble or disturbance, a close female friend, a godmother, and a female gossip.

10 This was known as the "osculum infame," literally the shameful kiss. Could this be from where we derive the insult "kiss my ass"?

Having made his "ungodly exhortations," the Devil spoke with great hostility against the king of Scotland.

The witches asked why he bore him such hatred. The Devil responded that the king was the greatest enemy he had in the world. This particular fact is stated in all the witches' confessions and depositions on record.[11]

After receiving the witches' oaths for their good and true service, the Devil then departed. The witches ventured back to sea and so to home.

Returning to Agnes Sampson again, it seemed her confessions were so various, strange, and miraculous that the king thought she and the others who had confessed must be lying. Agnes Sampson said she did not want the king to think her a liar.[12] To prove this, she took the king aside and told him the exact words that had passed between him and his new queen in Norway on the first night of their marriage.

The king was greatly amazed and swore by the living God that he believed all the devils in hell could not have discovered these words. Acknowledging her words to be true, he therefore gave more credit to the rest of the confessions.[13]

Agnes Thomson, meanwhile, was under the direction of the Devil himself to plan and execute the king's assassination. She confessed she took a black toad and hung it by the heels for three days, collecting

---

11 The (not so subtle) subtext here is that the king of Scotland must be exceedingly virtuous and godly if he is the Devil's greatest adversary. How lucky the people of Scotland are to have such a holy man to protect them from the Devil and his minions. And how lucky the English would be if he were to become their king too!

12 Quite why she would be so keen to prove herself a witch is not known.

13 Note the fact that the king of Scotland had put his credibility on the line by swearing to this, which meant that few would doubt the veracity of what was "confessed" by the witches. His royal seal of approval would surely change the mind of anyone who was in any doubt about the truth of them. The fact that he was the only one who could verify this story was of no moment.

Know Your Enemy, Part 1: *Newes from Scotland*

and gathering its venom as it dripped into an oyster shell. She kept the venom close and covered it until she could obtain a piece of "foul linen cloth"[14] belonging to the king, such as a shirt, handkerchief, or napkin. She attempted to get these items from John Kers, an old acquaintance who was an attendant in the king's chambers. He refused, saying he could not help her.

Agnes further confessed that had she obtained any such piece of linen cloth that the king had used, she would have bewitched him to death and put him to extraordinary pain, as if he had been lying on sharp thorns and the ends of needles.

Moreover, she testified that when His Majesty was in Denmark, she, along with those she had previously named, took a cat and christened it. Afterward, they bound to each part of that cat the "chieftest"[15] part of a dead man along with several joints of his body. The following night, the cat was taken into the middle of the sea by witches sailing in their sieves. They left the cat in front of the town of Leith in Scotland, and as a result, there arose a huge tempest at sea, the likes of which had never been seen before. This tempest caused the sinking of the boat coming from Burntisland (in Fife), which was carrying all the various jewels and rich gifts that should have been presented to the new queen of Scotland on her arrival at Leith.[16]

Agnes claimed that the aforementioned cat was the cause of the king's ship facing a headwind on his return from Denmark. The

---

14 The fouling of clothes is unlikely to have meant the king's soiled undergarments! Rather it meant any clothing or items he had worn or used.

15 If the chieftest part of a man is what we are imagining it is, that must have been pretty hard to attach.

16 Call us cynical, but it seems a little too convenient for a ship of riches and jewels to have disappeared in this way. Also, how fortunate it must have been for the captain of the Burntisland ship that, as with the Danish captain, all his problems at sea could be blamed on witchcraft!

king acknowledged it was true that the other ships in his flotilla had enjoyed a fair and good wind, whereas the wind continually blew against his own ship. Agnes further testified that His Majesty would never have come safely from the sea had his faith not prevailed above their intentions.[17]

Agnes was then asked to explain what the Devil would do with the witches when he was in their company. She said he received them as his servants and that he would "carnally use them, albeit to their little pleasure" due to his cold nature.[18] He would repeat this at various times as it suited him.

In respect of Dr. Fian, also known as John Cunningham, his testimony shows the great subtlety of the Devil. He was apprehended after Geillis Duncan's confession named him; she claimed he had been the register keeper for all the witches and that he was the only man called to the Devil's meetings.

The doctor was taken and imprisoned and subjected to the same torture as the others. First, they tried thrawing his head with rope, but he would not confess. Then, they tried to persuade him to confess "by fair means," but that did not work either. Finally, he was put to the most severe and cruel pain in the world, called bootikins.[19] After

---

17 Again: how virtuous and brave the king of Scotland is, whose faith is so strong it saved him from the Devil's fiendish plan to kill him, etc., etc. You get the idea.

18 Although the Devil's manner was probably not the warmest, this is not what the witches are speaking of when they describe his cold nature. At this time, it was known that the Devil was made of vapor, like a spirit. For him to take corporeal form, he had to compress that air. Such a transformation would leave him looking like a normal human being, but he would be cold to the touch.

19 Despite their nursery-rhyme name, bootikins were indeed a dreadful form of torture. They were wooden boards encasing the lower limbs and designed so that wedges could be hammered into them, crushing the ankle and foot. A bit like pilliwinks for the feet.

he had received three strokes, he was asked if he would now confess his damnable acts, but his tongue did not allow him to speak. The other witches present told the interrogators to search his tongue, under which were found two pins thrust up into his head. On this discovery, the witches said, "Now is the charm stinted [stunted]." The witches showed that those enchanted pins were the reason that he could not confess anything. At this revelation, he was immediately released from the bootikins and brought before the king, where his confession was taken.

First, he said that whenever the witches met, he was always present: he was clerk to all those who were in subjugation to the Devil's service. It was he who took their oaths of service to the Devil, and he wrote for them such matters as the Devil pleased to command him.[20]

Fian confessed that using his witchcraft, he had bewitched a gentleman who lived near Saltpans (where the doctor worked as a schoolteacher) because this gentleman was enamored of a woman whom the doctor also loved. By means of sorcery, witchcraft, and devilish practices, he caused the gentleman to fall into lunacy once every twelve hours, the madness lasting one whole hour each time. To prove the truth of the doctor's claims, the gentleman was brought before the king in His Majesty's chamber on December 24 last year. While he was there, the gentleman suddenly gave a great screech and fell into madness, sometimes bending himself over and sometimes stretching up so high that his head touched the ceiling of the chamber, to the great astonishment of His Majesty and the others present. All the gentlemen in the chamber were not able to hold him until they called for more help and together bound him hand and foot, and he had to lie bound until his fury passed.

---

20 It appears that the patriarchy is doing well in hell, what with the only man getting the desk job.

Within an hour, he became himself again. When the king asked him what he saw or did during that hour, the man replied that he had been asleep.

Fian also confessed that he had tried at various times to obtain his "purpose and wicked intent" with the gentlewoman, but he was not successful. Being thwarted in his intentions, he decided to use sorcery to obtain the outcome he desired. He did this in the following manner.

It so happened that this woman had a brother who went to Fian's school. The doctor called this boy to him and demanded to know his sleeping arrangements, in particular whether he shared a bed with his sister. The boy answered that he did. Fian thought that this would serve his purpose, so he secretly promised the boy that he would teach him without whipping him if he obtained three hairs from his sister's private parts when the opportunity presented itself. The boy promised to carry out this task faithfully and took from the doctor a piece of conjured paper to put the hairs in once he had obtained them. Thereafter the boy practiced nightly to try to carry out his master's instructions when his sister was asleep.

But God, who knows the secrets of all hearts and reveals all wicked and ungodly practices, would not suffer the intents of this devilish doctor's plan.[21] God declared that He was most gravely offended with this wicked scheme, and He worked through the gentlewoman to defeat it. One night when she was asleep next to her brother, she woke and suddenly cried out to her mother, declaring that her brother would not leave her alone to sleep. The quick-witted mother acted speedily; she very much suspected Fian's intention because she was a witch herself! She wanted to know what the boy had been

---

21 Here we see the omnipotence of God, even over the Devil's plans, and His willingness to intervene when an innocent young woman was preyed upon. We'll come to look at God's power and interventions later.

doing, and she beat him a number of times until eventually he told her the truth.

The mother, being well practiced in witchcraft, thought it would be clever to play the Devil at his own game. So she took the enchanted paper from the boy, went to a young heifer that had never borne a calf or been put to the bull, and with a pair of shears, she clipped off three hairs from the cow's udder and wrapped them in the paper. She gave the package to her son, telling him to give it to his master, which he immediately did.

As soon as Fian received the hairs, thinking them to be the maid's, he performed his sorcery on them, but no sooner had he done so than the heifer whose hairs had been clipped came to the door of the church where the doctor was and went in. The heifer made straight toward the doctor, leaping and dancing upon him and following him as he ran out of the church. The cow followed him everywhere he went, to the great astonishment of all the townspeople of Saltpans and all who beheld the sight.

The report of these extraordinary occurrences made all men believe that the Devil must have been behind them. From then on, the name of Dr. Fian—who was still a young man—became notorious among the people of Scotland, such that it was said he was a "notable conjurer."

Although at first he denied being a witch, after having felt the pain of the bootikins (and the charm stinted), he confessed that what had been said was true. In front of the king, Fian signed the confessions with his own hand, and the truth of this remains upon the record in Scotland.

After the depositions of Dr. Fian (alias Cunningham) had been taken, he was remanded in prison and given a cell by himself. There, he renounced the Devil, announcing that he was forsaking his wicked ways, acknowledging his previous ungodly life, and admitting that he had followed the allurements and enticements of Satan and had practiced his dark arts. He now vowed to lead the life of a Christian and seemed to be newly connected with God.

The day after his conversion, he stated that the Devil had appeared to him the night before, dressed all in black with a white wand in his hand, and had demanded to know if he was going to continue his service to him, as he had promised in his earlier oath. Fian declared that he utterly renounced the Devil to his face, saying to him, "Avoid, Satan, avoid, for I have listened too much unto thee, and by the same thou hast undone me, in respect whereof I utterly forsake thee." The Devil responded: "Once ere [before] thou die thou shalt be mine." As he said it, he broke the white wand and immediately vanished from sight.[22]

All that day, Fian spent time alone and seemed to be concerned about his soul. He called upon God, showing himself to be penitent for his wicked life. Nevertheless, that very night, he stole the key to his cell and the prison and escaped to Saltpans.

When the king became aware of Fian's sudden departure, he ordered him to be apprehended, and to aid this process, he sent public proclamations to all parts of the land. By means of "hot and hard" pursuit, Fian was soon recaptured and brought to prison where he was again called before the king and reinterrogated on his escape and all that had happened before.

But this doctor, despite his written confession having been taken in the presence of the king himself and a number of his counsel,[23] now denied its truth.

The king, seeing how stubborn Fian was, came up with the idea that during his time on the run, he must have entered into a new agreement

---

22 A white wand may be symbolic of the breaking of Dr. Fian's pact with the Devil. A broken wand appears similarly in other ceremonies; for example, at Queen Elizabeth II's funeral on September 19, 2022, the lord chamberlain broke a wand over her coffin to denote the end of his service to the queen.

23 The reference to the king and his counsel is where we get the term *King's Counsel* from. These were the senior lawyers/advisors who assisted the king.

with the Devil. If this had happened, he would have been newly marked, so Fian was closely searched once more. However, no mark could be found. As a result, a "most strange torment" was devised to make him confess.

First, the nails on all his fingers were riven and pulled off with an instrument that in old Scots is called a *turkas*, known in England as a pair of pincers. Then under every nail, two needles were thrust in up to their heads. These tortures notwithstanding, the doctor continued to refuse to confess to witchcraft.

With all due haste and on the commandment of the king, Fian was then subject to the torment of the bootikins once more, in which he continued to suffer for a long time. He withstood so many blows that his legs were crushed and beaten "as small as might be," and the bones and the flesh were so bruised that the blood and marrow spouted forth in great abundance, so that his feet were made useless forever. Notwithstanding all these terrible pains and cruel torments, he would not confess to anything. So deeply had the Devil entered his heart that he utterly denied all that he had vouched for before and would say nothing about his confession other than this: that all he had done and said earlier was due to him being tortured.[24]

The king and his counsel gave great thought to this, for as well as wanting to serve due justice upon such a detestable criminal, there was a need for an example to be made of him to strike terror in all others who might think to deal in the ungodly practice of witchcraft.[25] So Fian was soon arraigned, condemned, and adjudged by the law to die and then to be burned according to the law of the land.

---

24 Note that the idea he might have been telling the truth now and he had confessed before due to the torture is simply not entertained as a possibility.

25 Exemplary sentences are still used today to send messages to the public about the dangers of becoming involved in serious crimes. Thankfully in Scotland, we no longer have the death penalty, although other countries are not so fortunate.

He was strangled, after which his body was immediately put into a great fire that had been arranged for that purpose on Castle Hill in Edinburgh. This took place on a Saturday at the end of January 1591.

The rest of the witches that had not yet been executed remained in prison till further trial and in knowledge of the king's pleasure.[26]

THE CONCLUSION

Having heard this strange story, the reader may perhaps think the king would not risk himself in the presence of such notorious witches, as in doing so he might have faced great danger to himself and to Scotland. But let this answer suffice: First, it is well known that the king is the child and servant of God, and witches are mere servants to the Devil. He is the Lord's anointed and they but vessels of God's wrath. He is a true Christian and trusts in God; they are worse than infidels, for they trust only in the Devil, who brings them to utter destruction.

But here it is evident that the king possesses a truly magnanimous and undaunted mind. He was not afraid of the witches' enchantments; he was resolute in the knowledge that so long as God is with him, he has no fear of who is against him. Truly, this whole treatise makes plain the wonderful providence of the Almighty. If the king had not been defended by God's omnipotence and power, His Majesty would not have returned from Denmark, so there is no doubt God would defend him both on the land as He did on the sea, where the witches pretended their damnable practice.

So what can we take from this extraordinarily detailed document, other than that it was a very effective pitch for King James VI of Scotland to

---

26 The writing of the pamphlet was contemporaneous with the trials.

achieve his lifelong ambition of unifying the kingdoms of England and Scotland by becoming King James I of England?

It comes as no surprise that emphasis is put on the idea that if you are truly godly, then God will intervene in any plan the Devil seeks to carry out against you. So if a witch casts a spell on you and it works, then maybe you simply were not godly enough. Did your cow die after a witch cursed you? Maybe had you remembered to say your prayers, God would have intervened to stop it. The lesson is that the church provides safety from the Devil; the godlier you are, the less you have to fear.

Additionally, we learn that the Devil was very cunning at hiding his work. If you were accused but could somehow withstand the torture enough not to confess, that is because you had a Devil's mark somewhere on your body that had yet to be found. So confession or no confession—either way was proof you were a witch.

Finally, where you find one witch, there will doubtless be more. The Devil always ensures that if one witch is discovered and executed, he will have many more who can be called upon to do his satanic service.

By the time the Berwick witch trials were concluded, King James VI was an expert in witches. Happily, for our present purposes, he thought it important to record his expertise for others so they would be better prepared to deal with the problem themselves if/when it arose again. Thus, in 1597, he published a work titled *Daemonologie*—the king's own treatise on demons, spirits, witches, and all that is unholy.

PORTRAIT OF THE ACCUSED

Allison (or Margaret) Balfour

ORKNEY ISLANDS, 1594

Allison Balfour lived in the Stenness area on the Orkney Islands, off the north coast of Scotland, toward the end of the sixteenth century.

Orkney has quite a different history from the rest of Scotland, being officially still under Norwegian law until as late as 1611, although it had been ruled by Scottish earls from the late fifteenth century onward. In 1594, the archipelago was under the control of the second Earl of Orkney, Patrick Stewart, who was nicknamed "Black Patie" due to his tyrannical nature.

The paranoid earl was convinced that his three wee brothers, John, Robert, and James, were determined to kill him to seize the reins of power. Because of this, Patrick searched John's servants and, on finding poison among the belongings of one man, Thomas Paplay, he proceeded to torture the servant for eleven days. Paplay was placed in a "cashielaws," a metal cage that was gradually heated to cause horrific burns, then stripped and lashed with ropes. Somewhat unsurprisingly,

Paplay broke due to the torture and named, among others, a local natural healer called Allison Balfour as a coconspirator in the plot against Patrick.

Paplay confessed that the autumn before the accusations, Allison had been asked by the earl's brothers and their associates to cast a spell on Patrick. However, whatever spell she used didn't seem to have the intended outcome, as the earl was clearly in good physical health. Paplay was then executed, though he retracted his confession before he died.

In December 1594, entirely under the personal authority of the earl rather than under the usual legal commission, Allison was taken to Kirkwall Castle, where she was accused of witchcraft. She was questioned and tortured for two days by Henry Colville of Orphir, an ordained minister and the earl's close associate.

The torture involved Allison's legs being put into the cashielaws and burned, as Paplay had been. Every time she blacked out from the pain, they would revive her and repeat the treatment. Though what Allison was experiencing was absolutely hideous, it wasn't getting Colville the desired results. So after forty-eight hours with no confession, Allison's husband and small children were brought in and brutally tortured in front of her.

Colville began with her elderly husband, using something called "iron langs" for the torture. What exactly iron langs were is disputed, but they could've been a method of torture involving crushing the victim under fifty stones of weight. Despite this horror, Allison still did not confess. Colville then started on Allison's little boy, whose legs were put into an iron boot and mutilated by being smashed with a large hammer. Allison didn't give in. It was only when he tortured her seven-year-old daughter by crushing her fingers in thumbscrews that she finally broke and admitted to practicing witchcraft.

Allison had been told she wouldn't be executed if she confessed, but you're probably not surprised to hear this turned out to be a lie. She was tried, found guilty, and sentenced to death. On her day of execution, she (like Paplay) retracted her confession, instead telling the gathered crowd about the torture she and her family had suffered at the earl's hands.

Allison Ballfour was executed at Gallow Ha' in Kirkwall on December 16, 1594.

4

Know Your Enemy, Part 2: *Daemonologie*

The rare books section of Edinburgh's National Library of Scotland is, as you would expect, a quiet place. Readers sit at tables, manuscripts are spread about, books are piled up. So much antiquity in one room, with people beavering away, extracting history from the written word.

One Thursday afternoon, the two of us were brought into a quiet conference room and seated at a table. Though we had quite the view through the windows when we first arrived (of Arthur's Seat, the main peak of a group of hills that loom over Edinburgh), the view didn't last for long: metal blinds are fixed at the windows, ready to be closed so as to protect documents and ancient books from any dangerous sunshine. The blinds duly shut, one of the librarians checked that the air-conditioning was working, presumably so the books didn't spontaneously overheat and burst into flames.[1] Once we were fully air-conditioned, we were supplied with small beanbags to lay the books on to support their spines.

All these precautions having been taken, the librarian brought us in two books. Two versions of King James VI's book *Daemonologie*.

The first was dated 1597, a first edition copy of the text. The second was an edition from 1603, republished to coincide with James taking the English throne. Both were written in English, most likely so the king's words would have a wider reach. What immediately struck us both was that they were very small volumes, much smaller than a modern-day paperback. We had imagined that a book with a name like *Daemonologie* would be like a big bumper Disney book of spells à la *The Sorcerer's Apprentice*.[2] The smaller of the two, the London edition, is a little fancier than the other, with embossing on the front, gilt down the edges of the pages, and marbled endpapers, no doubt to suit the more refined tastes of a metropolitan London audience.[3] Both books are in very good condition.

The work itself is divided into three parts. Book One concerns itself with magic and, in particular, necromancy, the practice of speaking with the dead. Book Two covers sorcery and witchcraft, while Book Three is a discourse on all the remaining ghosts and spirits that bother folk. All three parts are presented in the form of a dialogue between two men, Philomathes and Epistemon. Philomathes (Greek

---

1 In all seriousness, it's commonplace for rare books such as this to be kept in dark and dry conditions with a steady temperature, ideally around 16°C–19°C (60°F–66°F).

2 The 1970s Disney one with Mickey Mouse as the hapless magic trainee, not the 2010 Nicolas Cage one where the book unfolds from a thin pamphlet to an enormous tome.

3 Plus ça change, eh?

for "lover of learning") is new to the subjects, curious and quite skeptical; Epistemon (Greek for "knowledgeable one"), on the other hand, is wise and clearly comprehends the real and present danger of the magics discussed throughout the books. We will focus on Book Two here, which is divided into seven chapters, each focusing on a question of witches and witchcraft.

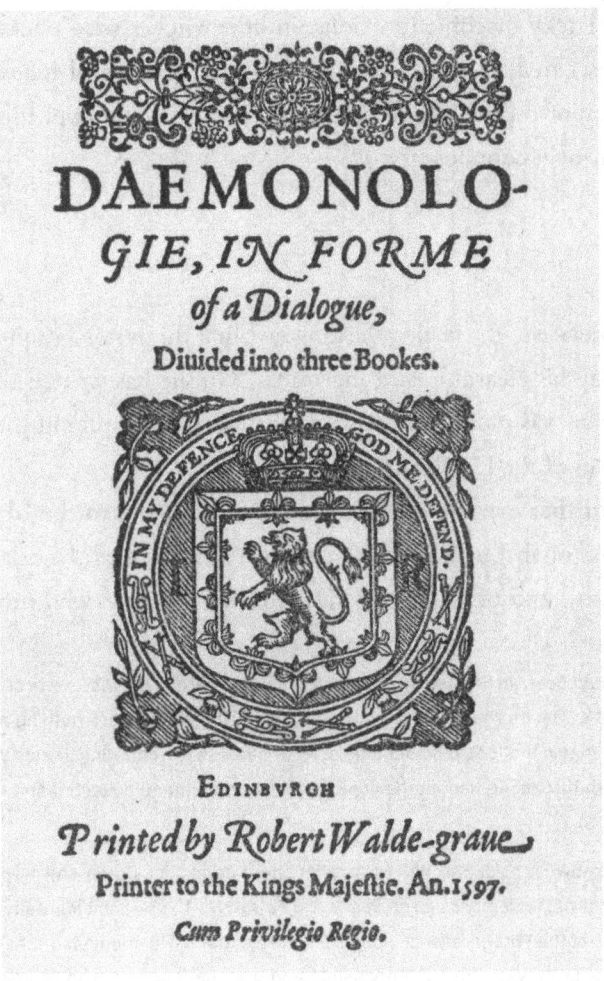

Daemonologie frontispiece, 1597

Approaching the volumes felt to some degree transgressive and dangerous. It is one thing to know—from our modern-day perspective—that witchcraft does not exist; it is another to be immersed in a world where it is entirely real. *Daemonologie* resurrects the beliefs of the times, inviting that dangerous history to come alive in the twenty-first century.

But here we could read King James VI's very own words. We could get a tantalizing insight into his mind. For anyone interested in how the patriarchy machine functions, in how witches were tracked down and prosecuted, *Daemonologie* is an essential text. What follows is our summary of the preface to the reader and of Book Two, interwoven with our own commentary.

In the preface to the reader, the king says that this is not a vanity project to display his "learning and ingenuity." No, he has written this book because he was moved by conscience to warn people about the detestable slaves of the Devil: witches.

He further explains that the book is a response to the "damnable opinions" of an Englishman named Scot, who denied the existence of witchcraft,[4] and of a German doctor called Wierus,[5] who proposed a

---

4   Reginald Scot, an English member of Parliament, wrote *The Discoverie of Witchcraft* in 1584, which proposed that most witchcraft and magic were nothing more than stage magic that could be debunked. Myth has it that when King James VI took the English throne, he had all the copies that could be found collected and thrown on the pyre.

5   Also known as Johann Weyer or Wier, he was in fact Dutch and wrote *On the Illusions of the Demons and on Spells and Poisons* in 1563—coincidentally the same year that the Witchcraft Act was passed in Scotland. He suggested that the crime of witchcraft was virtually impossible and that most people who confessed were mentally ill or "melancholic." As we will come to see, King James VI had no truck with this excuse.

Know Your Enemy, Part 2: *Daemonologie*

public apology for people accused of the crime and thus "plainly shows himself to be one of their profession."[6]

Speaking briefly on the structure of his work, James states that his use of a dialogue (between Philomathes and Epistemon, as we mentioned above) is "to make this treatise more pleasant and facile" and that he has divided his arguments into three books.

The king intends to prove two things: that the Devil and his witches are very real and that any servants of Satan deserve to be punished. He has attempted to describe what kinds of things are possible to perform using magic, although he admits the Devil's power is "infinite." Witches, he notes, have the power to cure or cause disease. From this, we can infer that the Devil has power over diseases in general, which can be seen in other ways, such as in "weakening the nature of some men, to make them unable for women," and in making this nature "abound in others, more than the ordinary course of nature would permit."[7]

The king signs off his introduction with a hearty farewell, recommending his goodwill to the reader's friendly approval.

Moving from there to Book Two, we now have to ask: What were the literally burning questions of the day?

Remember that from here on out, the chapters are written as a conversation between Philomathes and Epistemon, with Philomathes asking questions and Epistemon having the answers. As this is simply a method for James to portray his own arguments, we've simplified to him as the author.

---

6   Ahem, just for the avoidance of doubt, although some centuries later the Witches of Scotland campaigned for the public apology, we are not witches.

7   We pause to note how interesting it is that women are blamed here both for male impotence and for men being oversexed. It's almost as if women were blamed for things over which they had no power at all.

CHAPTER 1—Do Witches Actually Exist?

Naturally, this is the most important question. By this point, you will be unsurprised to learn that the answer, according to *Daemonologie*, is a resounding yes. But James still needs to prove this to the reader; thus, he presents (and subsequently refutes) three potential arguments that may be posed by those who think the so-called witches don't exist.

The first argument against their existence is that the scriptures don't speak of witches; rather they speak of magicians and necromancers. This is quickly dismissed by the author, as the Bible plainly prohibits anyone consulting with the Devil, whatever they are called. Second, are witches not, in truth, "simple raving creatures" suffering from "melancholique imaginations"? Again, no, and here we are given sixteenth-century medical theory as the reason. Apparently, those who have a "natural humour of the melancholie" are lean, pale, and "desire of solitude," but in sharp contrast, a great number of witches are "rich and worldly-wise, some of them fatte or corpulent in their bodies, and most part of them altogether given over to the pleasures of the flesh…which are thinges directly contrary to the symptoms of Melancholie."

Third and finally, if witches, through the power of the Devil, can kill people, why haven't they just killed everyone who is not a witch? The answer is simple: the Devil's powers are limited, as was established before the foundations of the world were laid. Ultimately, God has the power to rein in the acts of the Devil. The righteous have nothing to fear, as God will protect them.

This argument has important ramifications, not least of which is it gives us an explanation for why people stood by and allowed others to be executed: the woman on the pyre must be a witch, or God would surely have intervened to prevent an injustice from occurring.

So witches are real. What next?

Chapter 2—What Is a Witch, and How Do You Become One?

Sorcery, James tells us, is a Latin word, taken from the casting of the lot that determines fates. This makes sense, as the sorcerers' practices seem to be derived from lot or chance—knowing if someone would live or die, for example. The word has since come to be applied to the charms that are used for witchcraft. Both magicians and sorcerers (and, by extension, witches) serve the same master, i.e., the Devil.

How does the Devil ensnare a person to do his bidding? The Devil bases his decision on whether the prospective witch is "riche and of better accompt" or "poore and of basser degree." Perhaps unsurprisingly, to those in poverty, he promises "greate riches, and worldlie commoditie." For those who are rich (and therefore can't easily be swayed by money), he looks for another way in: revenge. He tempts them with "promises, to get their turne satisfied to their hartes contentment."[8]

But even if you are miserly poor or fabulously wealthy and filled with a desire for vengeance, the Devil still may not have sufficient leverage to ensnare you. You must also be an ungodly person. This is a central tenet of James's thinking—if you are conned by the Devil into becoming a witch, it's because your contempt for God created an easy route for him to get to you. Conversely, the godlier you are, the less likely it is the Devil will try to get you on his side.

When the Devil has found his target, what then? Displaying truly terrible behavior (as expected of this "old and craftie enemie of ours"), he fills his prospective witches with more and more despair until he finds the right time to show himself to them.[9] When he has them at

---

8 Note, he just promises them. So far in our research, we've not actually found one poor soul with whom the Devil has made good on his promise.

9 The ole "get 'em when they're down" trick. In fact, what follows we would probably now describe as the use of coercive control.

their lowest and weakest, he gets them alone—perhaps while walking in a field or lying in bed—and either by disembodied voice or in the likeness of a man, he inquires what troubles them. At this first meeting, he offers an immediate remedy to their problem, on the condition they follow his orders. Because of the target's low state of mind (and their ungodliness, greed, etc., etc.), they quickly agree to the deal and also set a time for a second meeting. Sneakily, the Devil doesn't identify who he is at the first meeting. It's only at that second meeting where he persuades them to give themselves to his service and reveals himself to be none other than Satan. Unfortunately, by this time, it's too late; the new witch has renounced their baptism. The Devil then places a mark on some secret part of their body, which remains unhealed until the third meeting. The pain the witches experience from that unhealed sore serves to not let them rest until the next meeting, for the Devil fears both that they may forget him (being new to their job as apprentices and not yet resolute in their "fiendlie follie") and that they may "skunner" [10] at the horrible promise they made him at their first meeting and try to take it back.

At last, the witches reach their third meeting with the Devil, where he takes all feeling away from the wound, regardless of whether it is "nipped or pricked." This is powerful proof that the Devil can hurt or heal them at will; their well-being is now wholly dependent on him. During this final meeting, the Devil makes a show of keeping his promise, either by teaching the witches ways to achieve their revenge or by teaching them how "they may obtain gaine and worldlie commoditie" through "unlawfull means," whichever is their preference.[11]

---

10 This is a great old Scots word still in use in the present day, meaning feeling aversion to something. "I'm scunnered with this weather" is, perhaps unsurprisingly, a relatively common phrase in Scotland.

11 The Devil appears to be an adherent of the three-date rule.

Chapter 3—How Do Witches Worship the Devil?

This chapter begins with a reiteration of what we've seen before: witches are in it for money or revenge, they have "cruell mindes" and "greedie desire," and, as with necromancers and magicians, their sole aim is "the enlargeing of Sathans tyrannie, and crossing of the propagation of the Kingdome of Christ."[12]

But then we get to the fun part: James moves on to how witches worship and how that contrasts with the followers of God. To understand this kind of worship, we must think of the Devil as "God's ape" ("ape" here meaning to mimic, often mockingly). God's ape requires service and adoration equal to that which God requires of His servants. Just as people go to church to worship God, witches convene to praise Satan, albeit in secret. To become one of God's servants, you have to be baptized, so to become one of the Devil's servants, you must receive his mark (as we've described above). Where ministers teach how to serve God in spirit and truth, the Devil teaches his disciples how to work all types of mischief.

James continues with the comparisons, but we think you get the gist.

Chapter 4—How Do Witches Travel?

Traveling anywhere during the sixteenth century was done on foot, hoof, or boat. Ordinary folk were unlikely to do much more than walk. There was a fascination, therefore, with how witches traveled to convene with each other and their evil master. Could they really teleport themselves to distant places?

Well, disappointing as it is, *Daemonologie* says no. James's argument

---

12 In *Daemonologie*, Satan is also referred to as Sathan, which has the unfortunate effect of making him sound more friendly.

is that although witches may *claim* to travel through more diverse means, this is not true—the witches' senses are simply deluded.

But just to be sure the reader really understands what witches can't do, we are treated to a few common misconceptions about them and their traveling methods.

1. Witches can't journey through "the force of the Spirite" over land and sea (essentially being carried by the wind to their destination). This one isn't written off immediately as absurd; James notes that in scripture, it's recorded that angels could carry people in this way,[13] so the Devil, by aping God's power, should be able to do an approximation of it. There is one drawback to this form of transport: they can only travel short distances, for the same length of time as they can hold their breath.[14]
   a. The witches also claim that the reason we don't see skies full of women holding their breath is that the Devil has made them invisible to all but each other. Well, there you have it.
2. Witches can't turn themselves into "the likeness of a little beast or foule," using that likeness to squeeze into any house or church, no matter if all ordinary passages are closed.
3. And witches can't lie in bed, verified by "witnesses that have seene their body lying senseles," while simultaneously having their spirit leave their body, free to roam from one country to another.[15]

---

13 James cites specifically the prophet Habakkuk being carried to Daniel's den by an angel.

14 This may be the origin of the superstition that you should hold your breath as you go through a tunnel.

15 The example of the witch lying in bed while at the same time being elsewhere was cited as evidence in the Salem witch trials, when one witch thought to prove her innocence by having witnesses swear they saw her asleep in bed. The menfolk of the parish saw right through that ruse.

We end the chapter with a warning that we can't let down our guard. Witches *do* exist, even if they can't perform these miraculous acts.

Chapter 5—What Things Can Witches Do, and Why Are They Mostly Women?

Witches usually convene for the "adoring" of the Devil in churches. When they meet him, they let him know what "wicked turne" ("turne" in this context meaning "action" or "plot") they propose to do for obtaining riches or revenge, after which he offers them advice and assistance with their plans. For the more "trifling turnes that women have ado with," the Devil tells the witches to dismember dead bodies and make powders from them for their magic. We're not certain what makes one plot "wicked" and another "trifling," but neither sounds very good.

Since we've brought up women, James asks the question outright: Why are there so many more women accused than men?

Daemonologie supplies the answer:

> The reason is easie, for as that sexe is frailer than man is, so is it easier to be intrapped in these grosse snares of the Devill, as was over well proved to be true, by the Serpents deceiving of Eva at the beginning, which makes him the homelier [more comfortable] with that sexe sensine [since then].

And this is all the book has to say on the subject. So short but so damning. In these few words, we see the roots of the patriarchy reaching far, far back through history: What better proof is there of women being the frailer sex than their deception at the beginning of time, when the Devil tempted Eve with the apple? It's only natural then that the Devil has found his closest allies in women.

So what does the Devil teach his witch women?

He teaches how to make images of people from wax or clay, which, when melted in a fire, will cause the person to suffer "continuall sicknesse." The Devil works his magic behind the scenes here, weakening the hapless victim's spirit and stopping their body from working correctly. Eventually, the person simply withers away and dies. To some witches, he gives stones and powders to help cure sickness and disease, while to others, he gives knowledge of strange poisons even medical professionals don't know about.

Witches can make men or women love or hate one another, as the Devil knows how to persuade the "corrupted affection of those whom God will permit him so to deale with." They can transfer the sickness of one person to another, which is again proven through scripture when God allowed Satan to lay a sickness on Job.

Witches can raise storms and tempests in the air, both on land and sea, within prescribed boundaries (as God permits). The storms can be easily differentiated from naturally occurring weather events as they are sudden, short, and violent. Of course, this is all possible because of the Devil's affinity with air—James reminds us that in scripture, the devil is known as the "Prince of the Aire."[16]

Witches can make folk become frenetic or manic,[17] which, being natural illnesses, the devil's power allows for (he is an "old practisian" and knows how to manipulate the human body). They can manipulate spirits into haunting certain people or houses. They can also cause possession in some cases, as is likewise possible for the Devil to do when sending his own "angells" to wreak havoc on the people of the earth.

---

16 In Ephesians 2:2, Satan is described as "the prince of the power of the air." This wording is found in the King James (yes, the same one) translation of the Bible.

17 We saw Dr. Fian cast such a spell on his love rival.

Know Your Enemy, Part 2: *Daemonologie*

Going through these witches' actions, we begin to see a few common themes. The Devil is the one behind everything; whatever the witches do, it is worked through his power. And the Devil can only do what God permits him to.

The book goes on to address another key issue: Will God allow witches to trouble anyone who believes in Him?

Apparently, there are three types of people whom God allows to be tempted or troubled: the wicked for their horrible sins, the godly who are weak in faith, and even some of His most holy to test their patience.[18]

Who then might be free from these practices?

The answer doesn't give much hope: "No man ought to presume so far as to promise anie impunitie to himselfe." Essentially, if God has preordained it, tough luck.

And there's more bad news. Readers might want to know, not unreasonably, if they could ask another witch to remove a spell cast on them? Again, the answer is clear: absolutely not. The only way to be lawfully cured is to pray even harder and amend your life—and by "sharp persewing" every witch to their death.

CHAPTER 6—What about the Witches in Prison?

If witches can do such terrible things to people, why are prosecutors immune from their spells? Or as *Daemonologie* puts it much more eloquently, "but who dare take upon him to punish them, if no man can be sure to be free from their unnaturall invasiones?"

James argues that just because the path of virtue is difficult does not mean it should not be pursued. He further clarifies that if you

---

18 On reflection, we can't help thinking it would just have been faster to say "everyone, but for different reasons."

are truly faithful and you are zealously pursuing witches, you *will* be protected.[19]

And what about when witches are in prison? Does their witchcraft work? Intriguingly, that depends on how they're detained. "If they be but apprehended and deteined by anie private person...their power no doubt either in escaping, or in doing hurte, is no lesse nor ever it was before." So if the witch is apprehended in what we now call a citizen's arrest—when a member of the public steps in to detain a criminal—then their power remains intact. But if they're detained by the lawful magistrate, witches will be robbed of their powers. In other words, leave it to the (very godly) lawmen.

Say we've justly captured a witch and thrown them in prison: Would the Devil ever visit his servant? Apparently so, but his response may depend on the state these "miserable wretches" are in. If he finds them "in anie comfort," he then tries to "fill them more and more with the vaine hope of some maner of reliefe." Alternatively, if he finds them in deep despair, he will encourage such thoughts and seek to "perswade them by some extraordinarie meanes to put themselues downe, which verie commonlie they doe." The only relief can be obtained by confession, after which "God will not permit [Satan] to trouble them anie more with his presence and allurementes."[20]

---

19 We paused to think of how important this philosophy must have been to a zealous minister, weeding out witches in the local community. What greater proof that he was doing the right thing than if he was immune to the powers of the witch whom he was accusing? We can see why those who investigated witches did so with such fervor: their own safety from the Devil depended on it, and not just their mortal body but their eternal soul.

20 Sadly, many women died during their prison stay due to the conditions they were kept in, their poor health, the torture, or more likely a combination of all three. Doubtless there were suicidal deaths attributed to the Devil that were much more man-made.

During these charming prison visits from Satan, what form does he take? Based on the diversity of confessions on this point, it seems he appears to different people in different forms.[21] To the less experienced (and more easily manipulated) witches, he conjures "vaine impressiones in the aire" to make himself seem more terrible so they are frightened into revering him all the more; to the craftier, more experienced witches, he becomes "les[s] monstrous and uncouthlike" so they aren't repelled or disgusted by his hideousness.

James now turns to his final question on this topic: What about the other people present in the prison at the time of the Devil's visit to his servants? Do they see him as well? The answer is inconclusive: "Sometimes they will, and some-times not, as it pleases God."

CHAPTER 7—Why Were Ghosts and Spirits More Commonly Seen Prior to the Reformation?

We've arrived at the last chapter of Book Two, where the main argument is this: during the time before the Protestant Reformation, people were seeing (and being bothered by) lots of ghosts and spirits; after the Reformation, there are far fewer ghosts and spirits and *way* more of those performing "unlawfull artes" (witches, necromancers, etc.). In both cases, the general population is being punished for their sins, only in different ways.

In the time of "blinde Papistrie,"[22] James says, ghosts and spirits

---

21 Sneaky work by the Devil here. Of course, the alternative explanation—not to be countenanced—is that everyone was making up what he looked like and that is why there are so many different descriptions.

22 James is using this opportunity to clearly express his rejection of the Catholic faith. Remember that his mother, Mary, had been a devout Catholic, and it would no doubt be important to emphasize his very different view.

had been seen more often. Why is this? "Our fathers erring grosselie, & through ignorance, that mist of errors overshaddowed the Devill to walke the more familiarlie among them." In other words: the ignorant (and religiously erring) Catholics had been deceived by the Devil into interacting with all kinds of spiritual apparitions.

On the other hand, though Protestants now have the "sounde of Religion," there are still some living contrary to their faith. Because of this "sinne of rebellion,"[23] evil acts of witchcraft and magic have flourished throughout the land.

What of people who deny the existence of spirits outright? That would seem the simplest option. It's a bit more complex than that, however. According to James, if you deny spirits, you deny the power of the Devil, and if you deny the power of the Devil, you also deny the power of God. And that, you simply can't do.

Thus James concludes his Q and A on witches.

Daemonologie is a remarkable document, written by the king about the most scandalous crimes (short of treason) of its day. The book was not an academic resource but a practical guide, meant to be used to keep the king's subjects safe. And it was King James VI's pitch for himself to be king of England.

Through *Daemonologie*, James portrayed himself as the envoy of God, so holy and divine that the Devil was attempting to bring him down. With God's grace and power, he could keep Scotland and England safe not only from witches but from all enemies. There was really only one choice for king of England.

---

23 James references 1 Samuel 15:23 here: "For rebellion is as the sin of witchcraft." Seems fitting.

Know Your Enemy, Part 2: *Daemonologie*

As we briefly mentioned at the beginning of this chapter, the English reprint of *Daemonologie* was published in 1603, the same year James took the English throne (as King James I). This was no coincidence; James wanted to quickly tackle the subject of witchcraft in his newly acquired country. Soon after his coronation, the English legislature passed the Witchcraft Act of 1603 as "An Act against Conjuration, Witchcraft and Dealing with Evil and Wicked Spirits." The aim of the act was to define witchcraft and its relation to the Devil more clearly and to ensure a "better restraining of said offenses, and more severe punishing of the same." There would be no mercy for witches either side of the border.

Reading *Daemonologie* was nothing short of transformational for us. We had, quite wrongly, thought the Devil and God were believed to be equal foes, with the same amount of power. It was quite the revelation to realize God was seen clearly as the strongest, omnipotent and infallible, and anything the Devil or witches did was only because He allowed it.

For instance, God may decide to test your holiness by sending witches to torment you, but if you are truly godly, He will protect you. This philosophy is true of the witch hunters and ministers: they need not fear witches, as by doing God's work, they cannot be harmed. But the same goes for the reverse: those people accused, convicted, and sentenced to death *must* have been witches, or else God would not have allowed their executions.

King James VI wrote his book in the sixteenth century to educate the public on the world of witches and magic, and here we were, standing in Edinburgh's National Library of Scotland in the twenty-first century, gaining new understanding from his words. After turning the last page, we headed out of the library and into the sun, our minds filled with images of these "wicked instrumentes" of the Devil and the terrible fates that befell them.

PORTRAIT OF THE ACCUSED

Janet Wishart

ABERDEEN, 1597

At midnight of Halloween 1596, a witches' sabbath was supposedly held in the city of Aberdeen, Scotland, at the site of an old fish market.[1] The witches sang, danced, played musical instruments, and met with the Devil. This event saw the beginning of a witch panic in the Aberdeen area, which led to the accusation and ultimate execution of twenty-three people, including Janet Wishart.

Janet was one of those accused of being at the midnight sabbath, as were her husband, son, and three daughters. A total of thirty-one accusations were eventually made against Janet, spanning an astonishing twenty-four years of her life.

These accusations came to light during her trial, including her involvement in an incident in 1572 where she was witnessed leaving her neighbor's yard in a suspicious manner in the middle of the night.

---

1   A witches' sabbath is simply a gathering of those who practice witchcraft.

When the witnesses confronted Janet about her actions, she cursed them. Later that day, two of the witnesses drowned.

Janet was further accused of using spells to make her victims fall ill, of killing people through her magic, of interfering with the weather, and of using a cat to invade people's dreams. Despite all this suspicious activity throughout the years, it wasn't until the fish market sabbath that Janet was formally accused of witchcraft.

Janet was found guilty of eighteen of the thirty-one accusations made against her and was likely executed that same day, February 17, 1597. Unusually, she was burned to death, rather than the much more common strangulation or hanging. The cost of Janet's execution was just over £11, which covered the costs of burning her plus the fee for the executioner.

Isobel Cockie and Janet's son were also found guilty, but her husband and daughters were deemed innocent; however, due to their association with her, they were banished from the area.

5

How to Believe in a Witch

Now that you're better prepared to understand the hyperbole, fervor, and theological justification for the trials, you may find yourself asking what made the public at large buy into these witch hunts. Was it simply a group of powerful elite working toward their own religious and political ends by abusing a largely illiterate population? Or was there something about the specific environment of sixteenth- to eighteenth-century Scotland that made it a fertile ground for accusation and persecution? These kinds of witch hunts are so alien to us today that it's difficult to understand how things got out of control so quickly. How were people content with letting these obvious injustices occur again and again?

And seriously—we keep returning to this question—why were so many of the accused women? Sure, we've heard King James VI's view, but was there more to it?

To help us answer these questions, we spoke (via Zoom) to

esteemed Scottish historian and one of the founders of the Survey of Scottish Witchcraft,[1] Doctor Louise Yeoman. Louise has written and researched extensively about the witch trials and has paved the way for many nonhistorians to become passionate about the subject. She also tells a great story; her speech is peppered with Scots language, and she made us feel as if she were gathering us in to tell us something special.

We began by asking her what ordinary folk would have believed at the time.

"An ordinary person in a fishing burgh like Pittenweem or Anstruther[2] might believe that people could do magical harm," she told us. "They could sink ships and bring ill luck on the men fishing."

Life, she continued, was often incredibly hard in the close-knit little villages that dot the northeast coast of Fife. Families made a precarious living from fishing the treacherous North Sea, and many superstitions and beliefs were woven into the fabric of the villagers' inner worlds. At the same time, the involvement of the church, or kirk, was incredibly important in these communities' lives, with the minister quite literally being seen as a direct connection to God. Everyone attended the kirk on Sunday, and communities were quick to point the finger of blame at anyone who deviated from societal norms.

If a villager had been paying close attention to the minister and perhaps even witnessed a witch trial, they would likely believe someone could sell their soul to the Devil and then use their newfound power maliciously against fishermen and their ships. In those days, men died

---

1 As previously mentioned, the Survey of Scottish Witchcraft is an online, interactive database with information on many Scottish witch trials and accused individuals. We cannot overstate how useful this painstaking resource is to those interested in the witch trials.

2 These coastal settlements are located in northeast Fife, where many witches were killed. This is where Zoe is from.

frequently at sea; in fact, many mariners refused to learn to swim, as they believed it was better to succumb to death if they fell in the water rather than fruitlessly battle against it. All the rage and grief villagers felt about losing fathers, husbands, and sons had to end up somewhere. Couple that with a culture where the church constructed a framework of belief as to why things happened and who should be blamed if something went wrong, and you end up with a perfect storm. As we see time and time again, people need scapegoats.

Louise elaborated. "If you lose your livelihood or if you're malting grain for brewing beer and it spoils,[3] this is bringing people into hunger and want and danger. And if you think an ill-willed neighbor can do that to you, you'd be very frightened."

There was no support system such as we (supposedly) have today. Life was brutal and short. Diseases and malnutrition routinely killed children, and people grieved their lost babies just as much as we do nowadays. If you believe someone deliberately hurt your loved ones, it makes sense to want to identify them and thereby punish them to the fullest extent of the law. And remember, this was all sanctioned—encouraged, even—by the king and the church, the two most powerful forces manipulating the ideas and actions of a society.

Louise told us the story of a woman called Anna Tait whom she had come across in her research. Anna was a miller's wife who lived in Haddington, a town near Edinburgh, in the seventeenth century.

"This case has always stuck with me. Anna is found trying to end her life. She is found trying to hang herself with the strings of her headdress. Of course, seventeenth-century society doesn't have compassion for people in these situations of despair. It thinks if you do that,

---

3   Leaving grain in water until it starts to germinate so it can be used in the production of beer or whisky. People often drank weak beer instead of water. Perhaps we should take this up again.

you're motivated by the Devil. Suicide is a terrible crime [in their eyes] and you'll not get a normal burial. They have really horrible beliefs on this. So once Anna is caught trying to kill herself, the first thing people say to her is, 'Did the Devil come to you?' And of course this is somebody in despair, so she says, 'Yes, yes, the Devil came to me,' but she also gives a horrifying, sad, tragic confession."

As we see time and time again, when a person is distressed, they often admit to anything to make the pain stop. Louise explained that during Anna's testimony, it seemed she took the opportunity to make a broader confession about things she'd done in her life, some of them quite shocking. First, she admitted to poisoning her first husband with foxglove leaves in order to marry her second husband. Then, when her daughter became pregnant, Anna helped her terminate the pregnancy, but tragically, her daughter died as a result. This was what led her to such distress.

Anna was arrested and imprisoned at the end of 1634 and executed soon after, but we do not have an exact date of her death.

While many witchcraft confessions have great similarities, Anna's confession is strikingly unusual. Generally, the confessions were formulaic, as the interrogators were looking for specific information, such as how the Devil approached the accused, what he said, what he promised, and what nefarious acts he and the witch then indulged in. In Anna's case, however, she unburdened herself of her very personal, very heartbreaking story, which, though criminal, was not exactly what the interrogators were interested in.

"These are not the kind of things the people interrogating you want to hear," said Louise. "The people who are interrogating you want to hear you made a pact with the Devil. You had sex with the Devil, the Devil gave you a mark, and then you went and did horrible things. They don't want to hear your life story."

Louise suggested that sometimes the accused thought they were going to die anyway, so they might as well use the opportunity to straighten things up with God.

"I know of another case where a woman talks about her young son dying and she talks about it in the context of fairy changelings. The fairies took the son, and they left a log in the cradle, and the log was thrown in the fire. You think, what actually happened to that wee boy?"

Louise has read many dozens of confessions to witchcraft, and she believes that often what is recorded is not the voice of the accused but the voice of the person asking the questions. Many of the confessions are so basic and similar they read like an early version of a "cut and paste" job.

When we do hear from the accused themselves, they often seem to be scrabbling for anything to say or, perhaps more likely, they just say anything to get the horror over with. In other cases, like in the story of the woman's deceased son, there is deeply personal information that is unlikely to have been made up by the interrogators. It's here where we may have the best insights into the genuine stories of women at the time. As Louise says, when a personal story breaks through, you know as a researcher that you're hearing the confessor's real voice.

Thinking on the stories of Anna Tait, the grieving mother, and the fishing villagers and on all the hardships found in their lives, it's really no wonder beliefs about witchcraft took such hold.

One thing we have discussed at length since the inception of the Witches of Scotland campaign is why so many more women than men were accused in Scotland (and in most other countries). It's true that in some places, namely parts of Scandinavia and Russia, witches were generally believed to be men, but this derived from specific local traditions. In the far north of Scandinavia, for example, shamans were all men, so it was they who were accused of working with the Devil.

However, in Scotland, the belief systems of the 1500s to the 1700s were particularly disposed to a patriarchal answer to the question of witches. Women were seen as weaker and therefore dangerously susceptible to the Devil's wicked and often sexy charms.[4] They were also more likely to misbehave and not follow God's (read: man's) rules, more likely to be grasping and greedy, more likely to be jealous and corrupt. In short, women were being stereotyped as perfect targets for the Devil.

What's particularly interesting to us is that back then, as is largely the case now, women weren't the ones wreaking havoc on battlefields or in street brawls. Women had no legal power or professional standing. They weren't sitting at the side of the king or presiding over legal cases. What we think this led to is men (with power) being desperately scared that those without power (women) would try to grasp it by any means possible. It's not that big a leap from there to the creation of a fantastical means by which they could keep the powerless down. Here, we would argue, is where Scotland found itself from the 1500s onward.

We return now to one of the most influential moral architects of the period, John Knox, a Protestant minister we met in chapter 2. Knox had a particular interest in women not holding power, believing that any woman in a position to rule was unnatural. If he had a hand in the creation of the Witchcraft Act of 1563—as Louise's colleague Julian Goodare argues—is there any evidence *he* drove this desire to accuse and punish women?

"No," said Louise. "John Knox is an interesting case. He's somebody who really loves and respects the women in his life. He spends endless

---

[4] Note that women alone weren't dangerous; they still needed a man to activate their dangerous tendencies.

time counseling them on their spiritual problems. He's somebody who, within what he thinks is the sphere for godly women, thinks women are great."

According to Louise, what bugged Knox the most wasn't women at all; it was idolatry. Idolatry—the worship of images, portraits, idols, and other such holy objects, very much part of the Catholic tradition—was seen by Knox and his contemporaries as a huge and important problem they needed to address. Protestants thoroughly condemned idolatry and had therefore thrown out their idols, instead choosing to worship God directly. They believed that the word of the Bible spoke against worshipping idols, and if you didn't follow the Bible to the letter, you could find yourself worshipping the Devil rather than God.

Because here was the crux of the issue: if people weren't worshipping correctly, they could bring the wrath of God down upon Scotland, upon the entire nation. For this reason, Knox concentrated—to the point of obsession—on people obeying what's written in scripture. This is shown in the wording of the Witchcraft Act: there must be absolutely no necromancers. *Everyone* must be following the rules of the Bible to the letter.

Despite Louise's take on Knox, his sexism, to us, runs deeply. In 1558, he published a tract with the ferocious title *The First Blast of the Trumpet Against the Monstrous Regiment of Women* ("monstrous" here meaning "unnatural," and "regiment" meaning "rule" or "government"). In it, Knox argues female monarchs are contrary to the Bible's teaching and an affront to God—a direct attack on the monarch of the time, Mary, Queen of Scots. It always struck us how Knox believed that although Mary was supposedly God's envoy on earth and had therefore been put into power by Him, the country would be better served with a male king. That seemed very bold, even treasonous. Perhaps it just again shows the temerity of men.

However, as is sometimes the case with this kind of grandstanding,

Knox gets caught bonny.[5] When the Protestant Queen Elizabeth I was crowned in England in 1559, Knox's colleagues received elevated positions in the Church of England, but Elizabeth refused to do the same for Knox. It is said that she never forgave him for what he wrote.

It's small comfort, but we'll take it.

We first came across the historian Marion Gibson on what was then known as Twitter, as she fiercely battled misinformation about the witch trials under her fantastic handle @witchesetc. Marion is a great communicator whose warmth and knowledge must surely make her popular with her students at the University of Exeter, where she is a professor of Renaissance and magical literatures.[6]

When Marion was herself a student at university, accounts of the witch trials drew her toward the field. As she learned more about the confessions of the witches and she thought about the women behind the stories, the truth about these persecuted individuals really began to matter to her.

As soon as you start reading confessions, you notice there are certain themes and ideas, even phrases, that get repeated. Was it a case of these stories permeating the national consciousness? Or were the accused simply repeating what their interrogators said to them? Did accurate accounts of what the accused said even exist? Perhaps most perplexingly for us as a modern audience is the question of why people confessed to witchcraft at all.

First, we have to think about how ideas become part of a culture.

Marion, speaking to us online, leaned toward her screen. "Why

---

5   A Scottish saying that means being caught in the act.

6   Imagine having "magical" in your job title!

did somebody one day decide that people might keep a small animal familiar[7] who was in fact a devil and that this would suck their blood? Who had that idea? That's a very strange idea indeed. But then when you think about how it enters into culture, you think about the rumors that fly around today—not only on social media but also in ordinary life."

It's true, of course: we often see today how obviously fabricated ideas or stories can become normalized the more they are shared. See the rise of conspiracy theories during the 2020 pandemic, flat-earthers, chemtrail believers, or those who deny the moon landings.

"Although coming to explain how these ideas originated is really difficult, how they spread is quite easily understood," Marion continued. "It is by gossip, but it is also by writing. The more people write these things down and the more people talk about them in court and then the more people print the confessions and the more people take the pamphlet down to the pub and they read it to their friends—you can see how once people got hold of these ideas, they circulated in the culture."

During the witch trials, publications appeared that were widely distributed, a bit like the penny dreadfuls of the Victorian era we're perhaps more familiar with.[8] As we've seen, the most famous of these was the *Newes from Scotland*, printed in England in 1591, then

---

7   Familiars are a small part of the Scottish witch trials story but a big part of the overarching idea of witches. A witch's familiar was an animal such as a cat, dog, or bird (sometimes it could even be a child) that would drink the witch's blood from their "witch's teat." One belief was that familiars suckled the witch as a kind of evil, female holy communion. The familiar would consume the blood, then "work" for the witch by doing evil deeds, such as killing people or livestock.

8   These were serialized stories that started being produced in the 1830s, so called because they cost a penny an issue. The stories focused on sensationalized murders and supernatural events.

circulated across the British Isles. While the advent of print is an indisputably positive development—the Age of Enlightenment could not have happened without it—it also had a darker side. One example of this is the broadening distribution of the idea that witches were hidden (or not so hidden) among the ordinary population. Seeing such stories written down legitimized the people's beliefs and encouraged communities to pursue witches as a way to keep themselves safe.

All this said, the vast majority of people in Scotland were still illiterate in the sixteenth century, leaving reading as a privilege of wealthy men (anyone seeing a pattern forming here?).[9] These elite men were powerful, educated, and in charge of the country. Their status and authority legitimized their views for the lower classes. No doubt servants would pick up snippets of information from their masters, and they would tell their friends, who would tell their friends. This spread of information provided ordinary folk both entertainment as well as a major source of news, the other dominating news source being, of course, the sermons of the minister at the kirk.

It seems the more things change, the more they stay the same. In modern times, we see nearly identical issues on platforms like X, Facebook, and TikTok, only on a much larger scale. Ideas—often harmful—are spread worldwide in seconds, and as humans have a tendency to be fearful and blame seeking, this is a perfect means of transmitting hate.

But it's not the mode of communication that's the problem. It's the humans who want to be scandalized by gossip and hear stories of aberration, which then creates a culture of accusation and punishment.

---

9   Scotland passed three education acts in 1616, 1633, and 1696 to try to establish schools, but a shortage of teachers and the expense of school fees meant literacy rates remained low, especially for girls.

"These are persistent human fascinations, and we can't get rid of them," Marion said. "We wouldn't have folklore and fantasy without these kinds of beliefs, but of course they also have these terrible consequences of persecution."

This leads us to a discussion of two often conflated undertakings of the time, both involving water—"ducking" and "swimming." Ducking (with the use of a "ducking stool") was a form of public punishment and humiliation that long precedes the witch trials, having been practiced since the thirteenth century. Women thought to be scolds or gossips were strapped to these ducking stools and repeatedly plunged into water to show them the error of their ways. Although ducking was not intended as a method of execution, it is said the practice occasionally proved fatal, when women would drown in the water or die from shock.

Where ducking was used to humiliate, King James VI deemed an adaptation (known as "swimming") a good test for witches. Swimming got rid of the stool entirely, instead simply binding the woman and tossing her in the water. If she floated, she was a witch; if she sank, lucky her—she wasn't a witch! Of course, she may yet drown before anyone can come to her rescue.[10]

You might ask yourself, what was the reasoning behind the swimming test? Well, it was actually fairly simple: no water will accept those who've rejected the sacred water of baptism. So if you've maintained your baptism, you would be accepted by the water— you'd sink. If you'd signed your soul to the Devil and therefore renounced your baptism, the water would refuse you entry, and you'd float. Despite the enduring image of witches being thrown

---

10 The water test is actually mentioned in *Daemonologie*: James states that finding the Devil's mark (and testing its insensitivity) and observing a suspected witch's "fleeting [floating] on the water" are both "good helpes that may be used for their trial."

into water, this particular test didn't happen nearly as often as is commonly thought.[11]

Along with ducking and swimming was another method to test for a witch: weighing the accused. Weigh stations—essentially large public scales in trade halls—existed across many towns in the medieval period for the purposes of commerce (grain, livestock, and so on). However, as witch hunt mania spread across parts of Europe in the 1600s, these stations were put to a different use, transforming into tools to determine whether someone was lighter than an honest woman and, therefore, a witch. Sadly, those who operated these weigh stations were often at worst corrupt, at best incompetent, and many people were found to be suspiciously light and then executed. One notable exception was at the Weighing House in Oudewater, the Netherlands, where the scales are reputed to have been deemed fair by Holy Roman Emperor Charles V himself. As a result, no one is thought to have been found guilty there; indeed, accused witches would make the (occasionally dangerous) trip to Oudewater just to prove their innocence. The scales were built in 1482 and, remarkably, still exist today, preserved in a museum. The museum offers the opportunity for visitors to be weighed on the scales, then receive a certificate proving they aren't a witch. An educational experience, if rather grim.

Another idea that permeated the culture of the time was the concept of good and evil as a paired set. Marion explained: "Their entire world was structured by this binary idea that there's God on one hand, with

---

11 The idea of witches floating in water may also be partially due to the famous scene in *Monty Python and the Holy Grail*: the villagers argue that because witches burn, like wood, and wood floats, like ducks, then if a woman weighs the same as a duck, she must be a witch. People don't remember the particulars of this scene outwith a mob shouting, "She's a witch!" and that it has something to do with witches floating, yet it is a part of our inherited knowledge about the witch trials and actually a great example of the transmission of nonsense.

His people, so on the other hand, there must be the Devil and his people. There must be witches, and they must have certain laws that apply to them, and they must have certain behaviors that are often a kind of parody or an inversion of Christianity."

For example, many witch confessions focus on their making a pact with the Devil. This is an inversion of the rite of confirmation, where baptized Protestants who have reached adulthood affirm their faith and commitment to the Christian community. Witches, by extension, would sign up to the dark side—they would make a covenant with the Devil. There are many variations on what this deal looked like, with the Devil offering money, sexual success, or revenge in return for the witch's soul. After the pact had been made, the witch could forge ahead with their harmful practices: ruining crops, killing neighbors, causing illnesses, manipulating weather.

Marion believes this binary thinking of God on one side and the Devil on the other (with absolutely no gray area in between) is what contributed to so many more women being accused than men. If the clever and morally strong men were on God's side, then who must be on the other side with the Devil? Silly, inferior women, that's who! Women in their gullibility would easily fall for the Devil's sophistication.

There was suspicion too when women spent time with other women. What did they talk about all day? Were they making plans to meet the Devil? Were they casting spells? Somehow, the reasoning was as simple as women can be malicious, and they gossip; therefore, they must be up to something. It's horrifying to think that thousands of people were scapegoated and murdered for such petty ideas.

"When I started off my career in academia," said Marion, "I thought, it can't be as simple as that. But it's one of the great truths. This is about people hating women, and it's really important to keep saying that. You can say all sorts of other things—it's about economic circumstance, and yes, that's important—but gender's part of that. Or you can say it's about domesticity and it's about people fighting over domestic spaces and boundaries, and yes, it is, but gender is a part of that. And you can say it's about medical knowledge and who's supposed to have it, yes, but gender's a part of that too. It's about gender. And I think we sometimes forget to say it because we're so busy looking for other explanations, which are contextually very important. But that central truth? It's about women."

We wonder whether we shy away from this truth because we modern women don't want to seem like harpies. It's the twenty-first century, and we're still banging on about gender equality? Yes. Yes, we are. And we're going to keep banging on about it until it's sorted. It's a massive disparity—85 percent of the people accused as witches were women. We feel terrible for the 15 percent who were men, but we have the feeling that many of them were dragged into it by the accused women. Quite often, the accused men were relatives of the women. Perhaps their mother or wife had been accused, and they were guilty by association, or perhaps they were being used to pressure the women into naming other witches.

Even the men who escaped direct accusation were harmed by the ordeal. "These men suffered terrible fates too," agreed Marion. "Imagine if you were one of the men left behind? Imagine if your wife is accused and you can't save her, you can't protect her? This is a universal tragedy."

It is indeed a terrible set of circumstances that tore families apart. But as Marion put it, "There is often a truth that you have to talk about, and then the other truths fall into place around it." And that truth is that this is about women, and as a result, it is a feminist issue.

The sexual dynamic to the accusations and confessions in Britain appears to be a key part of the witch trials. It's men who question and torture and examine the accused's bodies. It's men who decide their fates and then dispatch them. Once women are cast as witches in collusion with the male figure of the Devil, a sexual element to the confessions is inevitable. The witches meet up with the Devil, at night, in the woods or behind the town. What else would they be getting up to? The Devil is described as handsome and nicely dressed. He's charming and persuasive, a fantasy lover. Life was hard and short,[12] so who could blame a woman for having a little fantasy about someone who could take her away from all that? Women were viewed as difficult, foolish, *and* sexually dangerous[13]—a nasty mix that made them perfect targets for all society's fears.

One case with a strong sexual element was that of Isobel Duff from Inverness. Her trial took place on July 17, 1662, during one of the five peaks of witch-hunting.[14] In fact, Isobel had her trial during what's seen as the biggest peak of anti-witch fervor in Scotland; around six hundred people were accused, and nearly half that number executed.

Isobel's trial is so intriguing because it lays bare (so to speak) the underlying sexual dynamics of the pact with the Devil. Isobel's confession goes into detail about how the Devil tricked her into agreeing to have sex with him: he took the form of a man called Tailiour, a soldier with whom Isobel was having an affair. Apparently, Isobel could tell the difference between the Devil and Tailiour by "the length of his wand." Isobel also described the Devil as being unnaturally cold and not having any feet.[15] There are descriptions of the mechanics of

---

12 Rough estimates put life expectancy at around thirty-five during this period.

13 Riddle us this: men were morally stronger than women, but they also had to be on their guard not to be tempted to sexual impropriety by those sneaky sex pots.

14 Experts generally recognize the period of witch trials as occurring from 1590 to 1662, with peaks in 1590–91, 1597, 1628–31, 1649–50, and 1661–62.

15 The latter attribute would seem a pretty clear indication to us that he wasn't a human, but we suppose the difference in penis size made for a more interesting story.

the copulation as well, namely that the Devil penetrated her "after the manner of beasts" at Isobel's "back parts," which would seem to be either sex from behind or possibly anal sex.

At any rate, Isobel's confession clearly paints her as an immoral, sexually voracious woman, which was most strongly frowned upon at the time. Still is, some would argue. The confession goes on to record that Isobel agreed to be part of the Devil's coven as she wished to seek revenge on her local enemy, John Robertson (who later died of an illness). But her use of magic for evil purposes, or malefice, didn't stop there: besides Robertson, she was accused of being involved in the deaths of several local people. We also see in the confession a case of magical curing, stating that Isobel helped a child recover from whooping cough. Another child advised her to tie a ribbon around the affected child's neck; although this cured the sick child, the child who gave her the idea died soon after.

Isobel was tried and declared guilty, and why wouldn't she be, with such a sexually explicit and damning confession? The court instructed that Isobel "be taken to the usual burning hill beside Inverness…and there to be strangled to a stake…and thereafter your body to be burned to ashes as a notorious and known witch."[16]

Once again, we see the fear of female sexuality taken to its deadliest conclusion.

Why did Isobel Duff—and so many others like her—confess if they were innocent?

It's not hard to believe that eventually, after being tortured

---

16 These quotes have been taken from Isobel's trial, though we have modernized them a bit for ease of reading.

(whether by physical means or, in later years, with sleep deprivation), the vast majority of people will say anything to make the pain stop. However, Marion has a different theory for why some of the women gave false confessions.

"There's something in the stories that's satisfying to tell. If you're in a situation where you're tired and you've been physically assaulted or put under stress in some way, you're frightened and you want to go home, and this wealthy gentleman is asking you questions and you live in a society where your job is to agree with the wealthy gentleman, you can see why you might end up coming up with a story to please him. So you might say, 'Yes, I was a witch, and I quarreled with Goodie So-and-So next door, and I decided I wanted to hurt her. So one day, this strange man came to me and offered all this wealth and happiness. He said that I was special, and I was going to be his and that he would reward me if I took revenge on Goodie So-and-So, so I did and I felt fantastic about it. Now I can see that this was wrong. Please can you absolve me and then we can all go back to where we were?' But of course it doesn't work like that. By the time you've made the confession, you're in such deep trouble that you're probably not going to get out of it."

Yet we see a kind of agency in telling this story, in being able to threaten that you'd been in cahoots with the Devil, so people had better watch how they treat you, or something bad might happen to them. Women were given the opportunity to talk at length and have men—powerful men—listen and even write down what they had to say. On top of all that, these powerful men were often frightened of the women because of the power they thought they wielded.

As Marion put it, "That must have been a wonderfully satisfying position of power. Even if it only lasted for, say, half an hour. It must have been transformative."

PORTRAIT OF THE ACCUSED

Margaret Aitken

FIFE, 1597

Margaret Aitken, who later became known as the Great Witch of Scotland, was arrested in April 1597, triggering a devastating chain of events that led to hundreds of people's deaths.

Margaret came from a tiny village called Balwearie, located south of Kirkcaldy in Fife. The village had a long history of magic and superstition. According to one legend, many years before, in 1539, King James V suffered a disturbing nightmare during which he was visited by devils and the laird of Balwearie's son.

When Margaret was accused and arrested, she was tortured to induce a confession. Based on the record of the confession, it seems she concocted a story to save her life; she told her interrogators she had the uncanny ability to detect a witch just by looking into their eyes. This turned out to be a very in-demand skill. In May 1597, King James VI approved a commission for Margaret to be toured around Scottish towns in a kind of horrific judicial road show, picking out those she identified as witches. The commission even went so far as to utilize the rarely performed swimming test. Margaret and her clerical entourage eventually reached Glasgow, where things began to fall apart.

Initially, a minister named John Cowper (reputed to have been particularly unpleasant) was very keen to condemn any women based on Margaret's testimony. The number of accusations and executions stemming from Cowper and Margaret is suspected to have reached several hundred. But in August 1597, some sort of legal justice finally prevailed.[1] One of the prosecutors, unconvinced by Margaret's claims, arranged for a group of people she had condemned to be presented again the next day, only dressed in different clothing. Lo and behold, Margaret proclaimed them innocent this time, unwittingly sealing her own fate.

Margaret made one final confession where she admitted to fabricating her special powers and blamed Cowper for his part in the witchfinding frenzy. Marion Walker, a widow from Glasgow and an active resister of the witch hunts, printed and shared Margaret's confession, bringing this particular bout of witch trials to an end. Margaret was sentenced to death by burning at the stake and was taken back to Fife to face her fate.

Following this embarrassing disaster, King James VI stopped the commission. There were no further witch panics for more than thirty years—until they were renewed with a vengeance in the seventeenth century.

---

1 We know. We can't believe it either.

PART TWO

BUILDING A CASE

PORTRAIT OF THE ACCUSED

Agnes Finnie

EDINBURGH, 1644

Agnes Finnie was a notorious moneylender and shopkeeper who lived in Potterrow Port in Edinburgh in the mid-1600s. Unusually, according to writer Mary Craig in her book about Agnes, she described *herself* as a witch, and for many years, she conducted her business openly and bad-temperedly in her shop and the surrounding neighborhood. Despite her poor bedside manner, many locals consulted her to heal the sick, particularly children. However, as life became harder in these trying years, several of her customers and patients didn't recover, or indeed they fell ill or became injured following some of her characteristic harsh words. Eventually, Agnes's bad reputation caught up with her.

Craig argues that Agnes's denouncement functioned as a release for the community, who were under all the pressures of the time. Certainly, it was a thorough condemnation. On July 8, 1644, at around the age of forty-eight, Agnes was arrested and ultimately charged with over twenty offenses, spanning some sixteen years. It was said she was in "cumpany with the Devill, in consulting wi him," and that among other things, she "tried to remove witches' malice with a gift of ale." The records also indicate that her malice was partially caused by "social slight"—she sought revenge for a godchild not being named after her.

Agnes's prosecution dragged out for a long time, relative to other witch trials. The trial was on December 18, 1644, and she was held in Edinburgh's tolbooth[1] for five months beforehand. The case was then deliberated until February 8, 1645, and her date of execution was set a month later. In total, she was incarcerated for nearly nine months.

Finally, on March 6, 1645, Agnes Finnie was taken to Castle Hill, where she was strangled and her body burned.

---

1   A municipal building used for various city administration purposes as well as the city's main jail.

6

How to Accuse a Witch

You have a suspected witch in your community. What happens now?

One of the aspects of the witch trials that makes them so compelling to us is that these horrific events were not enacted by some out-of-control mob who were taking to the streets with pitchforks, as perhaps we might believe from portrayals in film and on TV. Rather, the whole process was considered, thought out, and organized by the two arms of society that should have been trying to keep people safe: the state and the church. We must do our best to understand that these laws and beliefs were seen as rational and approved by the king and God. The accusations and trials followed strict protocols, and communities that deviated from the law were punished.

Interestingly, from the time the witch trials began in Scotland, the execution rates in the lower courts were much higher than those of the higher courts. This changed somewhat in 1597, when the kirk sessions (local church courts) largely took over.[1] These kirk sessions consisted of local parish bigwigs and were far more open to abuses, such as attacking Catholics and the overly superstitious.

We spoke to independent scholar Judith Langlands-Scott about what happened in the kirk sessions. Judith is passionate, couthy,[2] and incredibly engaging. As a result of relentless detective work sifting through local archives, she has uncovered (and continues to uncover) more and more cases of the accused in the Forfar area.[3] It's fair to say that researching the witch trials in Forfar has become an all-consuming passion for her, so much so that she has a stylized rendering of one of the Forfar "witches," Girzell Simpson (accused and convicted in 1661), tattooed on her right arm. Alongside her co-researcher Shaun Wilson, Judith has galvanized local interest in the Forfar witches, discovered previously unknown names, headed up a local memorial, and more besides. There are many people in the area whose families have been there for hundreds of years, meaning they have a tangible relation to the accuseds' names. We believe thinking about and connecting to the real people, not just the historical details, is vital to engaging with history.

We were curious what it was like to be one of the accused, going through the trial process and up to the point of conviction and execution. Our understanding (garnered through representations in popular culture) was that the community would simply round on someone, literally pointing the finger. The reality was far more subtle.

---

1   Kirk sessions were run by the church. Local/lower courts were run by the state.

2   A Scots word meaning "likeable and friendly with no airs and graces."

3   Forfar is a small town in the county of Angus in eastern Scotland. It's only five miles from Glamis Castle, birthplace of the Queen Mother.

Forfar saw its first witch hunt from 1568 to 1569. This trial was terminated without conclusion for reasons unknown, but in July 1574, the Earl of Argyll held several more trials in which men and women were executed under the accusation of "common sorcery." Decades of relative peace followed until a spike in cases from 1649 to 1650[4] and then a much bigger peak from 1661 to 1662, where at least 53 people in Forfar and some 660 people across Scotland were accused in the space of sixteen months—more accusations than at any other time in Scottish history. It is believed around 120 people were burned during that time.[5]

This flood of cases occurred—not uncoincidentally—during a very unstable period in Scottish history. In the years prior to the events of 1661, there had been failed crops, a mini ice age, fatal illnesses, and the invasion of Oliver Cromwell's troops, which led to huge civil changes and unrest. Cromwell, a senior commander in the Parliamentarian army during the English Civil War,[6] had become head of the Commonwealth of England after King Charles I's execution in 1649. After the Scots proclaimed Charles I's son Charles II as king, Cromwell sent his forces up north to invade Scotland. He won battles at Dunbar and Worcester, ultimately leaving Scotland occupied by an English force until the Restoration of King Charles II in 1660.[7]

---

4   This followed the new Scottish Witchcraft Act in 1649, which essentially strengthened the powers of the original 1563 act and extended it to deal with consulters of "Devils and familiar spirits."

5   As a comparison, in the two centuries of England's witch hunt years (between 1541, when King Henry VIII made witchcraft a capital offense in England, and 1735, when the newest Witchcraft Act put an end to convictions of witchcraft across the whole of Great Britain), it is estimated that around five hundred people were executed. And of course, England has a much bigger population than Scotland.

6   Parliamentarians were supporters of the Parliament during the English Civil War, as opposed to those who supported the monarchy and King Charles I.

7   Cromwell died in 1658.

Again an independent kingdom, Scotland regained its system of law, parliament, and kirk. The Church of Scotland dominated all aspects of life, with as many as three services a day and hours-long sermons on Sundays. The biggest peak of the Forfar witchcraft trials took place against this background of intense religious focus.

Before church, the minister would meet with his twelve elders—the apostles to his Jesus—to hear any news of his parishioners.

"Imagine that you were an elder. You might feel a certain amount of pressure to have something juicy to tell the minister as, after all, your role is to enforce the religious code," said Judith. "It's your job to keep an eye on the parishioners and make sure they are toeing the line and living godly lives. You wouldn't want to appear to not be on top of things and not know everyone's business. Also, everyone in the town knows that the kirk session meets on a Sunday, so if anyone has an accusation, they'll bring it to an elder to tell the minister on their behalf."

See it, say it, sorcery.

Villages are notorious for being places where there's no such thing as a secret and everyone knows everyone else's business.[8] This was particularly true in 1600s Scotland, when everyone in society was a God-fearing Christian, expected to follow a strict moral code. It would be very easy, when heightened fears of the supernatural were added to the mix, to conclude that anyone who didn't comply with these societal rules was possessed by the Devil. Say someone was being a quarrelsome dame, cursing at people in the market, not attending church frequently enough, enjoying an inappropriate relationship, or maybe simply being different from the norm or from gender stereotypes or showing signs of mental illness, a learning disability, or alcoholism. If a woman's behavior is unacceptable or suspicious, could it be she's a witch?

---

8 This was true even in the olden days before the advent of Facebook.

Sure, there might be scurrilous gossip, but how did that gossip find its way from the minister in the kirk session to the local courts?

"Ah," said Judith. "It was because the elders weren't only in the church, but they were also the magistrates and the bailies. They had power at a civic level. It wasn't just the church court, but their other day selves were the law."

Bailies were civil officers working for the local government, and they essentially served as heavies for the minister, enforcing his edicts and decisions. From a modern perspective, it's shocking that there was no proper separation of powers. It begs the questions: Who kept a check on fairness or impartiality? And could any trials conducted in this manner be just?

"Exactly," said Judith. "They [the magistrates, bailies, and men of the church] elected each other. It wasn't put to a vote in the town. No one asked, 'Who do you want to be your magistrate?' These were men elected by other men. It was definitely not democratic."

Bailies weren't lawyers, but they held a great deal of power because everything was dealt with at a local level. They would hear accusations and decide if the kirk session should seek a commission from the Privy Council (which we'll hear more about in just a second) to proceed to a trial.

This was a particular weakness of the system, according to Judith. "If you were a bailie, it would be really easy to stitch someone up if you had a grudge. Think about how disliked politicians can be just now. If you think about what it was like back then, if someone was difficult toward a bailie, then the bailie had the power to punish them."

The kirk session met between sermons on Sundays. People were most often accused at the first session of the day, then questioned and pushed for a confession during subsequent sessions. Sometimes the accused would be humiliated in front of the congregation before they were taken away. Public humiliation was critically important, as it reminded the community of who was in charge and the consequences of not being obedient.

In 1661, Girzell Simpson of Forfar—the subject of Judith's tattoo—was accused of being a witch.

There are no records remaining that say exactly how old Girzell was, but she wasn't married and was not described as a "girl." As the average age of marriage for a woman was between twenty-two and twenty-six at the time,[9] Judith's hypothesis is that Girzell was probably in her late teens. After she was found guilty, she was hanged from the tolbooth window in August of that year.

There's an incredibly unusual aspect to Girzell's case: she was buried after her execution.[10] This may not seem unusual, but most convicted witches' remains were burned and destroyed rather than being buried. Judith realized this after finding evidence that Girzell's parents were called to collect her remains, eight days after her death. Judith believes this variation from the usual turn of events is down to the big gap that had occurred since the previous witch trials in 1650. We get the impression that perhaps there wasn't enough public appetite for witch-hunting to destroy Girzell's remains, and the townspeople were regretful after the deed was done.

No details remain of why Girzell was accused, and again, Judith

---

9 We were very surprised by this age range, as we had assumed that women in those days married much younger. However, Judith explained to us that the labor of unmarried girls played an important part of the financial security of many families (they might work on the family's smallholding and take produce to the market, for example), and the family might therefore be reluctant to relinquish that extra pair of hands any earlier than necessary.

10 As Judith's research develops, she will hopefully discover exactly where.

How to Accuse a Witch

has had to fill in the gaps using other pieces of evidence. She guesses that as Cromwell's troops had not long left the area, Girzell was probably accused of having taken part in dalliances or paid sex work with the soldiers. This would have been seen as completely immoral and unacceptable, although it was quite common in Scotland at the time.[11]

Following Girzell's execution, a flurry of new accusations followed, and several people were brought in for questioning. When the notorious witch pricker John Kincaid arrived in town, all the accused confessed.[12]

Agnes Spark, one of the first accused, had already faced public disgrace once before. She'd been paraded through town by her husband while wearing a scold's bridle,[13] her punishment for being a nagging wife. She's the perfect example of a quarrelsome dame who was disliked locally for being a woman with too much to say for herself—the type of person upon whom suspicion would naturally fall during times of strife.

Another woman accused in this group was Isobel Shyrie, an older woman who relied on the charity of the church to survive. When taxes were reintroduced after the English forces' withdrawal, a bailie, George

---

11 Any scandals would have sufficed to attract an accusation. Literally, "any scandals": Judith found this wording in the village archives of Inverarity, Angus. Women were accused of the following acts of witchcraft between 1661 and 1662 in Forfar: being beautiful; digging up a dead baby to eat in a pie to give themselves special, demonic powers; using cantrips (spells) and charms; cursing a cow so it no longer gives milk; cursing people to become ill or die. This list is by no means exhaustive.

12 See the chapter on witch pricking for a fuller picture of what this entailed and Kincaid's part in it.

13 A kind of iron face mask that functioned as a muzzle and was used for public humiliation. Sometimes also called a witch's bridle or a gossip's bridle.

Wood, demanded payment from Isobel. When she couldn't pay up, he took literally the only thing she owned—a cooking pot.[14] He would not relinquish the pot until he had his money. When Wood died some days later, Isobel was accused of witchcraft; people believed she'd cursed him in revenge.

As we see the number of accused begin to snowball, it's important to note that the community at the time would've believed no witch worked alone. Witches were said to operate as a coven of at least thirteen people, so the villagers would've always suspected another witch just around the corner.

Many of Forfar's accusations revolved around a woman named Helen Guthrie. Although she lived a tragic life, it sounds like it would've been difficult to have sympathy for her had you met her. She was socially problematic and roundly disliked by her whole community. Her role was central to the case, as it was her testimony that implicated so many of the other accused witches.

"I don't believe I would have liked her," said Judith. "It would be so easy to try and claim her as some sort of feminist hero, but she isn't."[15]

It seems Helen had accidentally fatally injured her sister as a child and, quite understandably, had never recovered from the tragedy. Her mother refused to forgive her, even on her deathbed, which perhaps hardened Helen into a difficult, cantankerous person who drank too much and caused a nuisance in the town.

---

14 She literally didn't have a pot to piss in. The origins of this phrase lie in the fact that the poor sometimes sold their urine to tanneries, so you must be truly poor if you didn't even have this means of making money. See also the phrase "piss-poor."

15 This is where we sometimes see the modern reclamation go awry—see, for example, the T-shirt slogan "We are the granddaughters of the women you couldn't burn." As well as being temporally wrong, this theory doesn't bear much scrutiny.

In today's terms, we would see Helen as someone who had experienced trauma as a young girl and would hopefully have some understanding for her anger and self-harm. However, in the early 1660s, all her issues were much more clearly linked to the Devil.

The number of accused only continued to grow. At this time in Forfar, there were approximately one thousand people living in town and another two thousand people spread out over the surrounding countryside.[16] A shocking fifty-two people ended up being accused, a significant percentage of the local population.

"Following the extraction of the confession, the town leaders would send for a commission to take the case further," explained Judith. "A commission wasn't merely a piece of paper; it was also a body of people—magistrates, bailies, and so on—who would then be involved in the case. A delegation, or sometimes an individual, would be dispatched by horse to Edinburgh to go to the Privy Council."

The Privy Council,[17] based out of Edinburgh, was in place from around 1490 until the start of the eighteenth century. It was created to advise the Scottish monarch and was heavily involved in the general running of Scotland, overseeing administration of the law in the kingdom and various other aspects of Scottish life, including dealing with outbreaks of the plague, regulating shipping and trade, banishing gypsies and beggars, tackling criminality in the further reaches of Scotland, and—crucially for our interests—managing witch epidemics.

Once at the Privy Council, the delegation would appeal to seek a commission so they could proceed to trial back home. The details of their case would be laid out, and they would communicate that a confession had been secured. Usually, the commission would name

---

16 These days, Forfar town's population is nearer thirteen to fifteen thousand.

17 We told you we'd come back to this!

only one or two accused, but this wasn't always the case; sometimes special circumstances were granted for a specified number of accused to be tried along with "others," allowing for a broader number. This effectively meant that anyone problematic could be swept up in the trial.

Meanwhile, back in Forfar in 1661–2, the accused were held in custody, awaiting their fate.

As neither the Privy Council nor the local court contributed anything financially, the family of the accused often had to pay for aspects of the trial such as paper, tobacco, and food and drink for the guards and questioners.

Life was hard for ordinary people at this time. In the latter half of the sixteenth century, the traditional wool trade declined; in response, Scotland increased its exports of salt, herring, and coal, all of which were hard, dirty, and dangerous industries. There were also numerous famines and outbreaks of plague. These factors meant that money was frequently tight.

If the accused's family couldn't afford to pay the costs of the imprisonment and interrogation, the debt would fall on the town council, and most likely the local burgesses would organize the payment. A burgess was something akin to a police commissioner, as besides handling money, they also had quasi-legal power. They had the power to arrest and were allowed to sit on a commission. Usually, they would've gained the position through having money and connections and by being voted in by their peers (though occasionally the position was hereditary). Judith said, "Burgesses received certain privileges in exchange for promising to protect the burgh and further its economic interests. It's likely that the position's clout and prestige

How to Accuse a Witch

would be why people did it. The guards [of the prison], however, were paid a salary in various areas as it was more of a regular job. The costs of the holding of the accused and their time in custody was listed in the accounts."

This is one of the areas that Judith studies to help her uncover new cases. She says she follows the money and finds that it's often these scrupulously kept parish financial records that reveal who was imprisoned and executed and when.[18] It's these financial accounts that have provided Judith with so much information about the logistic aspects of the trials.

And what of these trials? Once the commission has been arranged and the trial agreed upon, how did it actually proceed?

Generally, a minimum of five people was needed to be considered a commission. However, in the case of Helen Guthrie in Forfar in December 1662, thirty men sat on the commission. It seems all the men of status in town wanted to be involved in this high-profile case.

Judith explained, "People wanted their name put to it because they very much believed they were doing the Lord's work, and they wanted the world to know. Of course, being seen to be involved in ridding Scotland of witches would also help them curry favor from those in power—hopefully even the king."

Certainly, in this case, their work was very successful. In total, twenty-two witches were strangled and burned in Forfar, including Helen, who was the last woman to be executed in the town. Her thirteen-year-old daughter, Janet, who had also been accused, managed

---

18 In contrast, recordkeeping of confessions and court happenings is rare, and those that survived are usually incomplete or damaged. We believe in some cases records were deliberately destroyed to cover up what had become an embarrassment once the witch trials ended.

to escape the death sentence but was kept in prison for four more years. Her final fate is unknown.

As we've seen, more often than not, the witches' confessions led directly to their executions. The obvious question is how were these incriminating confessions extracted?

Enter the witch pricker.

7

How to Prick a Witch

In Scottish parishes and towns in the early modern period, two men held much of the authority in the local area.

The first was the magistrate, the man who would deal with prosaic crimes and misdemeanors such as poaching or fighting. The second, the minister, would uphold the spiritual and moral values of the parish, ensuring his flock toed the line.

However, there was another man who people feared much, much more than the magistrate or the minister. He would sweep into town and send the populace into an immediate and febrile state of fear.

Had you offended someone or acted suspiciously? Had you a reputation for being awkward in the marketplace or for scolding your husband? Did you drink too much or beg too often?

With this man in town, would you find the finger of suspicion pointing in your direction, and ultimately, would you pay with your life?

The witch pricker had arrived, and his power was absolute.

One of the most unsettling features of the witch trials was how guilt was "proved" by searching for and (almost always) finding the Devil's mark somewhere on the accused's body. People viewed this evidence the same way as we view DNA today, in that it was believed to be compelling proof of guilt. The idea of sin showing up physically on the body goes back to ancient times: you see it in medieval descriptions of "leprous" skin and in beliefs that warts and other skin irregularities were outward signs of evil. When Anne Boleyn was executed, there was much discussion about how many warts she had, and rumors abounded she had an extra finger (a certain sign of witchcraft). The prevailing belief was that God created us, and we were made in His perfect image; thus, if a person had a nonperfect body, it was a clear sign they'd been touched by the Devil.

If there was an inherent sexism in these judgments—with men inspecting women's bodies and finding them wanting—there were also issues of class and privilege at work. People of a better class had more nutritious diets and healthier lifestyles and would be less likely to suffer physical impairments than the lower classes, whose poor diet, sanitation, and working conditions would show in their physical health. Either way, for anyone whose body displayed any scars, calluses, unusual moles, extra nipples, or other "deformities," there was much to fear.

The concept of the Devil's marks was first seen in the sixteenth century and was taken up very enthusiastically in Scotland—much more so than in other countries. We would argue this is because different religions had different concepts of where witchcraft came from. In Catholic countries, witchcraft was believed to be a result of heresy; the Protestant Church of Scotland, on the other hand, was particularly obsessed with the Devil's relation to witches.

Certainly, the idea was strongly endorsed by King James VI, which only added to its popularity. When his book *Daemonologie* was published in 1597, one of its most compelling aspects was its description of how the Devil took people into his employ. James described the Devil performing a reverse baptism whereby the person would renounce their Christianity, and the Devil would make his mark on their body, an indelible sore only he could cause or heal:

> At which time, before he proceede any further with them, he first perswades them to addict themselves to his service: which being easely obteined, he then discovers what he is unto them: makes them to renunce their God and Baptisme directlie, and gives them his marke upon some secreit place of their bodie, which remaines soare unhealed, while his next meeting with them, and thereafter ever insensible, how soever it be nipped or pricked by any, as is dailie proved, to give them a proofe thereby, that as in that doing, hee could hurte and heale them; so all their ill and well doing thereafter, must depende upon him.
>
> JAMES VI, *DAEMONOLOGIE*, BOOK 2, CHAPTER 2

Given the Devil's mark's importance to the witch accusations and trial proceedings, it's unsurprising that a profession soon evolved to facilitate the search for it. A handful of individuals—known as "witchfinders" or "witch prickers"—were believed to have the power to identify and confirm the guilt of the accused. It's generally held that the role of witch prickers is largely responsible for the exponential growth in prosecutions and executions in Scotland and England during the seventeenth century.

Matthew Hopkins was born in England around 1620, and his demeanor and attitude embody how we think of a witchfinder today. Born in Suffolk, he was the son of a Puritan minister and thus had some childhood training in speechmaking and using the Bible to prove a point. Many thought he was a lawyer due to his writing and verbal prowess, but there's no evidence he ever trained as one. He must have spotted a gap in the market, given the demand for witch prickers at the time, and realized he could use his skills to make some serious money. His career really took off during the English Civil War; although he wasn't actually appointed by Parliament, he proclaimed himself the "witchfinder general" (a neat bit of early self-marketing) and proceeded to oversee an extraordinary fanatical witch hunt in East Anglia.

It's thought that over the three years of his witch-finding career (1644 to 1647), Hopkins was responsible for more witchcraft hangings than all the previous trials of the preceding century and a half—hundreds, in fact. It's Hopkins and his colleague John Stearne who are portrayed in the '60s cult classic film *Witchfinder General*, where they are shown sweeping into town and fashioning a reign of terror for their own ends.[1] Critic Adam Scovell, in an article marking the fiftieth anniversary of the film, described Hopkins and Stearne's behavior as "weaponized belief," in reference to how the prickers created such an atmosphere of fear among the communities they visited.

But paradoxically, they were seen as necessary for a stable society—how better to maintain order than by having a strong authority figure who can identify individuals working against the common good and rid society of their evil presence? All this while making a pretty penny

---

[1] Like Hopkins, John Stearne had grown up in rural Sussex. A staunch Puritan and a man of action, he was a decade older than Hopkins, and after the two met in Manningtree in Essex in 1645, they realized their future lay in collaboration. After Hopkins's death in 1647, Stearne retired and wrote a book called *A Confirmation and Discovery of Witchcraft* (1648).

How to Prick a Witch

too: the records at Stowmarket in Suffolk reveal Hopkins and Stearne charged the town £23 (equivalent to around £5,000 or $6,200 today) plus traveling expenses in exchange for their services.

When Hopkins was hired for a case, he and his assistants would begin their inspection by looking for the Devil's marks. The accused's body would be shaved and examined thoroughly. If the suspected witch had no visible marks, invisible ones could be discovered by pricking the skin (often called "brodding" in Scotland). The witchfinder would employ specialist "witch prickers"—instruments such as needles or sometimes knives—to pierce the accused's flesh. It was thought that a witch would have an area on her body that would not bleed—either because it was the place where the Devil had kissed her to seal their pact or because it was the spot where she suckled her familiars.[2] Whatever the reason, if the skin did not bleed after it had been pricked, this was "proof" of her guilt.

Hopkins is believed to have had a trick to help ensure success with this aspect of his craft: supposedly, he owned a special pin whose blade retracted into the handle when it met resistance. These "false bodkins" looked to all intents and purposes like the real things but could be used by unscrupulous witch prickers to "prove" the existence of a witch and collect their pay.[3]

---

[2] Here we see differing folkloric traditions to explain the same idea. Magic is the opposite of the bureaucratic process: it has no rules and regulations. Explanations and stories change and change again.

[3] We have tried in vain to find surviving bodkins, but there seem to be none in any public museums in Scotland. However, we were saddened to discover there are some people who make a hobby of collecting instruments of torture for their own private collections. We do not approve of this and think they should be held by bona fide museums just as ephemera from, say, concentration camps or notorious murders should be. They are historical artefacts and should not be used as entertainment or for commercial gain.

We spoke with Scottish historian and writer Mary Craig to see what light she could shed on the practice of witch pricking. Mary, a former Carnegie scholar, has written extensively about the history of Northern Europe from Mata Hari to Anne Frank. She also has a wry sense of humor and a gift for describing history in vivid, realistic terms. It was Mary who introduced us to the concept of "quarrelsome dames" and how this could be considered one of the first "tests" of being a witch. Mary herself would no doubt have been seen as a quarrelsome dame had she been alive in the seventeenth century, and we mean this as the highest of compliments.[4]

Surely, we suggested, pricking had a sexual element to it? After all, the accused were stripped naked, their heads shaved (thereby reducing their femininity), and searched in their most intimate areas by the men of their community (usually led by the minister) in an act almost guaranteed to prove them guilty of sin.

Mary nodded and drew the contrast between Witchfinder General Matthew Hopkins and his assistant John Stearne.

"John Stearne was a devout, religious man. He was terrified by the Devil, and he was out to find witches and condemn them to death. Matthew Hopkins was a sexual pervert who went about grabbing young girls and making as much money as he could. Matthew Hopkins didn't give a monkey's. John Stearne is mainly remembered only for the fact that in 1648, he wrote a book called *A Confirmation and Discovery of Witchcraft*. But Hopkins was great at self-promotion and called himself the Witchfinder General, so he has made a far greater impact on the public consciousness."

Hopkins was very young to have had such influence (he was

---

4   We would describe ourselves thus too, as anyone who listens to the podcast will know.

twenty-four when he began his witch-finding career) and was only around twenty-seven years old when he died. So could we view him as a seventeenth-century equivalent of the toxic male influencers of the twenty-first century?

"Yes," Mary answered. "Matthew Hopkins was having a great time to himself.[5] At the time, people genuinely were frightened of the Devil and were trying to find his handmaidens. But it's a system where anybody could just pitch up and say, 'I'm a witch pricker, and by the way, get your kit off so I can run my hands all over your body.'"

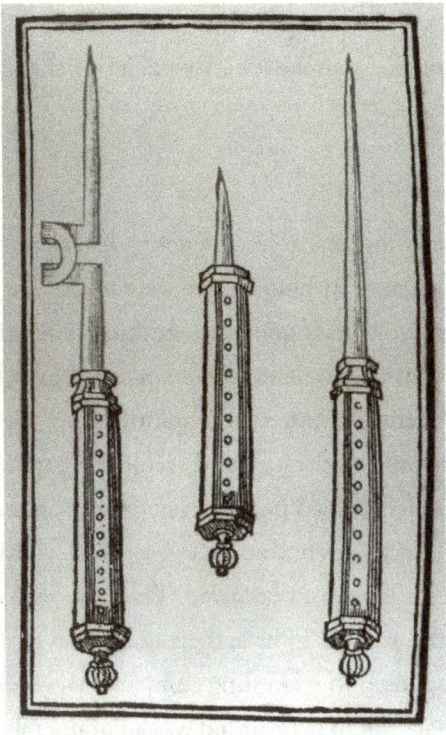

Engraving of retractable bodkins, from *The Discoverie of Witch-Craft* by Reginald Scot, 1584

---

5 Scots phrase meaning he was enjoying himself.

There *were* genuinely religious witch prickers who fervently believed they were doing the Lord's work. But others were driven by money and power and still others by sexual appetite or even sadism. Some will no doubt have been driven by a combination of all factors.

Money was certainly a corrupting influence. Because prickers were paid by the head, there was nothing to discourage the unscrupulous from deliberately inflating the numbers of those found guilty. Whatever the outcome, they would always be paid: their evidence was essential for the Privy Council to proceed legally. There was also that implicit threat that if the pricker wasn't paid, then the community would be at risk. Who's to say the next person to be accused of witchcraft (by an angry, unpaid pricker) wouldn't be…you? It was the ultimate racket.

We were curious how the role of witch prickers compared between England and Scotland. Although there were prickers in Scotland, there didn't seem to be anyone of quite the enduring reputation as Hopkins. The nearest Scottish equivalent was a man called John Kincaid, but he was quite a different creature from Hopkins.

In Scotland, more moderate and therefore perhaps more scrupulous prickers (or brodders) would put their hands only on the accused's head and neck, as that was where they believed the Devil would touch you or where the reverse baptism occurred. There are records that Kincaid would ask for the accused to have their heads shaved and their shoulders bared, as opposed to requesting complete nakedness.

However, that's not to say Kincaid was an honorable man. He made a great deal of money from his "profession." Very little is known about his background, but it appears he was illiterate, as any surviving records with which he was involved bear only his mark or initials. Literacy aside, Kincaid was obviously a compelling pricker. Over his career, he was involved in anywhere between 150 and 200 executions. During the height of popularity for witch prickers between 1648 and 1662, Kincaid was personally involved in two major surges (1649 to 1650 and 1661 to 1662).

Kincaid was based mostly in Tranent in East Lothian. Born somewhere between 1590 and 1600, he was already well into middle age when he first surfaces in the records in 1649, and evidence suggests he was already firmly established within his trade by that point. In June of that year, Kincaid was called to Dirleton Castle in North Berwick to investigate the accusations made against Patrick Watson and his wife, Menie Halliburton. It was the couple themselves who had requested Kincaid's presence to prick them, on the assumption that he was doing God's work and would therefore know they were innocent. Tragically, Kincaid announced he had found the Devil's marks on the couple, and when he pricked them, no blood appeared. Watson was executed, closely followed by Halliburton, who confessed to acts of witchcraft and to having sex with the Devil. Having been through questioning and a witness to her husband's execution, it's likely Halliburton was a broken woman; her "confession" then doesn't surprise us.

Kincaid mainly worked in the Lothian area, but he would travel as far north as Aberdeen when requested by magistrates. He has been identified brodding as far south as Newcastle, where he earned twenty shillings for every witch he identified. That significant a rate of pay would surely encourage prickers to find more witches, and Kincaid took every advantage of it. Records indicate that when he worked for the parish of Dunfermline, his accommodation costs were completely covered, and he was given a fee of twenty merks[6]

---

6 A merk was a silver coin that was worth two thirds of a Scottish pound. It comes from the word *mark*, the name given to the currency of several medieval European countries.

to work the case of one Bessie Mourton, who was found guilty and executed. He was paid by the Burncastle Estate for his role in the trial of a woman called Margaret Dunholm, who lived on the Scottish Borders and was also executed—£6, plus another £3 for food and wine for him and his assistant. It was nice work if you could get it.[7]

Fast-forward to 1659, and we come across the trial of Barbara Cochrane in Kincaid's hometown of Tranent. Kincaid found two marks on her back near her left shoulder. The marks didn't respond to his brodding, and Barbara was found guilty. It's said that when Kincaid declared her guilt, Barbara cried out, "Foul thief! Thou has deceived me!" Whether this recrimination was directed at Kincaid (to whom it's speculated she paid a sum of money) or at the Devil for forsaking her in her hour of need, we'll never know.

In 1659 Scotland, thirty-eight people were executed for witchcraft, nearly half of whom were in East Lothian—with Kincaid recorded as the pricker in many of these cases.

Still, Kincaid's work continued. Two years later, Beatrix Leslie, a midwife in her eighties from Newbattle in Midlothian, was accused of malefice and witchcraft. Two girls had died in a coal-pit accident after arguing with Beatrix over the killing of a cat; fingers naturally pointed at the old woman. Kincaid was called in to prick Beatrix, and as the case involved the death of two children, he also performed a peculiar practice called "bierricht" to assess her guilt.[8] This ancient ritual involved the accused being forced to touch the body of their

---

[7] It should be noted that Kincaid worked the Newcastle, Dunfermline, and Burncastle cases all in the same year as the Dirleton case.

[8] This is alternately spelled "bier-right," a bier being the name for the stand that carried a corpse or a coffin. The practice was also known as "cruentation" from the Latin word *cruentare*, meaning "to make bloody."

alleged victim. It was believed a corpse was still sentient for a short time after death, so when the murderer made contact, it would bleed or froth at the mouth. The girls' bodies supposedly bled when Beatrix was brought to them, and she was found guilty and executed on September 3, 1661.

In fact, 1661 was a busy year for Kincaid; he identified so many witches in Forfar, Angus (in the trials we discussed in the previous chapter), that he was given the freedom of the burgh as a reward, a prize that meant he could trade freely and thereafter held a more elevated position in the town.

Although Kincaid enjoyed a long period of prosperity and public approval, the tide turned on January 9, 1662, when the Privy Council received an application for his arrest. It seems the council had grown concerned about the lack of supervision in witchcraft trials, and word of Kincaid's abuses had reached their ears. This did not reflect well on them. By now an old man of sixty or seventy, Kincaid was imprisoned in the Old Tolbooth in Edinburgh, where he admitted he had not only been using deception when pricking for the Devil's marks but had also been practicing—almost more problematically from the authorities' point of view—without a Privy Council warrant. The official report submitted to the Privy Council concluded that Kincaid had strayed from his original religious fervor into cruelty and had harmed many innocents, stating, "There hath bein great abuses committed by John Kincaid."

After some time, incarcerated but not having been formally charged, the elderly Kincaid petitioned for his release. Upon posting a bail of £1,000 (equivalent to approximately £50,000 or $62,000 these days), Kincaid was released on the condition that he agreed not to work again without a warrant. However, seeing as he could afford such a huge bail fee, it seems he'd already made his fortune.

Despite the obvious miscarriage of justice that had occurred, there are no records of any appeals or releases for cases founded on his questionable evidence. Kincaid slipped back into historical obscurity, though his name does appear once more, in the records of a witch trial in 1690, where it's posthumously invoked as a threat. His reputation clearly left a long shadow in Scotland.

Not all prickers were men. Scotland's other most notorious brodder, Christian Caddell, was a woman, most likely in her late twenties or early thirties. In the early 1660s, Scotland was in such a frenzy over witch activity that work in witch finding was readily available for those who wanted it. It's believed Caddell was inspired to take on the profession when she saw Kincaid at work in Newburgh, Fife.[9] She may even have started off as his assistant.

Why would a woman want to do this work? The financial incentive was surely one reason—what other way could a woman earn such riches in this period? But also, witch pricking offered a certain amount of security in a febrile society. If you were the one pointing the finger at someone else, you were much less likely to be accused yourself. Arguably and ignoring the moral dubiety, it was pragmatic and even clever of Caddell to pursue this career. She was able to keep herself safe while making a very decent living out of others' misfortune.

There are, as it was with Kincaid, scant records of Caddell's career. What we do know is that she turned up in Elgin in March 1662, disguised as a man and calling herself John Dick or John Dickson. It appears no one knew she was a woman; after all, witch pricking was

---

9   This seems to be a story that has been passed down through oral history, as we've found no written record or evidence for it.

man's work. She'd been contracted by a John Innes, the bailie of Spynie in Moray. Innes signed Caddell/Dickson up for a year, where she was to be paid a generous daily rate of six shillings with a further six shillings per identified witch. Men in those days earned an average of about a shilling a day, so Caddell/Dickson was doing very well for herself. Not surprisingly, she "found" a great many witches. It's thought that Caddell identified perhaps the most famous of the Scottish witches, Isobel Gowdie, who was accused in Nairn in 1662. (We will come to her story in chapter 9.)

Caddell came close to exposure when she pricked a court messenger called John Hay in Tain. Hay's prestigious job bore the royal seal and, worse for Caddell, he had some legal knowledge and influence that he used to petition the government for his pricker's arrest. In his petition, he described his treatment: "Ane cheating fellow, named John Dick, to fix ane blott of perpetural infamie upon the petitioner by shaving all the parts of his body, and ther after pricking him to the great effusion of his blood and with much torture to his body."

There are no further records about what happened to Hay, although we are hopeful that due to his standing, he was not condemned. Caddell herself seems to have moved on elsewhere, despite her arrest warrant, and continued to ply her trade. In June 1662, she was working in Strathglass in the Northwest Highlands, where a commission had just been issued for the so-called Strathglass witches. It was this case that would prove her undoing.

The accusations were cynical and corrupt from the start. It seems a Strathglass landowner named Alexander Chisholm had formulated a plan to clear his land of a local tenant family called the Macleans, who'd been living there peacefully for the past two centuries. Chisholm contrived to have a group of Macleans charged and questioned; the accused, fourteen women and one man, were taken to the church at Wardlaw. There, Caddell, now using the name James Paterson (a.k.a.

Paterson the Pricker), shaved their heads in the churchyard, hid the hair in a stone dyke (a wall built from stones),[10] and set to work.

In the words of the minister of the Wardlaw church, Reverend James Fraser:

> There came then to Inverness one Mr Paterson who had run over the kingdom for trial of witches, and was ordinarily called the Pricker, because his way of trial was with a long brass pin. Stripping them naked, he alleged that the spell spot was seen and discovered. After rubbing over the whole body with his palms, he slipt in the pin, and, it seems, with shame and feare being dasht, they felt it not, but he left it in the flesh, deep to the head, and desired them to find and take it out.

A contemporary witness noted the accused were horribly tortured:

> ...by waking, hanging them up by the thombes, burning the soles of their feet at the fyre, drawing of others at horse tails and binding of them with widdies about the neck and feet and carrying them so alongst on horseback to prison, whereby and by other tortur one of them hath become distracted, another by their cruelt is departed this lyfe, and all of them have confest whatever they were pleasit to demand of them.

Faced with this torture, no wonder all the accused confessed. The Privy Council, satisfied with the confessions, deemed Chisholm's

---

10 Why was the hair hidden in the dyke? Perhaps it was to do with the old superstition whereby people would put bones, shoes, and bottles of urine in the walls of their homes to protect from witchcraft, the idea being that the witch would become distracted and would focus on the items rather than the inhabitants. Or maybe it was just an extra layer of humiliation and dehumanization.

application secure enough to award a commission to him, along with his brother and cousins, so they could conduct a trial.

However, the husband of one of the accused had the wherewithal to approach Sir Allan Maclean of Duart, a Maclean clan chief, who managed to convince the Privy Council that Chisholm was using the witchcraft accusations as a nonlegal means to remove his tenants. Finally, in October 1662, the Privy Council saw sense and sent a notary named John Neilson to examine the accused for evidence of torture. Neilson didn't end up asking the accused directly if they'd been tortured, and in a perhaps more unsettling turn of events, Caddell was allowed to stand at the door of the cell and watch the proceedings.

Nevertheless, Neilson must've had his suspicions; the accused were set free (though tragically, it seems some members of the Maclean family died while in custody). Caddell was arrested and sent to the Old Tolbooth in Edinburgh. There—surprise!—it was discovered that Paterson/Dickson/Dick was actually Miss Christian Caddell. One can only imagine how this revelation was received by the local grandees, who had unknowingly been trusting a mere woman to do their work for so long.

Caddell—presumably grasping at straws to save herself—then bizarrely claimed she had the power to detect witches by looking into their eyes. But this time, she was not believed. Her reign as Scotland's most notorious witch pricker had finally come to an end.

Unlike her victims, Caddell was not executed. Her punishment instead was to be transported to Barbados as an indentured servant. She would travel on the ship the *Mary of Leith*, where she would be held with a number of other convicts.

During her brief spell as a witch pricker, Caddell had become a rich woman. She was also responsible for the deaths of at least six innocent people, although it's suspected she was involved in at least ten convictions.

In a final, haunting coincidence, it's likely that on the day Caddell set sail, May 4, 1663, her two final victims, Isobel Elder and Isobel Simpson from Forres in the north of Scotland, were strangled and their bodies burned.

We wondered if it was clear to anyone that Caddell wasn't a man under her disguise or if it was a genuine shock when she was revealed as a fraudster woman.

"I think it was a case of the emperor's new clothes," said Mary. "Because would you want to take the risk of saying she [Caddell] was actually a woman? What if you were wrong? Or what if, in fact, you were then accused of being a witch for suggesting such a thing?"

As we have found again and again, the fear that ruled the land through the early modern period meant that many people kept their heads down and turned a blind eye to things that seemed wrong. It was an atmosphere perhaps akin to the days of postwar East Germany, when children were encouraged at school to report their own parents for misdeeds. The Maclean case encapsulates the terrible dangers of people capitalizing (literally) on fear. It's the clearest example we've come across of how witch accusations could be used completely immorally as a cover for personal gain, from the appalling greed of Chisholm to the horrific sadism of Caddell.

Given the degree of her fraudulence, not to mention the severity of her crimes in sending innocent people to death, how was it that Caddell got off so lightly after she was exposed? Mary thinks the reason is far from clear. "I find it really weird that Caddell wasn't executed," she said.

Claire speculates that perhaps because so much of Caddell's work had utilized the legal structures of the day, her exposure intrinsically undermined the whole system. How could the powers that be admit to her crimes after they'd been occurring for so long with their approval and without her being apprehended? Sending Caddell abroad meant the Privy Council could avoid the inevitably notorious show trial where it would be revealed that a woman (a woman!) had extremely publicly pulled the wool over the eyes of various magistrates and ministers and other men of good standing. Caddell had deceived the highest courts in the land and brought about the unlawful deaths of many people. Much simpler to just ship her off abroad where she would disappear from the sight and imagination of the Scottish public.

"That ties in with my theory about John Kincaid," said Mary. "He was just arrested and quietly released."

We considered how easy it was for Caddell to fool the Privy Council. After all, there were no formal qualifications for witch prickers.

"There are stories in parish records that witch prickers just appeared," said Mary. "You know, like Davy from the end of the street. So when John Kincaid first got going, he just started witch pricking before he had a warrant from the Privy Council. It was only when he started doing it and people said, 'Oh, he's really good,' that he started to get a reputation and approval from the Privy Council."

In the end, all these great men had been taken in by Caddell's self-assurance, ironically a trait more often associated with men than women. There must've been a certain element of showmanship to the pricker's art. People thought Matthew Hopkins was a lawyer because he spoke so well, though he very much was not. This type of confidence goes a long way—if you act like you're right, people will generally believe you, even without evidence. We need only to look at recent British and American politicians to see how this confidence trick continues to work.

It was all rather embarrassing. Much better to deal with the issue swiftly and quietly. The less said, the better.

In his book *Witch-Hunting in Scotland: Law, Politics and Religion*, historian Brian Levack argues that the Privy Council's decision to lock up Kincaid in 1662 for fraudulent and deceptive practices was a tipping point for the ending of the 1661 to 1662 witch hunts. Caddell's arrest the same year no doubt also played a part.

It seemed that the dark art of witch pricking was finally coming to an end, though the witch hunts themselves were still going strong, both in Scotland and abroad. In fact, across the Atlantic in America, a small town in Massachusetts was about to become the center of the most famous witch panic of all.

PORTRAIT OF THE ACCUSED

Tituba

SALEM, 1692

Tituba was the first woman to be accused of witchcraft during the witch trials in Salem, Massachusetts, in 1692. Our knowledge of Tituba is limited; what we do know is that she was an enslaved person, likely of Native American descent.[1] She'd worked on a plantation in Barbados, owned by a wealthy man named Samuel Parris, until he brought her to Salem when she was a teenager. In 1692, Parris became the Puritan minister of Salem Village.[2]

---

1. Tituba was described as "Indian" fifteen times in the court papers, although over time, she became Black in the public imagination. In 1952, the playwright Arthur Miller described her as a "Negro slave" when he wrote his account of the Salem witch trials, *The Crucible*. In reality, she may have been a native of South America, or she may have been brought from Barbados and therefore have had African roots. No one really knows.

2. Puritans were originally English Protestants committed to "purifying" the Church of England by ridding it of any practices they considered to be tinged with Catholicism—essentially, they believed the Reformation hadn't gone far enough. Salem had been colonized by Puritan settlers in 1626; they named the location Salem after Jerusalem, meaning "city of peace."

The trouble for Tituba started when Parris's daughter Betty and her cousin Abigail Williams (age nine and eleven, respectively) decided to play at fortune-telling, a popular pastime in Salem at that point but very much against Puritan rules. This had nothing to do with witchcraft and, more importantly, nothing to do with Tituba. The girls dropped an egg white into water and watched the shape the white took in the liquid; whatever it became would allow them to divine what was going to happen in the future. Unfortunately, what the children saw was the shape of a coffin. Immediately, the girls started barking, behaving hysterically, and having what looked like seizures. These incidents continued to occur over the next month with no medical explanation, so the work of witches became the obvious answer.

Upon questioning, the girls named three vulnerable women: Sarah Osborne, Sarah Good, and Tituba (Tituba had also tried to help the girls by making a "witch cake" out of rye flour and urine). When Parris discovered Tituba's involvement, he was furious, and he beat her to elicit a confession that she was practicing witchcraft. Tituba confessed to a detailed and fantastical number of things, including having familiars (rats, cats, hogs, wolves, dogs, and birds), signing the Devil's book, flying on a stick, and pinching the young girls of Salem. During her confession, she also claimed there were other witches in the town. This was enough to light the fuse of the infamous wave of paranoia and community panic known as the Salem witch trials. In total, over two hundred people were accused and twenty executed, with at least a further five dying in jail.

Tituba's involvement in the witch trials is interesting for several reasons. First, although she was accused of being a witch at least partially because of her ancestry, all her witch descriptions were of a European nature rather than Native American, Caribbean, or African. Second, Tituba was the only accused woman who wasn't white. And third, despite her extraordinary confession, when she finally went to trial fifteen months later, Tituba was not found guilty. Perhaps these last two facts are linked: there has been speculation that the Salem community didn't see witches as anything other than white.

Eventually, the general populace turned against the idea that witches had a stranglehold on Salem, and the governor ordered an end to the trials and accusations. When she was released from jail in 1693, Tituba recanted her confession, revealing Parris had beaten her to make her confess.

Little is known of what happened to Tituba after this, and sadly, as she was enslaved, owned no property, and had no rights and no one to speak for her, she slipped back into the shadows of history.

8

How to Kill a Witch the American Way

Sarah Good, Sarah Osborne, Tituba. The names are so familiar, the Salem witch trials having worked their way into our consciousness over the hundreds of years since the notorious events took place in 1692.

When people think about witch trials, they usually think of what happened in Salem. The common misconception is that this was "the big one"—the most hysterical, brutal, and iconic witch hunt of them all.

But the truth is that the trials in Europe, particularly in Scotland, were larger, more widespread, and bloodier, with much higher death tolls. Thankfully, due to the work of several excellent historians and the debate fired up by our own campaign and podcast—not to mention other small-scale campaigns in Scotland that have been developed since—this preeminence of Salem is at last being questioned.

But Salem was always an unusual case and has thus always attracted attention. In many ways, the Salem witch trials of 1692 were the exception to all the rules of colonial American witch trials. There had been trials of this nature in the English colonies before Salem, where a few people might have been executed, but this was of a different scale—albeit much smaller than the extreme purges of Scotland. Salem was a last gasp of superstition at the dawn of a new era.

What's fascinating about Salem is that these chilling events perfectly encapsulate the result of using a religious "solution" to address social disharmony and anxiety in an attempt to regain control. So while Salem was not a typical case, it's incredibly useful as a tool to illuminate how and why witch trials functioned as they did.

And arguably, Salem is the reason the modern positive reclamation of witches and magic has gained real traction. America took a grim episode in its history and in a way redirected it, both through swift recognition that there had been a miscarriage of justice and through a commercialization of the concept of witches and reframing the narrative.

When we spoke to Rachel Christ-Doane, the director of education for the Salem Witch Museum in Massachusetts, she laughingly told us that the museum frequently has Scottish visitors who are fascinated by Salem but are completely unaware of Scotland's much bigger and deadlier trials. It's clear the witch trials aren't given enough attention in Scottish schools, overshadowed as they are by world wars and the Industrial Revolution. Ask us anything you want about the benefits of farming Cheviot sheep after the Highland Clearances and we could name it. Witch trials? As school kids, we knew nothing. Thankfully, we are now frequently contacted by educators throughout the United Kingdom who are teaching about the witch trials and using our podcast as a resource. We're delighted by this turn of events and believe in the importance of understanding your own country's history, no matter how uncomfortable or fraught.

Yet Salem still exerts a real hold over the witch trial narrative. Why is this? And why are witch trials in general still so relevant in the twenty-first century?

We initially spoke to Rachel via Zoom when she was in her office at the museum. Rachel is a relaxed and warm figure. She brings a modern sensibility to what happened in Salem and what those trials say about human nature, particularly in times of social stress.

The Salem Witch Museum is usually incredibly busy, as is Salem itself. On the day of Halloween, the town, which normally has a population of less than forty-five thousand, welcomes approximately one hundred thousand visitors. Over the course of the year, Salem receives some two million visitors. This kind of tourism is a double-edged sword: it brings in much-needed revenue to the restaurants, bars, and witch-related attractions in the town, but it's also hugely disruptive for residents trying to go about their business. In fact, for many residents of "the Witch City," Salem becomes a no-go zone in October. Part of the issue is that the huge influx of visitors is not entering a custom-built theme park but a small town with a historic infrastructure of tiny streets and not enough parking for tens of thousands of people. Historians and those who know the real story of the trials find the Disneyfication of Salem problematic for their own reasons—they'd prefer (quite rightly, in our opinion) to focus on the miscarriage of justice and the people who lost their lives. Shouldn't the hordes of people descending on Salem for a fun time be more respectful to the accused of three hundred years ago? When over twenty people were unjustly killed?

The Salem Witch Museum is located on the land of the former home of the Reverend John Higginson, who was born in 1616 in England and came to Salem in 1629 with his father, Francis, the first minister of Salem. John Higginson took part in the Salem witch trials when he interviewed a four-year-old child, Dorothy Good, who had been sent to prison. The trials came much closer to home when Higginson's own adult daughter, Ann Dolliver, was accused of witchcraft for using poppets, small wax effigies. She admitted to owning the poppets but denied that she had meant to do any harm. Thankfully, she was released without trial and returned to live with her father.

In 1844, the imposing building that now houses the museum was built as the Second Unitarian Church of Salem. It's a brownstone-and-brick Gothic revival structure, and it remained a fully operational church until 1902. The museum opened in May 1972, its mission to connect the thousands of visitors with the real facts of the case and stimulate conversation about the ongoing issues of othering and justice.

"I've gotten really obsessed with why it's of such interest," said Rachel. "Gretchen Adams has written about how Salem became a 'critical metaphor' in the years after the trials. You so often hear people say, 'This is like the Salem witch trials.'" Adams, in her book, explains how Salem as a metaphor for mass hysteria began almost immediately after the events occurred.[1] Rachel continued, "You see people invoke the metaphor of Salem to criticize events of their time. It happens as early as the 1720s during a smallpox epidemic in Boston, and it happens again and again. We tend to think of Arthur Miller's play *The Crucible* as the first time this critical metaphor is used and, of course, with this play, he's criticizing McCarthyism and the Communist

---

1   See Adams's book, *The Specter of Salem: Remembering the Witch Trials in Nineteenth-Century America* (University of Chicago Press, 2008).

blacklist; American students learn that in high school.[2] But in truth it started much earlier than that."

In fact, during the American Civil War, the Confederates attacked the Unionists in propagandist pamphlets, saying the North should get off their moral high horses about slavery because they were no better: they had burned women at the stake. Although women were rarely killed in this manner (strangulation was by far the most common method of execution), this accusation stuck, becoming the basis for the popular trope of witches being burned alive.

It's all very messy. What did happen in Salem? What do we *really* know?

Let's start with the facts.

It all began in January 1692, when Betty Parris, the nine-year-old daughter of Samuel Parris, the then-minister of Salem, and her cousin, Abigail Williams, who was eleven, both became ill with a mysterious recurring ailment. What we would now likely call seizures struck both girls. They fell to the ground and made sounds that were described as "animal-like"—surely very frightening for the adults around them, who were powerless to stop it. Their families tried praying and fasting to help the girls, but a month later, the seizures were still occurring. A doctor was called in, but he couldn't find any medical explanation for what became to be known as "the affliction," instead suggesting it could be a case of witchcraft. In the late 1600s, just as in Scotland, Salem's inhabitants absolutely believed in the reality of the Devil and his ability to use witches to

---

2   It's also taught frequently in Scotland and partially explains why many Scots know about Salem but not their own connections to witch trials.

do his evil bidding. The townsfolk duly set about trying to identify who the witch was.

Betty and Abigail were questioned; they no doubt felt a certain amount of pressure to respond, perhaps believing this might end their suffering. They may have even enjoyed the attention. They offered three names: Sarah Osborne, Sarah Good, and Tituba. After their naming, these three people grew isolated and vulnerable. Sarah Osborne disgraced herself in the community's eyes after marrying below her station (she'd married a servant); she also hadn't been attending church as frequently as Puritan society demanded. Sarah Good was poor, rude, and aggressive; she would loudly curse those from whom she begged if she felt they were short-changing her.

And then there was the enslaved woman, Tituba, whom we've already met. Tituba was for all intents and purposes at the bottom of the pile in Salem society.

The three women were examined by the community's leaders. Osborne and Good denied any knowledge of witchcraft, but Tituba, for whatever reason, confessed. Moreover, she claimed there were other witches in Salem.[3]

Why did Tituba confess? Possibly because, as an enslaved person, she knew no one would help or defend her; more likely, she was beaten by her master, Samuel Parris, until she said what he wanted to hear. But whatever the reason, with the knowledge that there were other witches at large in Salem, proceedings kicked up a gear.

Rachel explained, "Things start to spiral out of control pretty quickly. Suddenly anybody you've had a problem with, anyone who you've had a border dispute with, anyone you think stole from you

---

[3] We're familiar with this in Scotland. Because the accusers believed there were always more witches, the accused would often give up other people's names, perhaps believing this might make the torture and questioning stop.

twenty years ago or broke social taboos like yelling at your husband publicly—these are the people who start to get targeted."

The Salem Witch Trials, Joseph E. Baker, 1892

Additionally, Salem had lost its charter in 1684. Charters were documents granted by the king of England that gave colonies in America the right to self-govern. If a charter was lost, the king would retake control of the colony. Without a charter, the town's leaders were in a state of flux while they waited to see how their legal system and courts would operate and who would be elected to office. Salem didn't regain its charter until 1692, making for an unsettling period for the townsfolk.

"They were in this weird legal limbo," said Rachel. "Without the charter, they didn't know what their government would look like. Would they have a royally appointed governor? Would they be allowed to appoint their own representatives, which they had been doing up until that point? What would their taxes look like? Would they increase? Would the king take back the land they had tilled and distributed so they would have to start again from scratch? You can see how this would be a period of extreme tension, especially for those ministers who came to Salem to start a city upon a hill where everything would be done right as they're God's chosen people. It really looked like it might all come crashing down."

The Salem ministers were fearful that their great Puritan experiment would not only fail but fail *humiliatingly* on their watch. And then, on top of all the political and religious uncertainty, comes a witchcraft outbreak.

"It's easy for them then to think the Devil has descended on Massachusetts and is waging war on them," said Rachel. "This is what they've been waiting for in some ways. The leaders are in a state of panic."

Although their charter had been newly granted in 1692, Salem's government and courts were still in a transitional period. With so many accused women already being held in custody awaiting their trials, an emergency court was put together to deal with them. Because of the rules of the emergency court, Salem was able to get away with importing some extraordinary legal practices from England and Scotland that were not normally used. The precedent used for the Salem trials was the trial of two English widows, Amy Denny and Rose Cullender, which took place in Bury St. Edmunds in Suffolk in 1662. The trial was presided over by Matthew Hale, later to become the lord chief justice of England.[4] Evidence was heard from several children who said they were attacked and threatened by invisible specters of the women. This was accepted as truth, and the two elderly widows were hanged.

---

4   If the name Matthew Hale is familiar, his opinion that abortion is a great crime was cited in a first draft opinion by Justice Samuel Alito in the case of *Dobbs v. Jackson Women's Health Organization* in 2022, the case that overturned *Roe v. Wade*.

Despite its obvious faults, "spectral evidence" was likewise admitted into the proceedings at Salem, a result of the Bury St. Edmunds precedent. Witnesses claimed both to see the specters of the accused practicing witchcraft and to be attacked by them in their spectral form. Just to be clear: it was accepted as evidence admissible in law for a witness to testify that they had had a dream or a vision of an accused person's spirit tormenting them, even though the accused's physical body was probably elsewhere.

As part of her confession and evidence in court, Tituba described her co-accused as having familiars no one else could see.[5] Other witnesses claimed to have seen the dead in ghost form and said that the ghosts had harassed them. Out of the total of 156 people accused and incarcerated, 79 of them had their charges based on spectral evidence alone.

It's hard for us to understand these days how this ever could have happened. Rachel agrees. "It didn't make sense even in the seventeenth century," she said. "There was discussion about using spectral evidence at the time. There were letters from ministers of the greater Boston area saying, 'We respect the court, but maybe don't use this evidence.'" But the court carried on using it; they had to find guilt where they could.

Bridget Bishop was the first person to be convicted during the Salem witch trials. She was hanged on June 10, 1692, on Gallows Hill in Salem Village. Nine days later, another five people were executed in the same place.[6] On August 19, a further five were executed. This group included George Burroughs, who had been a minister in Salem until 1683 and who recited the Lord's Prayer as he stood at the gallows preparing to meet his maker. As witch-hunt logic held that a real witch

---

5   Sarah Osborne's and Sarah Good's familiars were supposedly a yellow bird and two "grotesque creatures."

6   Included among them was one of the original accused, Sarah Good, who said that she was no more a witch than the judge was a wizard.

would be unable to utter God's word, we imagine this would've been very troubling to the skeptical in the community. But we must go forward, and on September 22, another eight convicted people were hanged. Among them was Martha Corey. Her eighty-one-year-old husband, Giles, having refused to confirm his wife's guilt, was accused of witchcraft himself, then subsequently arrested and pressed to death beneath stones. It took two days for him to die.

Tensions began to form between two groups of magistrates. One side was determined to see due process through to the end; the other side, the more moderate of the magistrates, was beginning to believe that while there may have been witches at one point, the rate at which they were executing meant innocent people were likely being killed as well.

The tide started to turn in October, when Lady Mary Phips, the wife of Sir William Phips, the governor of Massachusetts, was accused of being a witch. She had been named by one of the "victims" using spectral evidence.

The governor, knowing his wife wasn't a witch, finally realized that spectral evidence was unsound and moved to halt the court.[7] It took until the following January to organize a new formal court. Thankfully, this new court agreed that it did not accept spectral evidence. Most people still in custody ended up being acquitted, although a couple of prior guilty verdicts remained. The governor took decisive action, declared them all innocent, and (most) people were released from jail.[8]

---

7 It's funny that it was only when matters were brought to his own door that he finally said, "Wait a minute. Are we absolutely sure we're not killing innocent women?"

8 Though you couldn't leave until you paid your bill! You were charged for everything from food to clothes to chains. Some people, deeply in debt, could not afford to settle up and died innocent in jail.

How to Kill a Witch the American Way

The Salem witch hunt was over, but its story wasn't.

What happened next in Salem is crucial to its place in our popular culture.

As the seventeenth century came to a close, social change was in the air. The survivors started pushing for a public, formal acknowledgment of how badly they'd been treated.[9]

When Elizabeth Proctor was accused and convicted in Salem in 1692, she was pregnant. Her pregnancy saved her, as it was decided her execution would be delayed until after she'd given birth. Her husband, John Proctor, was not so fortunate and was executed. By the time Elizabeth's baby was born, the trials were over, but she was left in a peculiar position. She'd been found guilty of being a witch and thus remained a witch in the eyes of the law. She presented herself to the court and made her case, but there was nothing to be done—she was still legally a witch. Elizabeth knew she'd eventually need a court to fully clear her name; everyone knew that if you'd been found guilty of witchcraft, it was very likely you would be accused again—your name had been tainted within the community. Although she initially got nowhere, other survivors and her remaining family members came forward over the following years, asking for the accused to have their names cleared and to be paid reparations.[10] Collectively, their voices began to be heard.

---

9   This is in direct contrast to Scotland, where we are still campaigning, three hundred years later, for a legal pardon for those found guilty of witchcraft.

10 Since starting our campaign for a pardon in Scotland, some people have accused us of chasing reparations. This would be impossible in Scotland as, unlike in Salem, we cannot prove who the descendants of the victims are.

In Scotland, all the victims of the injustice, alive and dead, were swept under the judicial carpet. But within two decades of the trials in Salem, the government recognized the convictions had been wrongful.

"This was quickly understood to be a miscarriage of justice," said Rachel. "It wasn't just that there had been so many people in jail, but also important men of the colonies were saying, 'This is not right, or at the very least, the evidence used was wrong.'"

The public soon recognized that innocent people had been held because of insubstantial "evidence." Robert Calef's book, *More Wonders of the Invisible World*, was published in 1700 and was the first publication critical of the process of the trials.[11] In fact, the book came out during a ban on publications covering the Salem trials, an order from the governor. We can only guess that the governor had decided the trials were an embarrassment for the town, and everyone needed to move on from them, quickly.

Speaking of the survivors, what of Tituba? Did she ever get justice?

"Tituba was never pardoned because she was never actually convicted," said Rachel. "The only people who received pardons were those that were convicted. Tituba is a really interesting case as she was one of the first accused, and she confesses. Her confession is probably what saves her life because she's an important source of information. She languishes in jail through the whole trial. She was arrested in late February 1692 and not released until the spring of 1693. By the time of her trial, they're no longer using spectral evidence. They've essentially said, 'This whole matter is over and done with.'"

So even though Tituba confessed, she was acquitted at her trial.

"It seems as though Tituba is sold by Samuel Parris for the cost of

---

11 This title was a cheeky response to the famous Puritan minister Cotton Mather's book *Wonders of the Invisible World*, which was a defense of the trials and was published while they were ongoing.

her trial fees," Rachel explained. "But we don't know who she was sold to, and she just disappears. We have no idea where she goes after the trials."

Tituba is interesting to us as she's clearly the "other" in this setting. She's vulnerable and isolated, like the other accused, but her race and culture separated her from the group on such a drastic level.

"Tituba is one of the most fascinating people in the Salem witch trials," Rachel said, "probably partially because of Arthur Miller's portrayal of her in *The Crucible*. That portrayal is very inaccurate, and he doesn't do her justice at all, but he was basing his interpretation off older scholarship. When he was writing, that was the interpretation of her, that she was teaching the girls magic in the woods, and the guilt from [taking part in] the magic was what caused the affliction. We now know that's not substantiated by primary sources, but that was the original interpretation. But because she was one of the important characters in *The Crucible*, she's very well known to people, and she's fascinating because we don't know a lot about people of color from the colonial period. Enslaved people of the colonies lived their lives 'in the margins'; their names were literally often only recounted in the margins of papers, if recounted at all. The reason we know so much about her is because of the Salem witch trials. It's very unusual to hear a voice of a person of color of that time even though the voice is through a filter of the people who believed she was a witch."[12]

In 1711, some people's names were cleared, but this was purely down to certain families pushing for the cause. There were no automatic pardons. Following the American Revolution of 1765 to 1783, the cases were essentially shelved for nearly two hundred years, and it was only during the 1950s that the family of Ann Pudeator,

---

12 Despite the general belief at the time that witches were white, because of her race, Tituba was still considered suspicious.

executed in 1692, demanded formal recognition of her innocence. Finally, in 1957, the Massachusetts General Court declared that "Ann Pudeator and certain other persons" were cleared of all charges. As no other people are named, it took until 2001 (and a great deal of community activism) to clear the names of all but one of those convicted. That one, Elizabeth Johnson, had been missed, most likely because she was neither a wife nor a mother and therefore had no one willing to advocate for her at the time. Her exoneration was finally accomplished in May 2022 when an eighth-grade class in North Andover Middle School learned about her from their teacher, Carrie LaPierre. The students researched the case, realized the continued injustice, and called upon their state senator, Diana DiZoglio, who introduced legislation. Finally, 329 years after Elizabeth's conviction, her name was cleared.

As the bill was passed, Senator DiZoglio said, "Elizabeth's story and struggle continue to greatly resonate today. While we've come a long way since the horrors of the witch trials, women today still all too often find their rights challenged and concerns dismissed."

The schoolchildren's fascination and passion reflect the way the trials continue to capture the public's imagination. And this isn't just a modern phenomenon. People have been visiting Salem since as early as the 1700s. John Adams, the former president of the United States, visited what he called "Witch-hunt Hill" less than a hundred years after the trials.

"It speaks to what we call 'dark tourism,'[13] this fascination with tragedy and the macabre," said Rachel. "People have always been interested in sights of death and calamity. That's why people tour the Colosseum and the Catacombs and prison museums like Alcatraz.

---

13 Naturally, Scotland has a great deal of dark tourism, with all its castles, graveyards, battlefields, body snatching, and queen killing.

People find it fascinating because they are strange and disturbing. Salem held that draw from the beginning. People were coming to Salem and wanted to see where the hangings took place."

The first tourist guidebook to Salem was published in 1880. It instructed the reader not only on where the hangings took place but also where one could view the court documents. Sightseers came to Salem with the rise of train travel and would knock on locals' doors for information on the trials. The Spiritualism movement, so popular at the turn of the twentieth century, added to Salem's appeal, and the town's reputation only grew. In April 1906, Salem's name had become so ubiquitous that Harry Houdini[14] decided to visit, putting on shows of his various feats of escapology.

"Salem tourism kept growing throughout the twentieth century," said Rachel. "When *The Crucible* came out and when the television show *Bewitched* was filmed in Salem in 1970 in an episode where the characters are coming to a witches' convention—both those things upped the ante of interest. In the 1970s, you started to see modern witches moving to Salem like Laurie Cabot, who was very smart about publicity.[15] It all comes together at that time—the Salem Witchcraft Museum was inaugurated in 1972—but it was in the 1980s and '90s that we saw that huge influx of tourism. That was when Salem started holding the Haunted Happenings.[16] Salem is *the* witch reference in pop culture."

---

14 Real name Erik Weisz.

15 Among other things, Laurie Cabot opened the first Witch Shoppe in Salem, which garnered a great deal of national TV coverage.

16 This series of Halloween-themed events was originally held over two days, but now it lasts for the entire month of October.

Salem's story is amazingly well known, or at least *a* story is. As is often the case, with fame and popularity come disinformation, and even today, so much of the Salem witch trials is misunderstood.

Many believe that the accused were ducked in water and that they were burned at the stake. Neither happened. With the exception of Giles Corey, all the "witches" were hanged. And the ducking test was not applied here; instead, the two common tests were having the accused recite the Lord's Prayer (the belief being that the Devil and his consorts could not utter the words) and searching the accused for the Devil's marks, specifically a witch's teat the Devil could suckle from. This had the same inherent issue as the test in Scotland: scars, moles, skin tags, and so on could too easily be described as something evil rather than natural.

Perhaps the most prevalent piece of nonsense about Salem is the idea that the town was suffering from a collective psychedelic trip due to moldy wheat causing ergot poisoning. It's a convenient excuse for the accusers and prosecutors, absolving them from all responsibility, but there's just no evidence for it; researchers are confident that by the seventeenth century, farmers knew how to keep wheat dry and safe. In any event, the Salem accusations weren't a single, isolated incident but rather lasted for over a year between February 1692 and May 1693—far too long a period for no one to notice spoiled wheat.

Hyperbole and disinformation aside, Salem's legacy indirectly led to modern pop culture's embrace of witches, and the twenty-first century has seen a great rise in people (mostly women) identifying as them. Naturally, the modern interpretation of witches is not about gaining power from the Devil or practicing evil magic. The modern witch is generally someone who connects with nature, identifies as a feminist, and uses social media to connect with other witches worldwide. There have been examples of witches working together to try to bring about political change[17] and influence world events,[18] and it's heartening to see these positive connections and new directions. We're delighted to see women owning the word *witch* and deciding on their own definition of the term, and we're equally happy when witches contact and support us. They fully appreciate our distinction that while we support the modern person's right to identify however they wish, in the times of the witch trials (and in modern-day witch accusations), there was no such thing as a witch. As we say in our campaign—they were women, not witches.

Sadly, the reverse side of this positive move is that, of course, there will be some who cling to the old ideas and see themselves as antiwitch. The most obvious proponents of this are (surprise, surprise) right-wing religious types. Or at least people who declare themselves religious but are really just intent on controlling other people.[19] Greg Locke, a modern-day American pastor, has tried to make a name for himself as a worthy opponent of the Devil by, among other things, naming "witches" in his church. He also has a penchant for book burning and has burned so-called demonic novels like *Harry Potter* and *Twilight*. In February 2022, he was recorded addressing witches in a sermon, telling them to get out of the church or he would expose them. He even suggested that people who'd fallen sick in the congregation might've done so because they'd unknowingly befriended a witch.

Right-wing pundits and politicians also occasionally make use of the idea of witches, either to try to stir up a satanic panic (presumably

---

17 Witches once assembled to collectively hex an unpopular, destructive politician in American elections.

18 A group of Argentinian witches called La Brujineta worked twenty-three hours every day during the 2022 World Cup to send healing and protection to their team—who, of course, went on to win.

19 And by "other people," we mean almost exclusively women.

to frighten voters into supporting them) or by claiming themselves to be the victims of "witch hunts." Two of the men most known for using this phrase are Richard Nixon and Donald Trump. We believe that when politicians invoke this idea, usually what they're really objecting to is being held responsible for breaking the law or the code of moral decency. It's laughable nonsense to see a man in power putting himself on equal footing with someone accused of being a witch, facing execution.

The Salem Witch Museum team have gone to great lengths to create thought-provoking exhibits that encourage visitors to think about the causes of the witch hunts and link them to more modern issues.

"The last thing our visitors see as they leave the museum is called our 'witch-hunt wall,' and it's a formula we use to break down former witch hunts," said Rachel. "The formula is fear plus a trigger equals a scapegoat." Fear of the Devil was, in the case of Salem, triggered by a mysterious, incurable ailment that led to 150 people being scapegoated with accusations of witchcraft.

The museum curators also draw parallels with more contemporary American historical occurrences: what happened to Japanese Americans during World War II; the McCarthy hearings and blacklists during the Cold War; the scapegoating of the gay community during the AIDS epidemic in the 1980s. The good news for those who can't make it to the Salem Witch Museum in person is that there's an excellent online tour, which anyone can access—so long as they possess the heretical magic of Wi-Fi.

9

How to Gather Evidence Against a Witch

We know what witches are, how to round them up, how to prick them. But how do you prove their guilt in a court of law? How do you gather all the evidence you need to prosecute a witch? We know from *Daemonologie* that God protects those who hold witches to account, so we need not worry about the Devil interfering in our task, but what kind of proof and evidence are necessary for a trial?

For Claire, a student of the law, this is an endlessly fascinating subject. Let's try to take the superstition out of it (impossible, but even so) and dig deep into the legal system to expose the mechanics that led to the terrible, unjust deaths of thousands of people.

In 1833, a century or so after the final witch trials in Scotland, a man named Robert Pitcairn Esq., a Writer to the Signet,[1] decided to research and preserve details of trials held during the reign of King James VI in a book called *Ancient Criminal Trials in Scotland*. His work gives us excellent insight into the machinery of the trials on a very practical and legal basis.

There's a clear change, one hundred years after these events, in the way Pitcairn thought of witchcraft, apparent from the outset of his writing on the subject:

> AMONG the circumstances which peculiarly characterize the earlier Criminal proceedings...none are more prominent than the unmitigated rigour with which the profession as well as the practice of Witchcraft, Sorcery, and Necromancy, were punished. The hecatombs of innocent victims, whose lives were sacrificed to satisfy the gloomy superstitions of Nations termed Christian and civilized, but who, in reality, were only emerging from a state of semi-barbarism, sufficiently attest the justice of this observation.[2]

Times had certainly moved on. Pitcairn observed that after the Reformation, the countries that had embraced Protestantism were keen to outdo each other with their enthusiasm in "rooting out from the land every vestige of the professors of these works of darkness." As evidence, he cites a memorandum, saying it shows "proof of the nefarious wickedness which must have been perpetrated in Scotland."

---

1 A Writer to the Signet is a lawyer who draws up documents requiring the king's signet, or private seal.

2 Robert Pitcairn, *Ancient Criminal Trials in Scotland*, vol. 3, pt. 2, appendix VII (Edinburgh, 1833). The following quotes from Pitcairn all come from this appendix.

How to Gather Evidence Against a Witch

Those of a sensitive constitution may wish to skip the next couple of paragraphs.

> December 1, 1608,—THE ERLE OF MAR declairit to the COUNSALL, that fum wemen wer tane in Broichtoun, as Witches; and being put to ane Affyfe, and convict, albeit thay perfeverit constant in thair denyell to the end sit thay wer BURNIT QUICK, eftir sic ane crewell maner, that sum of theme deit in despair, renunceand and blasphemeand; and otheris, HALF BRUNT, brak out of the fyre, and wes caft in quick in it agune, quhill thay wer brunt to be deid.

In rough translation: a number of women were tried by baron bailie at Broughton,[3] and despite maintaining their innocence, they were convicted. Some were strangled before being burned, and some were set alight while conscious.[4] While dying, many of them renounced their baptisms and blasphemed. Horrifically, some of them broke out of the fire but were pushed back in to meet their deaths.

It's hard to get your head around this level of barbarity.

From the research Pitcairn conducted, he was able to conclude that only a very small number of the thousands of witchcraft trials were tried before the High Court of Justiciary, which was and is the place where the most serious criminal cases are tried in Scotland. Rather, the majority of trials were tried before either the lords of regality, the baron bailies, or the royal commissioners. These courts don't exist today, although their closest modern-day equivalent is probably the justice of the peace (JP) courts in Scotland, sometimes still described as "bailie courts." JP courts deal with the most minor

---

3 Broughton was at that time near Edinburgh but is now part of the center of the city.

4 We don't know why they weren't all strangled first. Perhaps the sheer numbers?

criminal cases in Scotland and are presided over by lay magistrates. It's strange to think a crime that could result in execution would be dealt with in anything but the highest court in the land, but this was indeed the case.

What begins a witchcraft accusation and prompts consideration of a commission is of course a claim that someone is a witch. This claim either comes from someone who says they've been affected by witchcraft or from a "witch" who, having already confessed to acts of witchcraft, is further prevailed upon to name others as witches. Accusation statements from those who bring the complaint against the witch are essential. The accuser begins their statement by identifying the accused, either by giving their description in writing or by pointing to them in the courtroom. Once the accused has been properly identified, the accuser offers evidence of what they'd done. There are few recordings of the accusations themselves, though most can be ascertained by reading the confessions.

Unlike in the modern trial process, an accused did not have the right to give evidence on their own behalf, although it has been noted in some rare cases. In any event, for most of the accused, because they were women, they wouldn't have been considered competent witnesses anyway.

Once the accusation was made, the next step was a commission. Pitcairn recorded that his research on the commissions took him to the work of Baron David Hume[5]. Hume wrote *Commentaries on the Law of Scotland*—the classical exposition of criminal law. His work is still quoted today by advocates presenting cases and by the court in giving decisions. Hume's work states that in one sitting of the Privy Council on November 7, 1661, "no fewer than fourteen Commissions" for trials of witches were granted for different

---

5   Not to be confused with David Hume the philosopher, Baron Hume's uncle!

quarters of the country. The commissions were a legal document that conferred power to commissioners for both examination and trial. They were granted by the Privy Council, a governing body in Scotland akin to the modern cabinet, which assisted the king in his decision-making.

The requirement of a commission was an attempt to keep some form of control over the wildly enthusiastic prosecution of witches. To obtain a commission, you needed to send a request to the Privy Council, along with some kind of proof to back it up. The bar for the Privy Council to grant your commission was not high, but you still needed to produce at least a modicum of evidence. However, what might have been more off-putting, especially for those in the Highlands of Scotland, would be the time and effort required to have to go to Edinburgh and present the argument for the commission in the first place. One of the potential reasons Scotland's witchcraft trials were more prevalent in the central belt was that it was just more convenient to get a commission if you lived nearby. A horse and rider cost the local jurisdiction time and money, which no doubt could have been spent elsewhere. Witchcraft trials were an expensive business.

On a related topic, Pitcairn explains that the part of the commission where the name of the accused was written had space for more names to be added if other people were later accused. Further, the jurisdiction of the commission—in other words, in which districts the Privy Council granted power for the commission to take place—was broad. This meant that the granting of a commission gave wide power to the commissioner. Pitcairn notes:

> As one unhappy creature was almost universally induced to accuse several others of the same crime for which he or she was to suffer, and as the evidence taken in one trial was held

to be conclusive in other cases, where the pannels[6] were thus proved to be "notour Witches,"[7] it was competent for these Commissioners to try any number of persons, and to "justify them to the death"; a practice which they were by no means slack of performing.

As we know, where you find one witch, you find many, and when one witch confesses, she is pressed to name more, and so on. No wonder they left such a big space for all the extra names that would end up being prosecuted. And usefully for them, once they'd proved the existence of one witch, that "proof" could be used in other trials.

So assuming someone has been granted a commission to examine and try a suspected witch, the next step is the examination. There were two favored forms of this: examining the mind of the accused and examining the body. We've already discussed the work of John Kincaid, the witch pricker extraordinaire, but how did his work become evidence that could be used in a trial? Well, he was required to sign a deposition, now referred to as an affidavit, setting out his expertise and then explaining what he had found. This official court document was used in lieu of Kincaid having to attend court himself and was of great practical importance. That said, he did give evidence in person when it was possible to do so. Who could resist attending a witchcraft trial and showing off their great and godly skills? (With all due humility, of course.)

Here is one of the depositions, translated by us:

---

6   The *pannel* is an old-fashioned word for the accused—some KCs still use the term in some official documents—although debate rages as to whether it is spelled with one *n* or two. No, we don't get out much. Thanks for asking.

7   A short version of the "notorious witches" spoken of in *Newes from Scotland*.

How to Gather Evidence Against a Witch

Deposition of John Kincaid (Witch-finder) relative to the Devil's mark found on Patrick Watson and Menie Halliburton.

At Dirleton, ... of ... [space left where the date would be inserted]. This day in the presence of Alexander Levington of Saltcoats, James Borthwick, chamberlain of Dirleton, John Stalker, baillie there, James Foirman, Drem, Mr James Acheson, in North Berwick, and William Daliell, notary, Patrick Watson of West Fenton and Menie Halliburton, his spouse, harboured and long suspected of witchcraft, of their own free will and uncompelled, hearing that I, John Kincaid, under subscribance, was in the town of Dirleton and had some skill and dexterity in trying of the Devil's mark, in the persons of such as were suspected to be witches, came to the Broadhall, in the Castle of Dirleton, and asked me, the said John Kincaid, to use my trial of them as I have done with others. Which, when I had done, I found the Devil's mark upon the backside of the said Patrick Watson, a little under the point of his left shoulder, and upon the left side of the said Menie Halliburton, on her neck a little above her left shoulder; whereof they were not sensible,[8] neither came forth from there any blood, after I had tried in exactly the same way as I had with any others. This I testify to be the truth, upon my credit[9] and conscience. In witness whereof, I have subscribed this in their presence with him hand, day, and place aforesaid, before the witnesses above specified.[10]

---

8   We think this means that these areas had no sensation.

9   His "credit" perhaps means his credibility.

10 Pitcairn, *Ancient Criminal Trials*.

Such a document would have been used in place of Kincaid giving evidence at trial if necessity meant he was not able to attend—a man who is so busy going around the country finding witches can't be expected to return to every district he's worked in and give evidence. Time is money after all.

While witch prickers were very much believed in the seventeenth century, as time went on, their influence began to wane, and by Pitcairn's time, views had changed so significantly he describes them as "worthless impostors." Using confessions as evidence, however, showed no such decline in favor.

A confession, being a statement against one's self-interest, is powerful evidence against an accused witch. Why would anyone admit to being a witch if they weren't one, knowing it would mean almost certain death? One reason was torture.

In the present day, if a confession was extracted from someone by keeping them awake for days on end and constantly interrogating them, it would be deemed inadmissible in law. The legal system at the time had no such compunction.

While the Privy Council specifically outlawed torture as a means of extracting a confession, it did not recognize sleep deprivation as a form of torture. Only now do we know that it's an incredibly insidious way to create psychological distress and likely to cause people to lose their minds. Such torture, said to have been designed by psychologists (although it could equally have been designed by anyone studying Scottish history), was used by the U.S. government as an "enhanced interrogation" technique at Guantanamo Bay. There's some irony in how studies showed the twenty-first-century technique being equally as bad at procuring reliable information as the sixteenth-century one.

How to Gather Evidence Against a Witch

As was not appreciated in the distant past—but should have been at Guantanamo—any evidence extracted from someone in the throes of sleep deprivation is likely to be completely fantastical, given that their ability to distinguish between reality and imagination would be lost.

Which brings us to arguably Pitcairn's most valuable contribution to historical knowledge of the witchcraft trials: the preservation of the record of the confessions—four in total—of Isobel Gowdie. The confessions of Isobel Gowdie are incredibly detailed, fantastical, and fascinating. Pitcairn calls them "by far the most unique and wonderful in the records of this and perhaps of any other country." We must thank him here for insisting on reproducing these confessions in his book, as his editor was against the idea.[11]

Pitcairn records that on April 13, 1662, in the presence of the "Minister of the Gospell at Aulderne" (modern-day Auldearn, a village in the Highlands), the "Shereffe deput of the shereffdom of Nairne" (the nearby town of Nairn), and nine other local men, the confession was "spoken from the mouth of Isobel Gowdie." She is described as the spouse of John Gilbert, both residing in Lochloy, a small hamlet by the coast. The document is signed on that day, in the presence of the notar public[12] and all the other aforementioned witnesses, and it states that Isobel Gowdie, "appearing penitent for her heinous acts of witchcraft, and that she had been over long in that service; without any compulsion, proceeded in her confession."[13]

---

11 As Pitcairn put it, "The Editor has been induced, in compliance with the repeated desire of literary friends, contrary to his own private opinion, to annex to this work the Confessions of these unhappy women and a few other similar examinations." If you are reading this, our editor has been similarly persuaded.

12 The old term for "notary public"—a qualified lawyer, usually required by folk who want documents validated.

13 This quote has been translated into modern English for ease of understanding.

Quite why this confession required eleven people to witness is not known.

The record notes that there was no compulsion for her to confess, which means she wasn't tortured, at least as torture was understood at the time. (Of course, just because the record *says* no compulsion was used doesn't mean it was true.) Because of this note, we can surmise that should the people hearing the confession know of any cajoling, threating, or any other kind of torture, they would've been less likely to accept it. Why this wasn't also the case for those extracting the confession is not wholly known, other than how their desire to uncover witchery may have superseded anything else.

The following first confession from Isobel Gowdie is the most detailed and lurid confession ever to have been recorded in Scotland. Again, we will summarize into more modern language, but the original is freely available online.

> As I was going between the towns of Drumdewin and the Heads, I met with the Devil, and there covenanted, in a manner, with him. And I promised to meet him in the nighttime in the Kirk of Auldearn, which I did. And the first thing I did there that night was I denied my baptism and I did put one of my hands to the crown of my head and the other to the sole of my foot, and then renounced all betwixt my two hands over to the Devil. He was at the lectern, a black book in his hand. Margaret Brodie, of Auldearn, held me up to the Devil to be baptized by him, and he marked me in the shoulder and sucked out my blood at that mark, and spouted it into his hand, and sprinkling it on my head, he said, "I baptize thee, Janet, in my own name." And within a while, we all went away.
>
> The next time I met with him was at the new Wards of Inshock and he had carnal copulation with me. He was a

How to Gather Evidence Against a Witch

meikle,[14] black, hairy man, very cold. I found his nature cold within me as spring well-water.[15] Sometimes he had boots and sometimes he had shoes on his foot, but still his feet were forked and cloven. He was sometimes like a deer, or a roe deer.

John Taylor, his wife Janet Breadheid of Belmakeith, [illegible] Douglas and I myself, met in the Kirkyard of Nairn and we raised an unchristened child out of its grave; and at the end of the cornfield, just opposite the Mill of Nairn, we took the said child, added the nails of our fingers and toes, pieces of grain and leaves of colwart, all chopped small and mixed together, and we put a part of it among the dung heaps of Breadley's land, and thereby took away all the fruit of his corns, and we parted it among two of our covens.[16] When we take corn at Lammas,[17] we take about two sheathes when the corn is full; or two heads of cabbage, and that gives us the fruit of the land or cabbage patch where they grew.[18] And we will be able to keep the yield till Christmas or Easter and then divide it among us. There are thirteen persons in my coven.

Pitcairn notes that the number thirteen was known as the Devil's

---

14 Scots word for "big" or "great."

15 The description of him as "black" did not relate to ethnicity but refers to his hair and/or clothing. As for his "nature"—her description of his semen inside her—it made sense that if the Devil appeared in human form as compressed air and therefore cold, his semen would also be cold as spring well water.

16 Pitcairn suggests in his footnotes the word *coven* might come from Latin *convenire*—to come together.

17 Lammas is a harvest celebration on August 1.

18 Stealing a symbolic amount of corn or cabbage allowed them to spirit away the whole crop.

Dozen in Scotland, although alas, this designation appears to have fallen out of use in the twenty-first century.

Isobel continued: "The last time that our coven met, we and another coven were dancing at the Hill of Earlseat [she also lists several other places] and after a time we went home to our howffs."[19] She then tells of the coven meeting in a field and yoking some frogs to a plough using long grass that served as chains (quite how that worked was left to the imagination), the frogs pulling the plough like oxen. The Devil himself held the plough. The blade of the plough was formed from the horn of a half-castrated ram. They went twice about the field, and the coven went up and down the length of the field with the plough, praying to the Devil for the fruit of that land and that thistles and briars that might grow there.

Isobel continued:

When we go to any house we take meat and drink, and fill up the barrels with our own piss, and we put brooms in our beds with our husbands till we return to them again. We were in the Earl of Moray's house in Dernway, going in through the windows, eating and drinking his best fare and taking some away with us. I had a little horse and would say, "Horse and Hattock[20] in the Devil's name!" and then we would fly away wherever we wanted to go, as straws fly upon the highways. We fly like straws when we please, wild straws and corn-straws will be horses to us, and we put them between our feet and say, "Horse and Hattock, in the Devil's name!"

---

19 "Howff" here probably means home or shelter. It's also used for graveyard.

20 "Hattock" is an old Scots word for a fairy's hat. "Horse and hattock" was said to be the phrase that fairies would cry when departing for their own world. Interestingly, given what Isobel went on to say about straw, it was also a regional word for a stack of corn.

And when anyone sees these straws in a whirlwind, and does not bless themselves, we may shoot[21] them dead at our pleasure. Any that are shot by us, their soul will go to heaven but their body will remain with us and will fly like horses to us, as small as straws.

Unlike many other confessions, Isobel Gowdie spoke in some detail of the fairy world: "I was in the Downie-Hills and got meat from the Queen of the Fairies, more than I could eat. The Queen is beautifully clothed in white linens, and in white and brown clothes, and the King of Fairies is a braw[22] man, well-built and of broad face. There were elf-bulls rutting and frolicking up and down and they gave me a fright."

Pitcairn notes here with obvious regret that he thinks Isobel's "gossiping" about the fairy world was purposefully cut short in favor of returning to her confessions of witchcraft, "which were obviously drawn out of her, and listened to with the utmost complacency by her reverend inquisitors."

Back on track again, Isobel went on to discuss how she used witchcraft to steal milk from a cow:

We pull the tow[23] and twine and plait it in the wrong way in the Devil's name, and we draw this handmade tether in between the cow's hind hoof, and everything between the cow's front and hind feet is taken in the Devil's name, and this is how we take all

---

21 There was a belief that the Devil gave witches "elf-shots," which were arrows fired at people using their thumbs rather than bows. There's some scholarly debate around whether these elf-shots were the act of "shooting" disease at a victim, thereby causing illness or pain in people or livestock, or were more tangible prehistoric flint arrowheads. Either way, they were a method used by witches to cause pain, illness, and, as here, death.

22 "Braw" is Scots for "good" or "excellent," probably coming from the word *brave*.

23 This likely means they take hairs from the tail of the cow.

the cow's milk. We even take sheep's milk too. The way to give back the milk again is to cut the tether. When we take away the strength of a person's ale and give it to another, we take a little quantity out of each barrel into a stowp[24] in the Devil's name: and with our own hands we put it among the other person's ale, which gives it the strength and substance and good health of his neighbor's ale. To keep the ale from us, bless it well, and we have no power over it. We get all the power from the Devil and when we take it from him, we call him "Our Lord."

Isobel then returned to a discussion of the work of other members of her coven:

John Taylor and his wife Janet Breadheid, Bessie Wilson in Auldearn, Margaret Wilson, wife of Donald Callam of Auldearn, and I made a picture of clay[25] to destroy the Laird of Parkis' [Parks] male children. John Taylor brought the clay in the corner of his plaid and his wife broke it up very small, powdered like meal. We sifted it with a sieve and poured water in it, in the Devil's name, and kneaded it into a hasty-pudding,[26] made of rye flour. From this we made a picture of the laird's sons. It had all the parts and makeup of a child, such as head, eyes, nose, hand, feet, mouth and little lips. It wanted none of a child's features: and its hands were folded down by its

---

24 "Stowp" is a Scots word for a bucket or drinking vessel, but it also means a basin for holy water.

25 A three-dimensional poppet rather than an actual picture.

26 This is Pitcairn's translation; we think he means a dough.

sides. It was like a large roll or a flayed suckling pig.[27] We laid it face first onto the fire till it shriveled with the heat, with a clear fire around it, and till it was red like a coal. After that we would roast it, now and then; each alternate day a piece of it would be well roasted. The Laird of Parkis' healthy male children will suffer because of it, both those that are born and those already dead already, if [the clay model] is not taken or broken. It was still being put in and taken out of the fire in the Devil's name. It was hung up on a knag.[28] It is still in John Taylor's house, and he has a cradle of clay around it. Only John Taylor and his wife Janet Breadheid, Bessie and Margaret Wilson in Auldearn, and Margaret Brodie and I were involved in the making of it. But all the multitude of our witches in all the covens knew of it all, at our next meeting after we had made it. And all the witches that are yet untaken[29] still have their own powers, as well as our powers which we had before we were taken.[30] But now I have no power at all.

Margaret Kylie in [illegible] is in one of the other covens. Meslie Hirdall, spouse to Alexander Ross in Loanhead, is one of them. Her skin is fiery. Isobel Nicoll in Lochley is one of my coven. Alexander Elder, in Earleseat, and Janet Finlay his wife are of my coven. Margaret Hasbein in Moynes is also one, as is Margaret Brodie in Auldearn, Bessie and Margaret Wilson

---

27 If you are having difficulty imagining what this looks like, rest assured it was also a bit of a puzzle to Pitcairn!

28 This is an old word for a wooden peg.

29 This means not yet arrested or taken by the authorities.

30 This is an interesting idea, if we're understanding it correctly: however many witches the authorities seize, their power is just transferred to the ones who are still free.

there, and Jean Martin there, and Elspeth Nishie, spouse to John Mathow there. The previously mentioned Jean Martin is Maiden of our coven. John Young in Mebestowne is our Officer.

Pitcairn notes that each coven appears to have had an "officer" for the men and a "maiden" for the women, "but whether the province of these personages was to preside over them or to act as messengers, to call them together, does not seem so certain."

Isobel went on to describe one particular escapade at a neighbor's dye house:

Elspeth Chisholme and Isobel More in Auldearn, Maggie Brodie [illegible] and I went into Alexander Cummings dye-house in Auldearn. I went in in the likeness of a jackdaw and the previously mentioned Elspeth Chisholm went in the shape of a cat. Isobel More was a hare and Maggie Brodie was a cat and [illegible]. We took a thread of each color of yarn that was in Alexander Cumming's dying-vat and tied three knots on each thread, in the Devil's name; and we put the threads in the vat, stirring it widdershins[31] in the Devil's name, and in this manner we took all the healthy strength of the vat away, so that it could only dye black, the color of the Devil, in whose name we took away the strength of the right colors that were in the vat!

---

[31] Counter Anticlockwise, although Pitcairn describes it as "contrary to the direction and ordinary course of the sun."

How to Gather Evidence Against a Witch

With the first confession having taken place on April 13, 1662, three more were to follow. The second confession was recorded on May 3 and tells the tale of the "Grand Meeting" of all the witch covens. Many spirits attended and are described in detail, including some of their rather bizarre nicknames: "Over the Dyke with It," "The Thief of Hell Wait Upon Herself," and the perhaps less complimentary "Able and Stout." She explains that "there would be many devils which wait upon the Master Devil, for he is bigger and more awful than the rest of the devils and they all revere him." In the second confession, there are also verses of poetry, one ending with the words, "And I shall go in the Devil's name, and soon I will come home again." Pitcairn's view on these pieces of poetry is that "the preceding and following rhymes are probably unique, even in the history of trials for witchcraft, and show, in a very forcible manner, the criminality of the bigoted, though learned and well-intentioned, individuals who dragged forward such wretches to public trial and ignominious death."

Pitcairn seems to believe the poetry was made up by the accusers. Pitcairn's editor had this to add to the discussion, as Pitcairn records:

> It has often been remarked by the Editor, in the course of the numerous witch trials which occur in this collection, that a great proportion of the charms, in use to be repeated by these unhappy women, were actually paraphrases of portions of the mass book—and in some cases…there appears to have been used doggerel versions of the Creed, etc.! Others were taken from ancient popular rhymes and songs.

Isobel's second confession is not complete. According to Pitcairn, the end had been "torn off."

The third confession of Isobel Gowdie was taken on May 15, 1662, and sets out the same story of meeting the Devil, having sex with him, and renouncing her baptism as before. However, this time, she gave a much more detailed description of sex with the Devil, describing how he would have "carnal dealings with all at every time he pleased." The witches would never refuse him. He came to Isobel's house in the shape of a crow, a deer, or any other shape, and on recognizing his voice, she would have sex with him. She also added, no doubt to the chagrin of the listening men, "The youngest and swiftest women will have very great pleasure in their carnal copulation with him, yea much more than with their own husbands." As if this wasn't enough, she followed it up with, "They have an exceedingly great desire of it with him, as much as he can have to them and more, and never think shame of it. He is abler for us that way than any man can be."[32] She described the Devil as "very heavy like a malt-sack; a huge nature and very cold, like ice."

Besides the sex, in this third confession, she described various shape-shifting episodes and also admitted to murder: "But that which troubles my conscience most, is the killing of several person with the arrows which I got from the Devil."

Isobel's fourth confession took place on May 25, 1662. Again, we have a reprise of her first confession, which, in our opinion, disproves the claim that these are Isobel's own words: clearly, she would not have kept saying the same thing over and over again. She also returned to her confession of murder using the arrows made by the Devil. She explained that one of her coven shot at a laird crossing a burn[33] but missed him. Pitcairn notes that the laird was beyond the reach of their

---

32 If we were to guess what parts of this confession were truly uttered by Isobel, it's probably this bit about the Devil being better at sex than men.

33 A "burn" is Scots for a little stream.

power when he crossed the water, as it was believed that bad spirits can't chase you across water.[34]

We believe Isobel Gowdie's confession was most likely the result of her being repeatedly asked questions until the desired answer was obtained or, otherwise, her words were simply fabricated by her questioners. But if you still need proof, the confession of her coven mate Janet Breadheid, spouse of John Taylor, provides it. There are startling similarities. They both described where the Devil sat when they met him (at the lectern) and said that he had a book in his hand, the baptism is identical, and Janet's description of having sex with the Devil is almost word for word Isobel's—down to the description of his "nature" within her, as cold as spring well water.

We can never be sure whether what we read are the words of the women themselves, words attributed to them by their interrogators, or a mixture of both. It's not impossible for many women, having been questioned for days on end and losing their minds from lack of sleep, to have made outlandish confessions. On the other end, the strong similarities between the accounts were probably a result of those doing the interrogating knowing exactly what they wanted from a confession: a meeting with the Devil, a renouncing of a baptism, and an act of witchcraft. Often, as we have seen, the confessions would include stories of "carnal connections" with the Devil and the names of other witches in their coven. It wasn't just the interrogators who knew what was required; the accused did too. Some may have confessed through fear, some through resignation, some not at all.

As we read these strange tales now, it's easy to lose sight of the visceral terror that lay behind the words. We tried to imagine the horror of the

---

[34] The witches that chased Tam o' Shanter in Robert Burns's poem of the same name were thwarted when his horse, Meg, gets him across a small river. But alas for poor Meg, the witches managed to snatch her tail before it crossed the water.

situation these poor women would have been in: a woman accused of witchcraft is likely to have been stripped, shaved, and searched by men looking for the Devil's marks. She would be in custody in dire conditions, not knowing when her incarceration would end. She would have no lawyer to help her. She would be kept awake day and night, questioned about when she met the Devil, what sex with him was like, and whether his semen was cold. She would be asked if she'd renounced her baptism. She would be asked who was in her coven— Was it her friend? Her neighbor? Her daughter? Her mother? All the while, her ability to distinguish between fact and fiction was slipping away from her. She would fear what she might say if she lost her mind, knowing that if she confessed, she would condemn herself to a most brutal death, knowing she would be burned, never given a proper burial on consecrated ground, and damned to spend eternity in hell, never to see her loved ones in the kingdom of God. We can only guess at how unwilling and afraid she must've been to admit to crimes that would consign her to such a fate.

The interrogators, however, have done their godly work: the witch has confessed by her own words. What is to be done now?

We have our case to prosecute a witch. We have an accuser, any physical objects that they may bring as proof,[35] the expert testimony of a witch pricker, and the confession.

Now we can begin the witch trial.

---

35 For example, a witch's charm found in the home of the accuser, placed there to work magic against the homeowner. These objects would be labeled and referred to as "productions" for the court.

PORTRAIT OF THE ACCUSED

The Paisley Witches

1697

In 1696, in the town of Paisley,[1] an eleven-year-old girl from a well-to-do family named Christian Shaw witnessed a family servant, Catherine Campbell, stealing a glass of milk. Catherine, upon discovering Christian had told her mother about the incident, allegedly cursed the child, entreating the Devil to "haul her soul through Hell."

A few days later, Christian encountered an old woman, Agnes Naismith, who was feared locally as a witch. The next day, Christian fell ill with symptoms eerily similar to those experienced by the Salem girls six years previously. Eventually, after Christian suffered violent fits and shaking for eight weeks, her parents had her examined by a top local doctor, Matthew Brisbane, who was unable to explain her illness. Although she then enjoyed a few days of relative health, she soon grew sick once more, enduring both the same fits as before and

---

1 A large town in the west central lowlands of Scotland near Glasgow.

now a kind of fugue state, where "she would become as stiff as a corpse and be senseless and motionless."[2] On her return visit to the doctor, she started producing strange items from her mouth such as hair balls, chicken feathers, coal, gravel, and straw. She supposedly also spoke to the air, entreating Catherine to be friendly with her again. As no rational explanation could be offered for her behavior, the doctor suggested its origin was demonic. Her father pushed for arrests, with Christian formally accusing both Catherine and Agnes Naismith. Although her initial accusation only included those two women, as events spiraled, she ultimately accused a total of thirty-five people.

In the end, seven individuals were charged with witchcraft: Margaret Lang, brothers John and James Lindsay, John Reid, Catherine Campbell, Margaret Fulton, and Agnes Naismith.

Dr. Matthew Brisbane testified that no natural causes could explain the girl's condition, and the minister, James Hutchison, sermonized to the court about witches' marks, casting doubt on those doctors who argued the marks could have innocent origins. In addition, the prosecutor threatened the jury, telling them that acquitting the defendants would align them with the Devil, making them "accessory to all the blasphemies, apostasies, murders, tortures, and seductions etc." Unsurprisingly, all seven were found guilty.

The executions took place on the Gallow Green in Paisley on June 10, 1697, where the convicted were hanged, then burned. By all accounts, this execution was particularly distressing. The original accused, Catherine Campbell, screamed, cursed, and tried to wrench herself free as she was carried to the gallows. The two convicted brothers, James and John Lindsay, heartbreakingly clutched each other's hands as they were hanged. Margaret Fulton was heard talking about

---

2   As described by Brian P. Levack in his *New Perspectives on Witchcraft*, vol. 3 (Routledge, 2001).

the land of the fairies as she faced her brutal death.[3] Margaret Lang supposedly confessed to the accusations being true but insisted she had since reconciled with God. Finally, Agnes Naismith cursed everyone present and their descendants. For many years afterward, every tragedy to befall the people of Paisley was blamed on Naismith's curse.

This was the last mass execution for witchcraft in western Europe.

There are elements of the Paisley witches story that seem almost filmic to modern eyes. For example, one of the convicted, John Reid, was found dead before they could execute him. He had a scarf around his neck (presumably like a garrote) that was tied to a stick placed in the fireplace, but he was still seated on a stool, and in any case, witnesses claimed the stick wouldn't have been strong enough to support his weight. It was deemed impossible he could have killed himself, yet his cell was locked, his window secured with boards.

In another ghoulishly cinematic touch, a contemporary statement about the executions insisted not all the convicted were dead when they were set on fire. A local man, Mark Canavan, had his walking stick taken by executioners to use in pushing flailing limbs back into the fire. Canavan refused to touch it after it had been in contact with witches.

Finally, sometime after the executions, someone discovered a hole in Christian's bedroom wall through which, it's been speculated, an accomplice passed the items Christian had regurgitated. Could she have known about the Salem case and fancied some notoriety for herself? She wouldn't be the first or last adolescent girl to cause a supernatural drama to gain attention.[4]

---

3   But remember, this is part of the magical mental landscape at this time.

4   See the case of the Fox sisters of upstate New York in 1848. They faked mysterious spiritual contact, which was instrumental in creating and popularizing the growing practice of Spiritualism.

Christian Shaw went on to become a successful businesswoman in the textile industry. The last recorded mention of her was her marriage to a businessman called William Livingstone in 1737.

Some modern-day psychiatrists believe she may have been dealing with conversion disorder when she was originally cursed by Catherine, and the anxiety she felt at the curse was then converted into her strange behavior and symptoms. But we will never know the truth.

In 2008, a memorial was placed in the ground at Maxwellton Cross in Paisley at the location where the witches' ashes were said to be buried. An inscription reads, "Pain inflicted, Suffering Endured, Injustice Done." Campaigners have been fighting for years to have those convicted pardoned, still without success.

10

How to Try a Witch

One of the most difficult elements of investigating witchcraft trials is that the records are very poor. The records in relation to Isobel Gowdie's personal history are even poorer. Save for the name of her husband and the fact that she hailed from Lochloy in the parish of Auldearn, we have very little information about her. From the Survey of Scottish Witchcraft, we know the grant of the commission from the Privy Council indicated there was to be no torture of the accused witch. We know Isobel gave a total of four confessions in April or May, two of them postdating the start of her trial, which began on April 13, 1662. We know she named eighteen other people as witches, fifteen of them women. We know that no fewer than nine commissioners (church men) and eleven investigators (senior and important men of the parish) were involved in the process. But that's where the trail goes cold.

It's particularly aggravating that despite four detailed confessions, we don't have the outcome of the trial. We (and you) could predict, given the evidence was against her, a likely conviction, but we don't know for certain. Extrapolating from the records of the witch trials we *do* have, we can see that approximately two-thirds of those accused of witchcraft were executed. We know a few were "banished" from the parish, although it's unclear why they avoided the usual witches' fate (as the official punishment was death). A small number were acquitted.

Given these numbers and the amount of evidence against her, surely she was executed?

Claire, looking at it with her experience of being a modern-day KC, considers this. Isobel confessed, which is pretty strong evidence that came directly from her. And she didn't just confess once; she gave four separate confessions over a period of about six weeks. We don't see anywhere that she renounced her confession. These would've been significant facts to be weighed up by a judge.

But let's get into the process. How exactly did judges decide who was guilty of witchcraft and who wasn't?

Court rules weren't nearly as regulated then as they are in the twenty-first century. Before 1926, when the Criminal Appeal (Scotland) Act was passed,[1] a court of appeal didn't exist in the country. Therefore, judges weren't obligated in criminal cases to write down their reasoning for how they reached their decision; there were no higher courts to

---

1   The Appeal Court in Scotland was founded after public outcry over the conviction of Oscar Slater, convicted in 1909 of the murder of Marion Gilchrist. The campaign to have him pardoned was lengthy, and its ultimate success was in part due to Sir Arthur Conan Doyle, author of the Sherlock Holmes novels, who became involved postconviction. He wrote a book called *The Case of Oscar Slater*, in which he argued that the prosecution was flawed and the trial had not been fair. It was not until 1927 that a Court of Appeal was instituted to hear his case. At the appeal, it was accepted that Slater's conviction had been a miscarriage of justice at trial, and his conviction and sentence were quashed.

check if they got it right, no appellate process, and no way to challenge a decision. What would've been the point in setting out the thinking of the court?

But just because we don't have a record of it doesn't mean the legal reasoning wasn't taking place. We can make an educated guess as to how that reasoning would have gone. Although laws and procedural rules have changed a great deal since the seventeenth century, it's likely the way a judge considered evidence and how he (it was always a "he," of course) came to a conclusion were similar to today's methods.

First, the judge would examine the charge. In Isobel Gowdie's case, the judge would've considered how she was alleged to have committed acts of witchcraft that came to light after her local minister became concerned about allegations that were circulating in the village of Auldearn.

The judge would then ask himself how the evidence before him might support such a charge. Evidence was then and still is now separated into categories, such as physical, eyewitness, and expert evidence.

In this case, he had the four confessions of Isobel Gowdie. Before the judge came to the contents of the confessions, he would've given consideration as to who had collected the statements and whether they could be trusted to have recorded everything correctly. In this case, the confessions were taken by the notary public, John Innes, who had been very careful to set out Isobel's words in great detail. In addition, they had been witnessed by ten other highly respected gentlemen.

Just as judges now ascertain that evidence has been lawfully obtained, a judge of the seventeenth century would also have been thinking about whether the circumstances in which the statement was taken were fair. Therefore, he absolutely would've noted how the confessions highlighted from the outset that on each occasion, the words were spoken directly by Isobel Gowdie, as witnessed by all those who signed the confessions, and that she'd said everything of her own free will, having not been compelled or tortured to confess.

From our modern-day perspective, we'll never know whether Isobel was talking from a state of sleep deprivation, somewhere between consciousness and unconsciousness; whether she was hallucinating or suffering from a mental illness; or whether one of her accusers made the whole thing up. The judge was presumably satisfied everything was proper and aboveboard, but we're suspicious, simply from the fact that the men recording the confessions felt the need to spell it out so deliberately and repeatedly.

Nevertheless, the judge would have weighed up her confession evidence by asking, "Do I find this evidence both credible and reliable?" The test of credibility is determined by whether you think you can believe the evidence given; reliability is whether that evidence can be depended upon. It's likely he would have answered yes in both cases.

Now the judge can dive into the actual content of each of these confessions. Isobel claimed she met with the Devil and willingly agreed to become his servant: to demonstrate her loyalty to him, she renounced her own baptism and engaged in a perversion of the sacrament. She said the Devil sooked[2] out the blood from her shoulder, leaving her with a visible mark there, and she engaged in carnal relations with him. This is a full house bingo card of confession essentials. Doubtless, the judge would've dealt with many witchcraft accusations and been aware of what witches and the Devil did when they met, so this confession would seem in line with the others. He may have thought some of the details Isobel supplied—for example, the Devil's "cold" nature, his cloven feet—wouldn't

---

2 Sucked.

have been known by a God-fearing woman unless she'd seen it with her own eyes. The Devil's mark could have been witnessed by the eyes of the judge himself, providing independent corroboration to the confession.

If the judge accepted the evidence in its entirety, he then needed to carry out a further assessment. The terms of the Witchcraft Act of 1563 made it clear that *being* a witch is itself not a crime: the crime is using your knowledge of witchcraft, sorcery, or necromancy to *perform* witchcraft. (The other crime of consulting a person to use witchcraft, sorcery, or necromancy does not apply in this case.)

Sadly for Isobel, this would've been an easy matter for the judge to rule on. From the four confessions, a judge almost certainly would've formed the opinion there was overwhelming evidence—from Isobel's own mouth—that she'd performed witchcraft.

Therefore, after assessing the charge and the evidence, along with the guidelines of the Witchcraft Act of 1563, it seems highly likely our judge or jury would've convicted Isobel Gowdie of witchcraft. After that, the court would've moved on to sentencing.

As the Bible confirms, "thou shalt not suffer a witch to live." This was taken literally in Scotland, and the only official punishment for acts of witchcraft was death. King James VI, in book 3, chapter 6 of *Daemonologie*, spoke of the sentence in the following terms:

> **Philomathes:** Then to make an ende of our conference, since I see it drawes late, what forme of punishment thinke ye merites these *Magicians a*nd Witches? For I see that ye account them to be all alike guiltie?
> **Epistemon:** They ought to be put to death according to the Law of God, the civill and imperial law, and municipall law of all Christian nations.
> **Phi:** But what kinde of death I pray you?

Epi: It is commonly used by fire, but that is an indifferent thing to be used in every cuntrie, according to the Law or custome thereof.
Phi: But ought no sexe, age nor ranck to be exempted?
Epi: None at al (being so used by the lawful Magistrate) for it is the highest poynt of Idolatrie, wherein no exception is admitted by the law of God.
Phi: Then bairnes[3] may not be spared?
Epi: Yea, not a haire the lesse of my conclusion.

Therefore, because she was convicted, Isobel Gowdie was probably sentenced to death for her acts of witchcraft. She's likely to have been strangled on a funeral pyre, her body burned to be sure the Devil couldn't bring her back to cause more mayhem.

So a confession extracted from a deliriously tired woman, together with a mark on her body, could find a woman convicted under the Witchcraft Act and executed by the state.

It didn't take much, clearly.

Despite what we may see as flimsy reasoning, it's important to remember that this was a proper legal trial, with evidence being put forward and the judge assessing it and carrying out legal tests. Some modern folk believe witchcraft trials were carried out by angry peasants waving pitchforks, and perhaps it's easier to think of them this way. No one wants to admit their judicial system, the system put in place to keep society fair and balanced, could get it so wrong. But it did, with catastrophic consequences for those accused.

After conviction and sentencing, the legal part of the process was over. The most gruesome part—the practicalities of killing the witch—was yet to come.

---

3   Children.

PORTRAIT OF THE ACCUSED

Janet Horne

DORNOCH, 1727

Janet Horne was the last person to be executed for witchcraft in Great Britain.

While there's a stone marking the location of her execution, it bears the incorrect date, something we find rather symbolic of the wrong perpetrated against her. We don't even know her real name, as Janet (or Jenny) Horne was a kind of catchall name for any women accused of witchcraft in Scotland at that time. Janet[1] lived with her daughter in Dornoch, in the county of Sutherland in the Highlands, and in 1727 (some sources say 1722), the two women were arrested and thrown in jail. It seems some of the towns-folk believed they were in league with the Devil, and following a rushed and almost certainly illegal trial led by the sheriff-depute

---

1   We'll keep calling her this as she can't be anonymous, and like it or not, it's what she's always called.

of Sutherland, Captain David Ross, it was ordered that the two be burned to death.

Janet was accused of turning her daughter into a pony; it was said her daughter, now a pony, was shod by the Devil himself. Sadly, there's a much more rational explanation for the accusations: Janet was probably suffering from dementia, while her daughter likely had a disability affecting her hands and feet. Contemporary witnesses of the execution described Janet being stripped, paraded through the town, covered in tar, and then laughing and warming her hands at "the bonnie fire" (as she called it) of the burning barrel she was to be executed in. There's no record of what happened to her daughter, so we can only hope she was spared.

When Janet Horne was executed in 1727, public sentiment was turning against witch hunts, and less than a decade later, the Scottish Witchcraft Act of 1563 was repealed.[2] It was replaced by the Witchcraft Act of 1735, which covered the whole of Great Britain and made it a crime for anyone to claim they could practice witchcraft. In other words, instead of starting from a premise that witches were real, the law now worked on the assumption that no one had magical powers and anyone who claimed otherwise was a charlatan. The law also abolished the hunting and execution of witches.

With this new act—enacted too late for Janet Horne—the age of the witch trials of the early modern period finally came to an end.

---

[2] The English Witchcraft Act was also repealed, although the Irish acts were not repealed until 1821.

11

How to Burn a Witch

The Howff,[1] a graveyard located in the heart of Dundee, is a place as familiar to us as it is alluring. In 1564, the land was granted to the burgh of Dundee for use as a burial ground by none other than Mary, Queen of Scots, and it now holds a remarkable collection of historical tombstones.[2] The reason we're such frequent visitors to the Howff is not solely Zoe's fascination with the human bones that often break the surface of the earth or Claire's enjoying a goth moment but the fact that the burial site has become inextricably

---

1 A Scots word meaning an enclosed, open space, like a yard.

2 The final burial took place in the Howff in 1878, and there are many thousands of people buried there. The oft-quoted number on the internet is eighty thousand, but given the small size of the place, we'd be surprised if that were so. Some of the more famous dead include James and Janet Keiller, who invented the famous Keiller marmalade, and James Chalmers, inventor of the adhesive postage stamp.

linked to a woman called Grissell Jaffray, who was burned as a witch in Dundee in 1669.

Very little is known about Grissell other than she was born in Aberdeen, where she married James Butchart in 1615. In 1669, the couple were accused of witchcraft, Grissell specifically of being a spaewife, a woman who could foretell the future. Their accusers were three Dundee ministers: John Guthrie, William Rait, and Harry Scrymgeour.[3] When Grissell was tortured, she named several others as witches, though no records exist of their names or fates. At her trial in November that year, the Dundee local court found her guilty, and she was strangled, then burned. According to local legend, upon returning to the city from some time at sea, her son saw the flames of his mother's pyre and fled Dundee, never to return.

No records exist to indicate where Grissell was executed, yet despite the scant details, her story is woven into the fabric of Dundee's history, and now a plaque and mosaic mark her tragic end.[4]

As is often the case, if a story intrigues but details are missing, people will fill in the gaps. This is where the link to the Howff comes in, as there is a stone post there—not a gravestone but rather a slim marker that reaches about mid height on an average woman—and this post has become known as the Witch's Stone. Considering this stone was actually a meeting point for local businessmen, we're not sure why people have become convinced it's Grissell's resting place; however, it has since taken on symbolic relevance and is usually decorated on its top with shells, coins, and little stones.

---

[3] This name lives on in Dundee, with the Dundee Law School being housed in the Scrymgeour Building.

[4] In a little cobbled lane close to the docks, there is a blue plaque and a mosaic depicting flames and waves. There's no great fanfare about this marker, and many people are surprised when their attention is drawn to it.

How to Burn a Witch

As the Witch's Stone is the only place near our homes with a witch connection (albeit an imagined one), we've conducted various interviews there with journalists from all around the world. Being in that space never fails to make us think about how an ordinary woman could so quickly find herself in a position from which she wouldn't escape with her life. We often take a moment to reflect on what it must've been like for Grissell (and the other accused) to be publicly executed and then for spectators to watch their remains be burned to ash.

As deeply unpleasant and upsetting as the execution aspect of the witch trials is, we must study and understand it, as it was a key driver in the war against witches. Fear of such a horrific death helped encourage people to keep a close eye on their neighbors and acquaintances and ultimately helped enforce public adherence to the laws of church and state.

It's generally thought that in Scotland, witches were strangled first, then had their bodies burned. There is some disagreement among historians on the mechanics of the strangling; some say they were hanged, some say strangit, strangld, or whirkened (an old Scots for strangled). Whatever the method, it's unlikely these executions were performed by hand, given how many women would've been executed in a day. Perhaps garrotes were used. Occasionally, witches were burned alive at the stake, and sometimes bodies were burned in barrels filled with tar. And people did all this legally, intentionally, and as a spectator event. However, these methods of dispatch were integral to how the public was educated and chastened about witchcraft and its consequences.

So why go through all the trouble? Once a witch is strangled, why burn them rather than bury them?

Put simply, it was to stop them from coming back. In the early modern period, there was a strongly held belief that the Devil was able to reanimate corpses and that, given half the chance, he would "revenir" the witches and have them continue their evildoing. People of the time truly thought that only by killing and then completely destroying the witch would they be protecting the community. So they burned the witch from the world, turning her to ash, leaving no trace she had ever existed.

We're so familiar with the idea that witches were burned at the stake that the reality of it has little meaning for us. People sometimes talk quite glibly about this perhaps because it happened so long ago, and they prefer to distance themselves. But we wanted to know To that end, we spoke with world-renowned fire expert Niamh Nic Daeid, who we knew could explain what physically happened when witches were burned and could therefore evoke some sense of what it was really like.

Niamh was an early supporter of our Witches of Scotland campaign and is someone with whom we never tire of talking. She's a professor of forensic science and the director of the Leverhulme Research Centre for Forensic Science at the University of Dundee. She specializes in fire investigation and is the person you go to if you want to know anything about fire. In fact, Niamh was called as an expert witness in the Grenfell inquiry.[5] She is originally from Ireland and has the uncanny ability to speak about horrendous and distressing subjects in a way that's both fascinating and informative, all in a soft, warm accent. Niamh never lets you feel as if you're asking stupid or weird questions, even when they patently are.

So how would burning a witch's body to ash work in reality?

Niamh explained, "If you think of the body as a solid fuel, you heat up that fuel and you cause the materials within it to thermally decompose and produce gases. That's the first thing. The fuel that burns isn't the solid. It's the gaseous products that come off the fuel."

---

[5] An appalling tragedy where seventy-two people were killed when a block of flats in London caught fire in 2017.

How to Burn a Witch

Therefore, if you have a witch's body being burned, the body itself will act as further fuel. Then, as the body heats up, it begins to thermally decompose and release gases that in turn keep the fire going.

Niamh continued: "If the person is clothed, then the clothing may be the first thing to start to thermally decompose—the molecules of the material literally just starting to break apart. Because the fire is imparting lots of energy and lots of heat, the heat causes the molecules to break apart from each other, and they produce the gas. It's a process called pyrolysis."

The amount of thermal decomposition depends on both the fuel (the body) and the temperature. In a modern crematorium, the deceased is laid flat, and the temperature around them is between approximately 1,800°F and 2400°F. When a corpse is in those very controlled circumstances, it takes around an hour and a half to burn, after which it's allowed to cool for an hour or so, then moved to a cremulator to reduce the remaining ashes to a fine powder.

By contrast, during the witch burnings, there was a much less scientific approach.

Witch burning engraving, 1555

The main issue was that when you tied someone to a stake, the body was usually upright. This created a situation where the flame was flickering rather than consistently static, leading to inconsistent temperatures (very unlike within a crematorium).

"That means it's going to take a longer period of time for that person to burn to ash and bone," said Niamh.

This lengthy burning time was something of a headache for early modern executioners. As we mentioned above, they sometimes placed the accused inside tar-filled barrels, then lit the tar on fire. This was done in an effort to speed up the process. But despite how good an idea it seemed to them, we know now that it was *less* efficient. Getting tar ignited is not as easy as you might think,[6] and once lit, the flames (and heat) will only reach whatever fuel is above the tar's surface.

"If you're in a tank submerged in tar up to your neck or waist, it's only the surface of the tar in the barrel that burns," Niamh explained. "The material beneath the surface is still cool. It could be much more prolonged, albeit in the immediate environment of where that surface tar is burning, the temperature would get very hot. It could again take a considerable amount of time for the body to burn down completely."

As terrible as it would've been to see a burning body, your sight wouldn't have been the only sense that was shocked. The smell of burning flesh or, as we now know, the smell of the oils from burning flesh, would've been all-pervading for the town or village where the execution was taking place. There would've been no escaping the carnage as the putrid, sweet smell would twist around the town and even snake into the houses of the inhabitants.

Throughout the long hours burning at the stake, the body likely would've moved and changed position. The tendons and ligaments, especially in the arms, legs, and hands, would've contracted and

---

6 Claire: "I've literally never given it a moment's thought, but Zoe clearly has."

possibly pulled up into what is known as the "pugilistic stance" by pathologists, in which the corpse takes on a posture as if they're raising their fists to fight. This is a purely physical reaction to the fire and doesn't mean the person was fighting or alive during the burning, but it must've made for quite the viewing experience and probably added to ideas about the power of witches.

For those of us who have scattered ashes by hand, we know that cremains[7] are dusty ashes but with slightly bigger bits of bone in them. In contemporary crematoriums, remains are gone over with a little hammer to reduce bigger bone fragments into more dustlike matter. Under the less controlled conditions of the witch trials, the resulting remains would've been much more irregular. Turns out bones are pretty strong, and under the circumstances we're describing, there would've been several reasonably large pieces left.

We've read some accounts saying the ashes were just left to blow away, but it sounds as if those running the execution would've had to get involved with the remains that weren't small or fine enough to be left to nature.

"Let me show you something," said Niamh, getting up and going to her bookshelf, which is, naturally, stuffed with academic texts. She brought back a book and, flicking through, found an image of different bits of bone that had survived a person's being cremated. Niamh pointed at a chunk of bone that was the joint at the top of a leg. Although the photo didn't depict a bone from the witch trials, it backed up the theory that there would've been relatively large fragments left over from the executions, and those pieces may only have become ashes (as we think of them) if someone had intervened and smashed them up.

As bones are exposed to higher temperatures, they change color from white to gray to silvery and eventually become brittle. But again,

---

7   As they're known in the business.

this all takes time and occurs only in very high temperatures, something made even more difficult to achieve with the body upright, tied to a stake.

We've been told that in the Scalloway Museum in Shetland, there's a collection of ashes taken from a place where guilty people were burned. Though no scientific testing has been done on these ashes, many believe they're actually "witches' ashes." It's possible, and even if they're not, we're sure the sight of them in the museum only aids the mind in contemplating the trials. The power of human imagination is strong and, indeed, necessary for acknowledging the full obscenity of what occurred.

But back to the burning. We wondered what the spectators who stood and watched would have actually seen.

"In terms of the way the individual will be positioned, they will start by standing upward,"[8] said Niamh. "When the body burns, the soft tissues go first, exposing muscle and fat underneath. Those will gradually disintegrate from heat exposure, eventually revealing bone, which will also begin to degrade."

There may be a point where the body might disarticulate and collapse into pieces. If the head and limbs came off, those organizing the execution could find themselves in the position of having to move body parts back into the fire. As mentioned earlier, there are contemporary reports during the Paisley witch trials of a bystander's walking cane being used for exactly this purpose.

The skin would blacken[9] just as chicken on a barbecue would cook.[10] Because women have a higher fat content than men, there's a possibility

---

8   If they are still alive of course. Otherwise, the body would have been propped up by the stake.

9   As we're talking about the Scottish witch trials in this scenario, we mean pale skin.

10 Sorry.

they might've burned faster. However, Niamh said it wouldn't be enough to make any great difference, since it would take such a considerable time for anyone to burn to bone and ash. Besides gender, there are also some differences to consider based on body mass, in that it may take larger people longer to burn, depending on the circumstances.

Another variable would be what materials the person was wearing. If someone had on a more protective layer such as leather or wool, it could certainly prolong the process. Natural fabrics also hold their shape longer when burning compared to modern, artificial materials.

"If you set fire to a wool jumper, it holds its shape for some time. The clothing that they wore would provide some level of a barrier that would slow things down. Their hair would catch on fire, and hair changes color when it's burned."

Although it was rarer for witches to be burned alive, it did happen sometimes. Thankfully, while this is terrible, the victim wouldn't have had the long, drawn-out death that you might imagine—they more than likely would've died of shock, smoke inhalation, or heart failure, none of which take very long.

There are some stories of well-meaning people putting gunpowder in the witch's clothing to speed up the process and help the person die more quickly. However, Niamh thinks it's unlikely this would make much difference, because unless gunpowder was put into a closed, confined container, it would cause only a quick, localized effect somewhat similar to that of a sparkler and wouldn't move the process along in any meaningful way.

Some contemporary reports recorded that when a witch's corpse was burned, it would let out a gasp. Which means, of course, it wasn't some supernatural event, but back then, it surely would've been seen as more proof the guilty person was nonhuman.

But they *were* human; they were real people. When we visit the Howff, we're forced to think about how, in so many locations across

Scotland, we go about our normal, daily lives on the same ground where these horrific scenes took place just a few hundred years ago.

We must make the connection from our history to the present day. Think of these innocent people who were subjected to the most awful punishment. Think of someone like Grissell Jaffray, who was plucked from her normal life and made an example of. And think of how that was done to her in a city where thousands of people now go about their lives, never realizing they are perhaps passing over the spot where Grissell's strangled body was burned beyond recognition to keep the Devil at bay. No matter how terrible, history must be learned from and remembered.

PORTRAIT OF THE ACCUSED

Katherine MacKinnon

SKYE, 1747

In 1747, Katherine MacKinnon went begging at the door of a man called Rudy or Ruaridh[1] Mac Iain McDonald in the village of Camuscross on the south end of Skye. It was a fatal mistake; Katherine, an elderly woman, died a horrible death at McDonald's hands. Seven years later, he was accused of her "barbarous and cruel" murder in Inverness in August 1754.

Recently uncovered archives have revealed the sad case of Katherine—the first and only recorded incidence of a witch accusation on the Isle of Skye in the Inner Hebrides. Ironically, Skye's oral history is rich with tales of witches. For example, according to legend, the imposing, jagged Cuillin Hills on Skye were formed by them. Despite the legends and folklore, unlike most of the rest of Scotland,

---

1   He is referred to as both names in the archives. The records were discovered by Skye archivist Catherine MacPhee, whose interest was piqued when she came across the words "as a witch" in pencil in the margins of the original eighteenth-century papers describing the case.

Skye didn't suffer from the same appetite for accusing and executing witches. It had an easier relationship with the supernatural, possibly because it's a Gaelic-speaking area (as mentioned earlier, Ireland and other Gaelic areas had a stronger acceptance of the Otherworld).

One of the great tragedies of Katherine's murder is that it came more than ten years after the Witchcraft Act of 1563 was repealed. It was also perpetrated by a man known locally for being difficult and cruel. He'd previously been accused of various violent acts, including an assault on a family member. But as a tacksman[2] of Clan MacDonald[3] of Armadale, he was a powerful local figure.

McDonald alleged the destitute Katherine had poisoned some of his men and was intent on causing mischief when she arrived at his house. He tied her hands behind her back and then held her feet over a fire in an attempt to force her to confess she was a witch. Katherine's feet were badly damaged, and after escaping from McDonald's property and finding her way to a neighboring house in Duisdale Beag, she succumbed to her injuries nearly two weeks later.

During McDonald's subsequent trial for Katherine's murder, he denied the accusations made against him, calling them "false and malicious." He was acquitted of the murder. Perhaps poor Katherine was simply in the wrong place at the wrong time, and McDonald used the accusation of witchcraft as a means of legitimizing his desire to inflict pain on those who crossed him. Sadly, McDonald wasn't the only person to use the fear of witches as cover for murderous leanings.

---

2 A tacksman was someone who held land and sublet it to other parties. Often, they were closely related to the chief. It was a title often used in the Highlands in the 1700s.

3 Due to low literacy levels at the time, names were spelled phonetically. Therefore, there are often different versions of names and generally, there is no way to know which variant is correct. A great example of this within the witch trials is the various spellings of Jonet/Janet/Jonnet—names which turn up in records frequently with every possible permutation of spelling.

12

How to Bury a Witch

The witch had been troublesome enough in life, but she was even more bother in death. Which left the Reverend Allan Logan with quite the problem: he had to find a way to dispose of her corpse so that she *stayed* dead.

Reverend Logan was the first Presbyterian minister at Torryburn, ordained in 1695 just a few years earlier. He was a youthful and energetic minister, determined to make his mark on the small village kirk. He'd written several well-received books on church discipline, and it was important he put into practice what he'd preached. He was a man whose hard work and dedication to the Lord had seen him gain a good reputation in the church, where he was considered an intellectual. It hadn't hurt his public standing that he'd married into a local minor aristocratic family.

On this day, he would get rid of the troublesome witch once and for all.

With its kirk sessions and parish elders, the Church of Scotland today retains the same structure as it did when it was first formed, although now women are allowed to sit as elders too. Even with the similarities, it might be difficult to imagine how central the reverend (and therefore the church) was to every part of his parishioners' lives at the beginning of the 1700s. Think eighteenth-century religious helicopter parenting, and you would be getting close: it was the minister's job to guard the morals of the parish, rigorously apply the word of God, and ensure the continuance of all things God and godly in his parish. Returning to Torryburn, there was no part of the lives of the people that Reverend Logan did not have the right to enter into and opine on. Drinking, fornicating, swearing, stealing, lying—their business was his business, because ultimately, it was God's business.

For his local flock in Torryburn, a small fishing village in Fife that probably consisted of two hundred or so souls, life was not easy. The weather was usually cold and wet. It's probable that when the men worked at sea or tried to mine sea coal from the shore, the women of the village worked in the salt-panning industry. Although that might conjure up an image of ladies sitting by the water's edge genteelly sifting the sea salt, the reality was drastically different. During the evaporation process to extract the salt, the blood of cattle was added to the heated water to collect any impurities, which could then be skimmed off. The village would no doubt have regularly been covered in a haze of foul-smelling boiling blood. Furthermore, food was in short supply, and medical treatments for any ailments were rudimentary.

It's hardly surprising the villagers wanted to find some ways to brighten up their dismal lives, and it was here, in monitoring their behavior, that Reverend Logan needed to be the most vigilant. To keep God's laws, he had to remind the locals (frequently) that the sins of the flesh and drinking were gateway behaviors to the Devil himself. To the modern eye, it may seem God wasn't much fun if He insistently cracked down on what small amount of pleasure could be had in such difficult times, but Reverend Logan would've been confident he was helping to save the villagers' immortal souls.

Like most men of his time, Reverend Logan was, in 1704, wholly seized by the unshakable, genuine belief that the Devil was alive and a threat to his flock. To allow infractions of God's law in the village was to invite Satan himself to visit. The Devil's business was to tempt away the vulnerable, make them his witches, and use them to bring misery on the good, law-abiding folk—stealing from the devout, ruining their food, afflicting them with terrible ailments, even killing them. Reverend Logan was not going to let this happen to his parishioners, not on his watch.

From the start of his career in Torryburn, he'd been scrupulous enough to ensure that aside from those who drank a little too much and the odd adulterous allegation, God's laws were properly observed. As a result, Satan had not infiltrated the parish. Sadly, that streak was to end quite suddenly on July 30, 1704. That we know so much about the allegations that arose and what happened in the following months is in large part due to Reverend Logan himself, as he was a man of punctilious kirk-session minute keeping.

His notes reveal he was very much concerned on that particular summer's day—he'd just heard an allegation of witchcraft. What fear he must have felt in that moment, knowing that despite his best efforts, Satan had managed to get a cloven-hoofed foothold in his hamlet. It's clear Reverend Logan treated the matter with the utmost seriousness, as he immediately convened an emergency sitting of the kirk. After discussion with the elders, it was agreed that to properly deal with an accusation of this sort, a public court hearing would need to take place. Witnesses would be called to appear, and evidence would be taken from them so the reverend could assess the seriousness of the situation.

Imagine the stir such a hearing would've caused in a small hamlet where nothing much of *any* sort took place, where the only entertainment that didn't fall wholly foul of God's rules was gossip, and presumably gossip about a witch in the parish would be the very sort of gossip God would want to encourage, to warn everyone the Devil was in town.

The first witness called to give evidence was a woman who lived about half a mile outside Torryburn, Jean Bissett of the parish. She was the initial source of the witchcraft accusation. She said she'd left her house with her child on the previous Tuesday morning (when all the good folk would normally be working) and joined a group of six or so women and two men, all of whom began socializing, moving from house to house, chatting with neighbors and friends. The reverend's fears that drink had been taken were confirmed when she admitted ale had been drunk by all. The evidence of Jean Bissett as part of this group of socializers can hardly have impressed Logan, but equally, if the Devil was to get anyone over to his side, the idle drinkers of the parish would be the very sort vulnerable to temptation.

Jean explained that she and her friends had visited three or four houses over the course of the day and that by about 9 p.m., she'd fallen into a deep sleep. She woke from this sleep disoriented. Her friends who were with her, also called to give evidence, described her as ranting, havering, talking nonsense. Of this Jean was certain though—an old woman in the parish called Lilias Adie had used witchcraft and put a spell on her. She also claimed Janet White, another local woman, was involved in bewitching her. According to the eyewitnesses of the revelry, Jean said about Lilias, "She's done for me, her and the Devil." She also said to those who were still sober enough to listen, "I think, and Janet White as well, she's put the spell on me." Jean knew Janet White from a previous interaction where Jean had borrowed money for ale from her and had yet to pay her back.

From what can be gleaned from the evidence of others, the partying continued for a good few hours thereafter, with no one paying much attention to Jean. At around midnight, she left, her child still in tow, and returned home. It was said she was acting out of sorts during the walk home—jumping and skipping and suchlike. The next day, a friend of Jean's traveled to her house at Craigmill to see how she was and found her very ill. She was feverish, had a headache, and felt awful. This sickness lasted for a whole day.

What's happening here then?

Well, the more doubting among us might think that far from suffering the effects of a satanic spell, it's possible Jean was merely horribly hungover and looking for someone to blame. In a small village in the eighteenth century, it would certainly have been frowned on for a woman to be seen careering around the village late at night, drunk and definitely not taking care of her maternal duties. The gossips would've been in overdrive about this wild, ungodly woman—unless of course none of this was Jean's fault. Unless Jean had been the victim of a terrible witch or two. It was coincidence, surely, that she owed one of them money and a well-timed allegation would delay, if not disappear, an outstanding debt.

There was one person who didn't believe witchcraft caused Jean's illness—Jean's husband, John Tanahay. He seemed to take her allegations of witchcraft as the nonsense ramblings of a woman who'd had too much to drink. He provided a damning character assessment of his wife to the kirk session, opining to them that she was far too given to keeping bad company and, yes, she drank too much. The minutes record that he stated, "Gie her to me and I'll ding the Devil out of her." Perhaps because of these observations, or perhaps because

Reverend Logan discovered Janet White was a creditor of Jean Bissett, he was satisfied enough to conclude that the allegation of witchcraft was without merit, and the matter could be neatly brought to an end. Neither of the accused women was brought before the minister and his elders to answer the allegation.

It may be the history of witchcraft in Torryburn would've ended there, and the investigation into witchcraft accusations against Lilias Adie and Janet White would've been no more than a short, forgotten entry in the kirk session minutes, except for what happened next, the effect of which was to make one of the accused, Lilias Adie, into the most famous woman accused of witchcraft in Scotland, if not, at one time, the world.

Four weeks later, on August 30, there was another accusation.

This time, a villager named Jean Neilson accused Lilias Adie of putting a spell on her and making her ill. Unfortunately for our purposes, the minutes don't record any further details about the allegations. What might've happened, purely our own conjecture, is the tendency for gossip to congeal into rumor and then to solidify to fact. Although Reverend Logan may have been persuaded that the allegations of Jean Bissett were nonsense, the parishioners, reveling in the excitement of a witchcraft allegation, may have formed their own opinions on whether there was a fellow villager in the Devil's employ.

Unfortunately for Lilias, she was probably more vulnerable to accusations of witchcraft than others. From what we can glean from the kirk session minutes, Lilias was an old woman, at least sixty years old and possibly as old as eighty. At a time when life expectancy was much lower than it is now, even the lower estimate was a considerable age. The minutes don't disclose any family—no husband, son, or daughter to advocate for her or try to protect her from the allegations. For reasons that will become clear, we know a lot about what Lilias looked like, and she was not a physically conventional woman. She was very tall—probably over six feet—and we know she had a smaller than normal head with an oddly shaped skull and significantly protruding front teeth. In short: an old woman, without family support, who looked physically different from the rest of the villagers. If the Devil was to choose a woman to do his evil work, who better than this old crone?

Reverend Logan was once again quick to act on the allegation. His minutes tell us he immediately instructed his assistant, Bailie Williamson, to take Lilias into custody. Although it was not explicitly stated, we can be fairly certain Lilias was taken to the strong room in the parish church, to await interrogation the next day.[1]

The next day, Lilias was interrogated by the reverend. She'd no doubt been kept in poor conditions, but there was little time for her to have been tortured, and there's no evidence to suggest she'd been kept awake overnight to deprive her of sleep. Yet when asked if she was a witch, she responded in the most emphatic terms that yes, she indeed was. She described the Devil and what they did, stating in detail about how he caused her to renounce her baptism, that "the Devil lay with her carnally; and that his skin was cold and his color black and pale, he had a hat on his head, and his feet was cloven like the feet of a stirk." She went on to detail several meetings, including dancing in the moonlight (and in no moonlight) and revelry "whereof none are now living but herself." She confirmed she had been a witch for many years, but due to her infirmity in old age, she wasn't able to do as much of

---

1 The church currently in Torryburn is a nineteenth-century replacement of that original seventeenth-century church. Reverend Allan Logan's house remains intact from the seventeenth century, and you'll also find a nod to his legacy in the form of Logan Road.

the Devil's work as she used to, and she explained that she had been a witch since what she described as the second burnings of witches, so it's likely that she remembered the trial of a woman, among others, named Anderson in 1666 and the trials before that in 1640.

Due to her confession, over the next month, Lilias was kept in terrible conditions, treated badly, and probably kept awake for days on end, her health probably declining all the while. There was a delay in obtaining a trial date, likely because the local court couldn't consider a case without a warrant from the Privy Council in Edinburgh. On September 29, she was interrogated again and pressed to give up further information about the Devil—in particular about who else in the village had been converted to Satan. Lilias duly accused two local women, Agnes Curry and Elspeth Williamson. Immediately, they too were hauled up in front of the kirk session and interrogated. The minutes state Lilias remained emphatic in her confession, recording that she claimed, "what I am to say shall be as true as the sun is in the firmament."

Then, on September 30, three months after she was first taken into custody, the minutes fall completely silent. Lilias, an elderly, infirm, self-confessed witch—in a turn of events that was deeply worrying for the reverend—had died in custody before she could be brought to trial.

What do you do if you're certain a woman is a witch, but she dies before you have a chance to mete out her punishment in accordance with the law and the appropriate witch-destroying practices of the day? This situation left the reverend with a very real problem. Lilias's death didn't end the agency of the Devil. Logan knew as well as anyone that unless very significant steps were taken to stop the Devil, he could reanimate Lilias's body to wreak her satanic revenge on the villagers, the elders, and himself.

It would be highly likely the reverend would've heard of these "revenants"[2] who return from the dead and terrorize the community. He couldn't take that kind of risk with Lilias.

This problem was unique to Lilias's circumstances. While she had confessed to witchcraft, she hadn't been convicted in a court of law. In the ordinary course of events, the disposal of the body of a witch was done by burning because it was well known the Devil couldn't reanimate ashes. But could the reverend burn the body of someone who hadn't had a lawful trial? And could he deny her a Christian burial? This was a terrible dilemma for a man of God, both legally and morally.

After some considerable thought, the reverend designed what he imagined was a foolproof plan. He took this problem extremely seriously, evidenced by the amount of money and effort spent to put his plan into place.

It was, of course, completely out of the question to bury Lilias's body on consecrated church ground. Instead, the reverend took the decision to bury her in the Torryburn foreshore, where for most of the day, her wooden coffin would be covered in water. As the undead couldn't cross water, this would effectively trap her soul. However, this was not enough on its own: with the changing tides, Lilias's grave wouldn't have remained underwater all day. The reverend therefore decided on an expensive but wholly (he believed) necessary solution. He hired a local stonemason to provide a vast sandstone slab, six feet by three feet and probably about half a ton in weight, to place over her coffin to keep her remains firmly below the water line. Installing the block above her watery grave would've been difficult and expensive but worth it in every sense to ensure that the good folk of Torryburn could sleep safe at night, knowing the Devil's revenant envoy was not afoot.

---

2   Revenants—yes, the undead. Zombies.

And there lay Lilias Adie in her watery resting place on the Torryburn shore, trapped for ever more.

Or so the villagers thought.

It was on this foreshore some three hundred years later where we spoke to Douglas Speirs,[3] a local archaeologist. Doug, as he asked us to call him, arrived resplendent in tweed, just as a gentleman archaeologist should dress.

Some years before our meeting, Doug had been contacted by witchcraft expert turned broadcaster Louise Yeoman (whom we met in chapter 4), who had asked him if he was aware of the story of Lilias Adie and of the unusual underwater gravesite. She said there were numerous historical references to Lilias being buried in the Torryburn foreshore. Doug didn't know the story, but in listening to Louise, he became fascinated by Lilias's case and, more importantly for our present purposes, obsessed with finding her grave.

Doug took a scientific route to the search. "I immediately made an excuse to go and look for it. My colleague Steven Liscoe and I searched the Torryburn foreshore for the grave. Torryburn Bay is a big area, and the geology is very distinctive because it is whinstone, a hard blue stone, and what we were looking for was very different—a huge doorstep-shaped block of sandstone. For three long days, we walked up and down looking but found nothing. We were looking at the intertidal space—not quite land, not quite sea. On the last day, heading

---

3   Doug Speirs (Dug Spears) is about as good a name for an archaeologist as you can get. Having met us in Culross in Fife for the opening of the Witches Walk memorial and talked to us about Lilias, Doug was kind enough to speak to us again at length on our podcast. His words quoted here are an amalgam of these meetings.

back into shore, we saw a large, rectangular-looking block, covered in seaweed. It was only about two meters from the edge of land—we had been searching far out in the bay—but we quickly scraped off the seaweed, and there it was: a three-foot-by-six-foot, large, rectangular, sandstone block. It was probably about a quarter of a ton, with a dimple in the middle, showing it had been lifted from a quarry. It was completely alien to the rocks of the bay. We had found the site of Lilias's grave."

Meanwhile and separately, Louise was carrying out her own, somewhat more haphazard investigations. When did *she* discover the grave?

"Well, I never like to use the word 'discovery' because my point would be if you went and asked the right people in that community, they'd always kent[4] about it," said Louise when we spoke with her. "In a way, it was knowledge that was always there, and people in the community would have known it. What I basically did was jump up and down about it!"

In truth, Louise did more than that; she put on her wellies and waded out into the sea to the spot where Lilias's intertidal grave can be found.

Louise laughed her lovely, hearty laugh and said, "I was recording with A. L. Kennedy and the fantastic Scottish historian Dr. Martha McGill, and I was the mug who put on her wellies. There's always silty mud there. The thing is my background is as a historian and manuscript curator. Show me a sixteenth-century document, and I'll have a good go at reading it. I know about documents. I know nothing about stones! I was just armed with all this local history and was thinking it ought to be around here. I'll just have to wade out and have a look at it. I saw this gray, rectangular stone. One of the local histories had described it as being like a giant doorstep. That's got to be it!"

---

4   Scots for "known."

Now we stood on the pavement at the foreshore, staring at the large, gray sandstone slab only a couple meters away from us. The seawater lapped around it. The land all around the slab was sludgy and gray. The sort of mud that you could easily lose a Wellington boot to.

Doug explained that a horse and cart, or a "yanker"—a wheeled cart employed to move big stones—would've been used to haul the heavy stone to its destination. It would've been far from an easy job.

We fell to talking about Lilias herself. We know the accusation against her was made-up nonsense, but we wondered why on earth she confessed.

"I don't think she did confess," said Doug, who has studied the case in a great deal of depth. "On June 30, she has spent one night in custody, and she's interrogated for the first time. The minute records that Lilias is being exhorted to declare the truth and nothing but the truth. She is alleged to have replied, 'Be this as true as the sun is in the firmament.' This declaration that everything she is going to say is true immediately makes me think that these minutes have been faked. Who speaks like that when they're panicking and frightened and in custody? It's recorded that she admitted she was in compact with the Devil and that she had been so since before the second burning of the witches in this place. She further declared that the first time she met with the Devil was at a small local river between Torryburn and Newmills, in the harvest time before the sunset. He caused her to renounce her baptism by putting one hand on the crown of her head and the other on the soles of feet and declaring that all was the Devil's betwixt the crown of her head and the soles of her feet. Then the Devil lay with her carnally, and his skin was cold, his color was black and pale,[5] and he had a hat on his head."

---

5   As in black hair and clothing, pale skin.

So as Doug explained, "On the very first day, at 9 a.m., after being taken into custody, Lilias is interrogated and apparently those are her first words, or certainly that's what the minister in the kirk session recorded. And of course, what we see is there's a very clear black-and-white confession of evildoings with the Devil. With almost no prompting, Lilias confessed that she was a witch. She renounced Christian baptism; she had had sex with the Devil; she had willingly entered into an evil satanic baptism."

As we've seen with other confessions—this is all very familiar from Isobel Gowdie's case, for example—it's conveniently all there. "And of course," Doug continued, "she knew, and anybody would have known fine well at this point that when you confess to witchcraft, it's certain death. So it seems very suspicious that somebody would sit and make such a self-condemning confession on the first morning."

Our interpretation is that rather than the confession being faked, Lilias might've just confessed due to fear of torture, as she would've known that confessing meant she wouldn't be tortured in the future. Or she could've caved from the psychological pressure. It's surprising, but Claire finds in her work that people often confess to things they haven't done, even when no pressure is being put on them. There are all sorts of procedural safeguards against this in modern criminal law, such as having a lawyer present or being given the "right to remain silent" caution. But no such safeguards existed then, and we know people regularly confessed to things that weren't true. We wondered why Doug was so sure the whole confession was fabricated by Reverend Logan and not just Lilias trying to avoid torture.

"Ah, well, firstly, as I said, she makes a cast-iron confession of guilt. She makes a very clear declaration she is telling the truth. She goes into detail about renouncing her baptism. Today we're not terribly worried about that, but back then, baptism was a fundamentally important prerequisite of entry into heaven, so this was really, really, important. You couldn't get a bigger deal than confessing to having renounced your baptism. Not only that, but then it's said that she immediately confesses to taking part in a satanic baptism. And of course then to add to all of this and to rubbish her character as a woman and as a person, she gives details of sealing that compact by having sex—fornication in a field with the Devil! I mean, goodness! In a single statement, she manages to absolutely condemn herself. Beyond any question. Are these really the words of an elderly woman in a tiny little backwater parish in 1704? I would say what we're seeing here is complete fabrication of the minutes. What makes me utterly convinced that she did not say any of this, what is most compelling, is that if we study the kirk records of witchcraft in Fife, we find that in 1649, Margaret Martin in Inverkeithing confessed in exactly the same way about the satanic baptism. Is it likely that fifty-five years before these events, somebody would have used almost exactly the same words? This is a word-for-word copy. Now we can conclude one of two things. Either the Devil is real, and he was operating in West Fife from the seventeenth century, having sex with women and forcing them to renounce their baptism. Or we have an institution, in this case the church, which basically has a preconceived idea and is forcing it on those that it considered guilty."[6]

But for Doug, the copied confession isn't the only issue. As he explained, "If I needed to make the case any more clearly that this was a fixed record, when we really drill down into the minutes, we actually find that there are many entries in the minutes that describe events that

---

[6] We have seen similar examples of the word-for-word copies in the case of Isobel Gowdie and Janet Breadheid, but there are much more recent examples too. In the 1980s "Ice Cream Wars" case, which, despite the name, concerned gang turf wars in Glasgow, convictions for murder were quashed on appeal when the court decided it was not likely that a number of police officers could remember one of the accused's statements word for word.

don't happen until a week or a few days after the date of the minutes. So clearly these minutes should have been written up immediately *after* the event. But the fact that they include certain references to events that didn't happen for another two weeks gives us some kind of idea that these minutes weren't written up at the time as things were being said or even the next day or that night. They could have been written up to two to three weeks afterward in some cases. So this is clearly an account of what the court wanted recorded and probably not an accurate account of what actually happened. So for example, in the minutes, it says that June 20 is a Tuesday. But when you actually consult the historical calendars, you find out that that was a Friday. In 1704, when people's schedules were regulated by the kirk and observance of church events on the sabbath were part of every diary, it's not likely that, had the minutes been written on June 20, the writer would've mistaken the day. Which points to a far more likely cause—that these minutes were written up some time later, when memory of which day events had taken place was distorted."

Could these minutes have been a retrospective back-covering exercise? Did the reverend panic because Lilias had died in custody? Did he want to show his belief that despite her odd death, a terrible old witch had gotten her comeuppance, so he overegged it a bit, used a bit of artistic license, and copied the confession from previous minutes?

After a long, reflective pause, Doug answered, "My view of things is that there are pages and pages and pages in the Torryburn kirk session minutes from mid-June 1704 to September 3, 1704, about this case, and then suddenly nothing was mentioned after that for four weeks. Remember, the suspected witch Lilias has been incarcerated and interrogated. She has spilled the beans on another three women at least. They are then brought in and interrogated, and they start pointing the finger too. Other women and witches are being discovered everywhere. So from nowhere, a single accusation has snowballed into this.

A localized parish witch hunt within a month has gone from one witch to witches absolutely everywhere. And then, suddenly overnight, the case closes, and there's no further record or mention of anything or any charges or cases against anyone ever again. Now, how do we account for this? Well, my view—and it's only a personal view, not substantiated—I think two things happened. I think one is that the Reverend Allan Logan and his elders and bailie got carried away, and they've treated Lilias so badly that she's died in custody. And when the kirk session and the minister have approached the civil authorities and asked for a mandate for a legal commission to try the remaining witches, the civil authorities have denied the warrant and effectively said, 'Stop being so silly and stop torturing your poor old residents like this with trumped-up, ridiculous charges.' So knowing that they couldn't get a proper legal trial as they wouldn't be granted a warrant, they've just been told to pretty much drop the case. I think that's probably what's happened. Secondly, I think we have to appreciate the death was essentially an illegal killing in the sense that there wasn't a legal mandate for it. While there were powers for the church to investigate this case and to take confessions and so on, there was no legal basis to actually bring about a death without due and proper authority."

Doug means, of course, that there had been no trial, that her death before trial, possibly a result of the way in which she'd been kept or what she'd had to endure, was an as-yet-unsubstantiated allegation. It was not a good look for the authorities.

So after her death in custody, the minutes make no further reference to witches, witchcraft, or compacts with the Devil. Which begs the question: What happened to Agnes Curry and Elspeth Williamson, who'd been accused by Lilias?

"There is just no further mention of it, like it never happened. It supports my theory that after Lilias's death, everyone wanted to just forget about it. There's one last piece of information the minutes reveal, which seals the deal as far as I'm concerned that the Reverend Allan Logan was up to no good in relation to Lilias's 'confession.' In 1715, the reverend left Torryburn Parish as the minister there, and he got moved up the road to Culross. There is a record of him writing back to his former parish, and guess what he was asking for? Of all the things, he wanted the minutes of Lilias Adie's case. Why did he want these minutes all these many years later? My feeling is he wanted to rewrite history and to get rid of that record for some reason.[7] Again, we don't have enough evidence to be sure of this, but why else would he want those minutes? Thankfully, for whatever reason, he didn't get them, which is why we know Lilias's story today."

We watched the sea come in, now almost covering the huge slab of stone under which Lilias's casket lay. So, is this where Lilias Adie lies to this day?

"Oh no," said Doug. "Lilias did indeed revenant, although it wasn't the Devil who brought her back."

---

7   Doug believes that in later years, the reverend wanted to erase the record of the minutes because he wasn't so certain on the issue of witchcraft and wanted his involvement in the whole business removed. Doug stresses that this is only his suspicion, however.

PART THREE

A THING OF THE PAST?

13

How to Lose a Witch

"Her grave was robbed," said Doug Speirs.

"By witches?"

"Nope, by locals."

The water lapped around our feet as we watched Lilias Adie's grave be swallowed up in the incoming tide.

"So wait, are you meaning to tell us the same poor woman who died in custody and was locked in a box and buried at sea in an effort to stop her coming back was then in fact brought back by the folk who had put her there?"

"Not quite," said Doug.

In actuality, the mastermind of the grave robbing wasn't born until 1797, some sixty-two years after the revocation of the Scottish Witchcraft Act. Joseph Neil Paton was, as was common of men of his time, deeply religious.[1] While belief in witches had waned, belief in

---

1 The son of a Unitarian, he joined the Presbyterian Church as a youth, then turned Methodist, then Quaker, before finally settling into Swedenborgianism, a type of Restorationist Christianity.

God had not. More uncommon was his religious fervor, so strong he built a chapel on the grounds of his land so he could deliver sermons from his very own pulpit.

Not just anyone could afford a project like that, but Paton had done very well in business. His trade was weaving, a common business of the time, which he combined with a natural gift as an artist to create intricate and delicate designs in damask. His cloth was so admired that after his death in 1872, the Victoria and Albert Museum bought over seven hundred of his designs. He was married to folklorist Catherine MacDiarmid, who hailed from the Highlands, and they lived together in Dunfermline, a town a couple of miles inland from the Firth of Forth, in a grand family home.

But what does this religious artist have to do with grave robbing? Well, besides Paton's interest in all things religious, he also dug deep into hobbies of practicing phrenology and collecting witchcraft artifacts, which led him to Lilias Adie.

Phrenology was the brainchild of a man named Franz Joseph Gall, an eighteenth-century German doctor who believed he could tell the mental traits and character of a person simply by studying their skull; the theory was that the various areas of the brain were bigger or smaller in each individual according to their character traits, which would result in different skull shapes. Later "scientists" in this field, Johann Spurzheim and George Combe, went on to create the well-known picture of a human skull split up into different areas, which many would later associate with this now wholly discredited field of study.

Need we mention how racist and sexist this "science" was? Phrenology naturally played off the stereotypes and biases of the day. It provided the opportunity for anyone with confidence, fingertips, and a measuring tape to feel a human skull and proclaim knowledge of that person's character. How unsurprising it is then that phrenology affirmed the belief of European superiority and revealed women excelled at childcare, but their brains were underdeveloped when it came to science, art, and pretty much everything else.[2]

Living in Dunfermline, only five miles from Torryburn, with a wife who collected folktales, Paton was no doubt aware of the story of Lilias Adie and her revenant grave. As intersections go, a witch's skull would be the apex of twin obsessions with witchcraft and phrenology. So with the unfettered ambition of a typical Victorian collector, he decided he had to have it.

To turn his desire into reality, he contacted Robert Baxter Brimer, grave robber for hire.

The crime of grave robbing, or to give it its official name, "violation of a sepulcher," was all the rage for criminals in the eighteenth and nineteenth centuries. For those with a disregard for superstition and a strong stomach, graves were sources of jewelry and artifacts that could be obtained for little work. In Scotland, stealing corpses to sell to anatomists was particularly common, as Edinburgh was a leading center of anatomical study, and Scottish law had no strict controls about which corpses could be used for medical research. It was a simple case of supply and demand.[3] Violating sepulchers became such a frequent occurrence that iron "mortsafe" cages were bolted above graves in the hopes of deterring those who sought to tomb raid. Mortsafes could be

---

[2] Phrenologists divided the brain up into twenty-seven parts, each section denoting some human sentiment. The difficulty was—and perhaps here was the clue that this was not a legitimate science—hardly anyone could agree on what each of these twenty-seven parts signified. What *was* clear was that this nonsense abounded with misogyny and racism.

[3] The most infamous criminals associated with this period are William Burke and William Hare, who took this trend to its logical conclusion. In 1828, they committed a series of sixteen murders in order to sell the corpses to an anatomy lecturer for dissection, crimes for which Burke was hanged (though Hare was later released, as he'd given evidence against his former partner). Contrary to popular belief, it appears they didn't actually rob any graves themselves.

rented either for a certain amount of time, to allow the body to decompose in dignified peace, or could be installed permanently. Many graveyards also appointed watchmen to ensure that the grounds stayed as quiet as, well, the grave. By the middle of the nineteenth century, the tide was turning against the "resurrection men."

Back to Joseph Neil Paton and his grave robber, Robert Baxter Brimer. For Brimer, a young man in his early twenties in 1852, the grave of Lilias Adie provided some interesting challenges. It wouldn't be easy robbing a grave half-buried underwater, particularly in the dead of night. Added to that, as the grave belonged to a witch, this wasn't so much an illegal endeavor—the ground wasn't consecrated—as one that might threaten his mortal soul and those of the local villagers.

Brimer found the grave with surprising ease. The local folklore made it quite clear that under an enormous cut stone in the Torryburn Bay lay the box that held the witch's mortal remains. As we've seen with the twenty-first-century efforts to locate the slab, it's still visible at low tide. In the nineteenth century, it presumably would've been even easier to find, as less time had elapsed since it'd first been laid there.

So Brimer gathered up a crew and located the incongruous slab, and he and his accomplices set to work gaining entry. They knew they had to move quickly before the tide returned or the locals woke, but moving a six-foot-by-three-foot stone under ordinary circumstances is challenging enough; add to that the boggy mud in which they stood, and matters were complicated all the more. It was only dogged determination and the promise of Paton's purse that enabled Brimer and company to succeed in their grisly endeavor. Once they'd removed the slab and revealed the box, the men doubtless caught their breath for a second before breaking open the lid sealed a century before. Inside, among the sludgy silt, were the disarrayed remains of the now revenant witch, Lilias Adie.

Working quickly, the grave robbers exhumed their bony treasure. They carried away the skull, ribs, and a femur. Brimer, probably realizing the interest in such a curio, also took some wood from the box itself. Then he and his accomplices resealed the lid of the coffin and replaced the stone slab atop it, where they lie to this day.

In his collector's zeal, Paton had ordered a number of grave robberies across Fife, but this particular assignment held more than the usual promise of phrenological interest. Once Brimer returned with Lilias's remains, what did Paton do with his haul? Given his interest in phrenology and religion, it seems likely he carefully studied poor Lilias's skull to see what knowledge he could glean from it. By the time of his investigations, few people believed in witchcraft anymore, but Paton's strong religious beliefs may have led to a traditional approach to his study. It seems reasonable to assume he asked himself: Can I tell this woman had been evil from her skull? Had the Devil left his mark not only on her body and soul but in her brain?

Records indicate that the highheidyins who visited Paton in Dunfermline would be treated to a display of Adie's skull, which was kept in Paton's private collection until his death in 1874. Paton left a detailed will, revealing that Lilias's skull is likely to have gone to his firstborn son, Joseph Noel Paton.

Joseph Noel Paton (1821–1901) was a gifted and famous Scottish artist, his art often depicting images of witches, demons, and fairies. He received a knighthood later in life, and some of his works can be seen today in the National Gallery of Scotland and the Kelvingrove Art Gallery and Museum.

"You can see his father's artifacts in his paintings," explained Doug. "Swords and such. I have a theory that you can even see Lilias's skull in a couple of them. If you look at the painting *Luther at Erfurt* [1861], there is a skull in the background. I think there is a reasonable chance it's the skull of Lilias Adie."

Sure enough, the painting shows a tortured Luther poring over his texts at the University of Erfurt,[4] and there, lurking on the corner of his desk, is a skull. Could this be Lilias? And if it was there in 1861, where is she now?

In 1884, Paton Junior passed Lilias's skull to a Dr. William Dow of the Fife Medical Association. In that same year, Dow conducted a detailed examination of the skull, after which he wrote a paper and gave lectures on his findings. Several years later, the skull was given to the University of St. Andrews's collection of anatomical artefacts. It was still there in 1901, when a member of the Dunfermline press photographed it for an article on Lilias's case.

But Doug had some bad news for us. "In 2014 when I discovered her grave, the first thing I did was to contact the university to ask to see her skull. To my surprise, they couldn't find it!"

Doug thereafter undertook a painstaking search for any mention of her skull in documentary evidence that was available from that time. Almost miraculously, he found a small item in a local newspaper from Falkirk in 1938, which had a throwaway reference to the Empire Exhibition in Glasgow, where readers could view the skull of a real witch, Lilias Adie.

---

4   This Luther being of course Martin Luther, former disillusioned Catholic priest, founder of Protestantism, and author of the *Ninety-five Theses*.

The Empire Exhibition of 1938, a presentation intended to showcase Scotland on an international stage, was based on the Great Exhibition of 1851 in London. Little did the planners know the success of their exhibition would outstrip London's by far: in total, it received an amazing 12,800,000 visitors—every one of whom had the opportunity to see Lilias's skull.

Sadly, from 1938 on, the trail runs cold, and as of this moment, there have been no further mentions or sightings of Lilias's skull.

If the skull is gone, what about the rest of Lilias's remains beneath the huge slab? Could there be bones underneath? Robbers aren't the best at completing inventories, so we can't be sure of the answer, but Doug believes it's likely some part of Lilias's body is still there.

What of the other items removed along with her skull? Her femur and the pieces of wood taken from her box?

"For that," said Doug, "you'll need to go to Dunfermline."

Robert Baxter Brimer, erstwhile grave robber, had moved on since his early days as a tomb raider for hire. He'd left the shores of Torryburn far behind and had long since emigrated to Ontario, Canada, where he'd become a successful man of business. His youthful high jinks in Torryburn were long gone, though not forgotten.

On November 11, 1871, an incredibly successful man, Andrew Carnegie, visited Ontario and Robert Baxter Brimer. Carnegie, a Scottish industrialist, made his money from the steel industry; he was, at the time, one of the richest men in the world—if not *the* richest. His visit presented Brimer with an unusual problem: What gift could you give a man who has literally everything? And then it came to him. He had the perfect, most unique, most unforgettable gift—a memento from the old country.

How to Kill a Witch

We traveled to Dunfermline on a dreich Tuesday afternoon to meet Jennifer Jones, the comanager of the Andrew Carnegie Birthplace Museum.

Dawn: Luther at Erfurt, Sir Joseph Noel Paton, 1861

The museum is made up of two buildings. One building is a small, unassuming cottage with a plaque on the wall that boasts of, you guessed it, being the birthplace of the philanthropist and businessman. The other, a larger, more ornate building with a big hall tells the incredible story of Carnegie's life and is filled with historical artifacts gathered by him and his wife.

As much as we wanted to stay in that hall and discover what connected Carnegie and Big Bird from *Sesame Street* (whom we saw nesting in a glass box along with puppet pals Ernie and Bert[5]), we dutifully followed Jennifer to an office up the stairs. There, on the desk, lay what looked like an unassuming wooden walking cane.

Jennifer carefully picked up the cane and handed it to us. As we examined it more closely, we saw there was very faded, carved handwriting that ran down its length. We couldn't make out what had been written, but Jennifer helpfully showed us a typed museum label, which read:

A walking stick with a grisly history which reminds us that dark deeds were carried out only a few centuries ago, often in ignorance, against women who were deemed to be witches. Written in ink on the straight, wooden cane is the following inscription:

"This is made from part of the coffin of Lillian Eadie, who was burned for a witch[6] and buried within the sea mouth of Torryburn, Fifeshire, Scotland, and dug up by James Bonner[7] and

---

5 In 1911, Andrew Carnegie established the Carnegie Corporation of New York, which promoted knowledge and understanding by providing grants to deserving causes. One such grant was given to fund a groundbreaking TV show that desired to aid in the education of children—*Sesame Street*!

6 As we can see, the inscription isn't entirely accurate in respect of her name or her manner of death.

7 Presumably an accomplice of Brimer's.

others about 1860. The skull and some of the bones and parts of the coffin are now either in the British Museum, London, or Saint Andrews, sent there by Mr. Paton, father of Sir Noel Paton.

Presented to Mr. Carnegie by R. B. Brimer, Toronto, 11th November 1871."

It was the very wood from the box in which Lilias Adie was buried. Knowing about history is one thing; seeing and touching history is a very different feeling. The power of a historical artifact is huge. We don't believe it's a coincidence that in war, enemy invaders target both vital utilities as well as treasures of history and locations of historical importance.

Just think: this nondescript piece of wood had been part of the box that once held the body of a woman accused of witchcraft, had traveled to Canada as the loot of a tomb raider, and had been gifted to the world's richest man, only for it to return home to Fife and land in our hands. It was all so extraordinary—a tangible connection to the past that left us humbled and amazed.

In 2017, Lilias Adie's connection to the present took another extraordinary step when forensic artist Dr. Christopher Rynn worked with the University of Dundee Leverhulme Research Centre to reconstruct her face from the photographs and measurements that had been taken of her skull before it was lost.

The face of Lilias Adie shows a kindly woman with a half smile, a little bemused at the fame she never could've imagined she'd achieve after her death.

We may not have her skull, but we can remember Lilias for who she was as a person: a poor, old, probably ostracized, and lonely woman who was accused of something for which she wasn't guilty; a woman imprisoned and harassed by the very society that ought to have protected her; and someone who, even in death, was further exploited for the entertainment of wealthy men. Her story and life are important to hold in our memories—both out of respect for her and in hopes what happened to her will never be repeated.

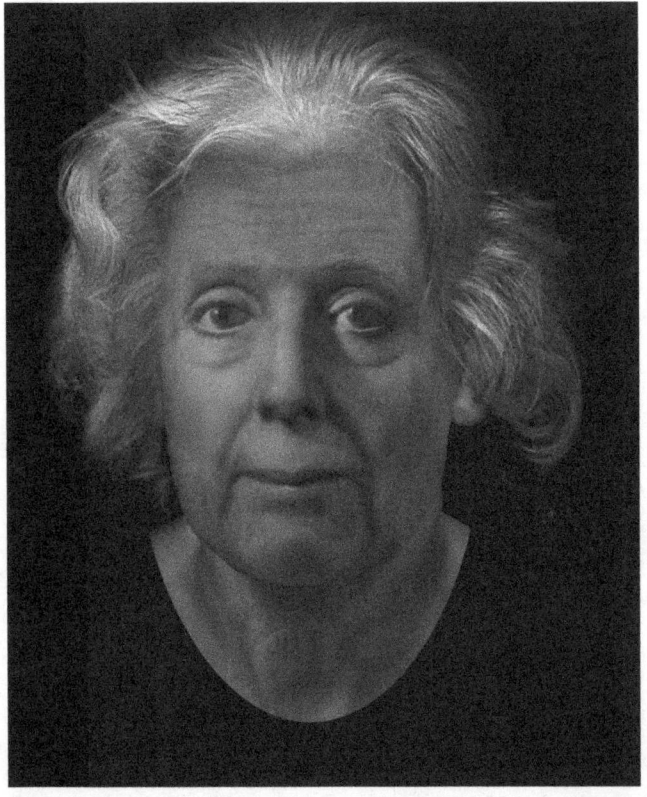

Reconstruction of Lilias Adie's face by forensic scientist Dr. Christopher Rynn, 2017

PORTRAIT OF THE ACCUSED

Helen Duncan

LONDON, 1944

Victoria Helen MacFarlane was born in the autumn of 1897 in Callander, Perthshire. She was one of eight children. Despite coming from a typical Presbyterian background, Helen (as she was known) was given to bouts of high drama and terrifying her friends with tales of the supernatural. She believed she could prophesize the future: she told people about dangers they should avoid and claimed she had psychic abilities. It was at primary school where she was given the nickname "Hellish Nell," which still clings to her now.

When she left school, Helen moved to Dundee, a much bigger town, where she gained work first in a munitions factory, then as a nurse at Dundee Royal Infirmary. On May 27, 1916, she married a cabinet maker and war veteran named Henry Duncan. The couple had twelve children, but sadly, only six survived. As well as rearing the children, Helen had to take up part-time, arduous work in a bleach factory to make the family's ends meet, as her husband's ill health made full-time work impossible.

Helen and Henry both claimed they'd had visions of each other before they met, and Henry, who came from a family who purported to have the gift of second sight, encouraged Helen to develop her psychic abilities. Helen began to hold séances for the wider public and in more intimate, private settings, and she steadily gained a tremendous reputation for her readings. Séances would take place in various settings, including Spiritualist churches and people's homes; she would commune with the dead, often reassuring the bereaved that there was life after death and loved ones were watching from beyond the grave.

By the mid-1920s, Helen had developed her skills and reputation to such an extent that she was in demand all over Great Britain and was becoming well known in Spiritualist circles. With so many families suffering devastating losses from the First World War, many saw Spiritualism as a way of keeping in touch with their dead sons and husbands or, at the very least, of being reassured they were in a better place.

At one of Helen's Spiritualist sittings, the attendees sat in a dark room in a semicircle, gathered around a large "cabinet" with curtains covering it. Helen would be searched to confirm she wasn't hiding any tricks or gadgets, and then she would step into the cabinet. (Henry usually sat at the back of the room during the sitting.) She would enter a trance, and a spirit would speak through her, deliver messages, and talk to other spirits who'd come to visit the attendees. Helen had a particular spirit guide named Albert Stuart who, although originally from Dundee, had emigrated to and died in Australia. His voice came from Helen's mouth, and he supposedly spoke with less of a Scottish accent than the one Helen usually had. Stuart would introduce the other spirits present for the sitting. The curtains on the cabinet would then be opened, and ectoplasm—so-called spiritual energy—would come streaming from Helen's nose and mouth. Sitters often thought the ectoplasm (actually white cloth) resembled their deceased loved ones.

Throughout her career, Helen's work was frequently investigated. In 1931, the great psychic researcher and skeptic Harry Price[1] gave his opinion after having Helen do five sittings for him. The ectoplasm he witnessed was photographed, scientifically examined, and subsequently exposed as being cheesecloth. Price discovered Helen had other various tricks up her sleeve, such as waving around a cut-out picture of a child's face to simulate a head appearing and using safety pins to shape the ectoplasm. Price's conclusion was that Helen's skills were far from genuine, calling her a "fat female crook." But his goal was to expose Helen, not criminalize her, and even with all the tricks, some people still believed there were unexplainable parts of Helen's sittings.

Helen was first convicted in 1933 of fraudulent mediumship and fined £10. Despite this, her reputation grew, and she remained in great demand. At the height of the Second World War in November 1941, Helen held a séance in Portsmouth where her performance included her "seeing" a sailor who'd died in the sinking of the HMS *Barham* a short while previously, a tragedy in which 862 crewmen had lost their lives. The issue with this particular séance was there happened to be a strict hush-hush policy on the ship's destruction for reasons of national security—no one was supposed to know. Of course, with the number of sailors who died and all their families duly informed, hundreds of people *did* know about the sinking. Nevertheless, because of her supposed revelation of state secrets, the powers that be began to keep an eye on Helen.

---

[1] Harry Price (1881–1948) was a British psychic researcher and author who found fame debunking various fake mediums, although he did endorse those whom he believed to be genuine. He was involved in several famous cases including that of the Borley Rectory ("the most haunted house in England"), the Battersea Poltergeist, and Gef the talking mongoose, along with many others.

In 1944,[2] two naval men, Lieutenant Worth and Surgeon-Lieutenant Fowler, saw Helen at a sitting organized by a local couple, Mr. and Mrs. Homer. The two men were suspicious about some of the details coming from Helen and reported her to the police.[3] Worth attended a second sitting (this time with a plainclothes policeman) where a white-shrouded vision appeared; rather pathetically, this turned out to be Helen covered in a sheet. Helen was attempting to hide the sheet when she was apprehended. She, the Homers, and a lady named Mrs. Brown were all arrested.

Normally in England, this sort of fraudulent mediumship was dealt with under the Vagrancy Act of 1824, but as the authorities wished to deal harshly with Helen (perhaps to make an example of her), she was also later charged, rather sensationally, under the Witchcraft Act of 1735. Prime Minister Winston Churchill was unimpressed with what he viewed as the "obsolete tomfoolery" of the charge, but the case ran, and after a seven-day trial, she was found guilty and sentenced to nine months in prison.

Helen Duncan died in 1956 after a police raid on one of her séances. Her supporters claimed her death was caused by the "shocked" ectoplasm returning too quickly to her body. She was, however, known to suffer from heart trouble—a more likely cause of death. She was the last person to be convicted under the Witchcraft Act of 1735. There have been various recent campaigns to pardon her, but all have failed.

The Witchcraft Act of 1735 was repealed in 1951.

---

[2] We believe the time gap between Helen's séance of the dead sailor and her arrest is due to the heightened paranoia leading up to the Normandy landings of 1944.

[3] Helen had claimed to be in contact with a woman who wasn't yet dead.

14

How to Accuse a Modern-Day Witch, Part 1: The Twentieth Century

The very last witch trial in England[1] was toward the end of the Second World War in 1944, a full 217 years after Janet Horne's execution in 1727.[2] Unlike the traditional witchcraft accusations, this story is markedly different, not least because we can much more easily identify with the people of this period. However, some key points remain the same. A woman causes anxiety—in this case by revealing state secrets about a sunken ship that was supposedly under wraps—and falls out of favor during a difficult time for the country. The woman must be made an example of and suitably punished.

---

1   Technically speaking, it was a "pretended" witch trial, as the crime of witchcraft had been changed to that of "pretended witchcraft" to reflect the fact that witchcraft did not exist.

2   Janet Horne was the last witch executed in Scotland.

When Helen Duncan was brought to trial, the judge addressed the court and said very clearly, especially to the assembled journalists who were hungry for lurid headlines, "Though we are using the Witchcraft Act, Mrs. Duncan is not on trial for witchcraft. This is not a witch trial—this is an accusation of fraud."

Yet inevitably, by choosing to prosecute under the Witchcraft Act of 1735,[3] the authorities ensured the trial had all those connotations firmly embedded. In Scotland, when the Witchcraft Acts of 1563 and 1649 were repealed and the Witchcraft Act of 1735 put in place, the crime of witchcraft as defined by the earlier acts was firmly rejected in favor of the crime of "pretended witchcraft"—so ironically, the charge was that she was *not* a witch and instead was pretending to have powers she didn't have.

Despite this legal distinction, the public saw the whole circus as a salacious witch trial, and it firmly grabbed everyone's imagination for several weeks during the seemingly interminable war.

We spoke to historian Malcolm Gaskill, who has written various books on witch trials and a stand-alone book on Helen Duncan.[4] Malcolm is an emeritus professor at the University of East Anglia. We love speaking to Malcolm; he's not only very knowledgeable but also great fun.

The first thing we wanted to clarify was why on earth did the Crown charge Helen Duncan with such an antiquated crime?[5] Malcolm told us the Spiritualists who were defending her in the case

---

3 Specifically, Section 4 of the Witchcraft Act of 1735, which covers anyone who "pretend[s] to exercise or use any kind of Witchcraft, Sorcery, Inchantment, or Conjuration, or undertake[s] to tell Fortunes."

4 Malcolm Gaskill, *Hellish Nell: Last of Britain's Witches* (Fourth Estate, 2001).

5 "The Crown Office" aka "the Crown" prosecutes criminal cases in the public interest on behalf of the people.

had asked the same question. It turns out the Crown also charged her with the pretended witchcraft crime "in the alternative," which was and is a perfectly acceptable thing to do in law. A person may be charged with more than one crime if the Crown thinks one charge isn't quite guaranteed, or the evidence may be stronger in favor of one charge than another. In the case of Helen Duncan, she was originally accused of the much more straightforward crime of fraud under the Vagrancy Act,[6] which includes the crimes of "pretending or professing to tell fortunes, or using any subtle craft, means, or device, by palmistry or otherwise, to deceive and impose on any of his Majesty's subjects," and was also charged under the common law of public mischief. It seems the witchcraft charge was added because the Crown wanted to make an example of her behavior, which they didn't consider good for the war effort. Her colleagues Ernest and Elizabeth Homer, who ran the psychic center in Portsmouth, and her agent, Frances Brown, were also charged.

"Helen is charged under Section 4 of the 1824 Vagrancy Act, which is mainly for exactly this kind of fraud," said Malcolm. "It was introduced after the Napoleonic Wars, particularly to stop returning soldiers fleecing people by becoming palmists."

After the Napoleonic Wars of 1803–1815, many soldiers were coming back injured and unable to earn an "honest" living and were therefore forced to turn to other means to survive. Fast-forward around 120 years, and the law was still being used in England and Wales but now for Spiritualists and mediums taking advantage of distressed people who'd lost loved ones in the two world wars.

As Malcolm pointed out to us, it's always been the case that poverty and witchcraft are closely intertwined. We've seen how people with

---

[6] Section 4 of the Vagrancy Act of 1824 has the raffish title "Persons committing certain offenses to be deemed rogues and vagabonds."

less power are usually viewed with suspicion and may fall out with neighbors due to the kinds of issues that often surround poverty, such as alcohol abuse or antisocial behavior.

In the 1940s, someone charged with the Vagrancy Act for this kind of fraud would've simply received a fine for fraudulent crimes, as other Spiritualists had in the past. But when Helen's case came to trial, her vagrancy charges were dropped, and the Crown only proceeded on the Witchcraft Act charge. The authorities were keen to stamp out the trend of Spiritualism by any means necessary.

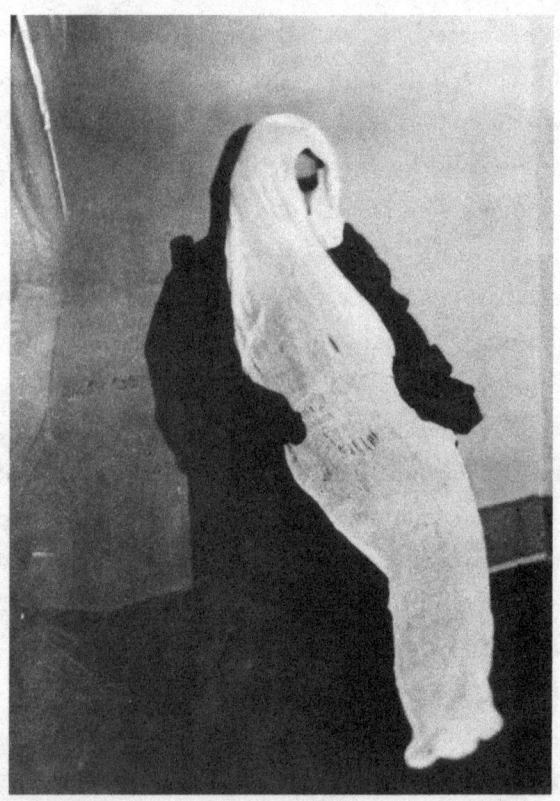

Contemporary photograph of Helen Duncan with muslin "ectoplasm," published in the *Daily Mirror*, 9 October 1933

On the opposite side from the Crown, because Helen was a

high-profile medium, the Spiritualists' National Union (SNU) decided they were going to use her case essentially as a show trial to try to prove that Spiritualism was real. Yes, you read that right: Spiritualists had their own union as well as dozens of Spiritualist organizations, clubs, associations, and publications across Britain. The movement was enjoying a huge wave of popularity at the time, and it had many influential people on board. As a result, there was a great deal of money available to push for the legitimization of Spiritualism in the public arena.

Malcolm elaborated: "The world of Spiritualism one hundred years ago is not the world of old ladies in Spiritualist churches in back streets in small towns. This is a very powerful, important part of British religious and social culture between the wars."

It's no wonder there was a strong resurgence of a desire to communicate with the dead at the end of the war years. The psychological damage wrought on the country after the losses of World War I was bad enough in isolation, but to have another conflict with such high casualties a mere twenty-one years later—a single generation—was soul-crushing. When we're talking about spiritual beliefs, we always need to factor in the emotional temperature of the nation. Britain in 1944 was reeling from its losses and was therefore searching for something to cling to psychologically and spiritually. One could argue Spiritualism is a fairly logical response, considering the circumstances.

"It's respectable. It's not a crank movement," said Malcolm. "All these Spiritualist organizations have a relationship with psychical research, which is another respectable enterprise that's going on in Britain and Western Europe at this time. They're often in tension with each other, but psychical research has some very respectable scientists who have money to spend on trying to prove the reality of mediums contacting the spirit world."

With Helen's trial, the SNU saw a golden opportunity to bolster their reputation and reach the masses. They engaged Charles Loseby KC—a Spiritualist himself—for Helen's defense and were convinced they would win the case.

Meanwhile, the Crown engaged John Maude KC. He was, besides being a lawyer, an MI5 officer whose specialist area during the war was shipping security.[7] The Spiritualist KC and the sea security KC were apt opponents for this trial. If Helen had just accepted the charge of fraud, all the commotion might've quietly gone away. However, with Helen denying the charges, the case took on circus-like dimensions, and the stage was set for a very public showdown.[8]

Malcolm thinks Helen's part in the process was fairly passive, but the SNU were determined they were going to use her case to make people understand what Spiritualists did. At the same time, the Crown was utilizing the proceedings to force people to comply with wartime rules: the powers that be were alarmed by Helen's revelation of classified information regarding the HMS *Barham* sinking, and they wanted to make sure there were no repeat incidents.

It is easy to feel sympathy for Helen Duncan. She'd found a fairly lucrative way to look after her large family in very difficult circumstances. The money not only became better over her career,[9] but she'd found something she was very good at. She seemed (despite the tricks) to genuinely believe she was in touch with the dead and was

---

7   A KC, or King's Counsel, is a special type of top lawyer. Claire is a KC, though not an MI5 officer. Doubtless, that's what John Maude KC would've said at the time too. "I'm not," says Claire.

8   Interestingly, at the same time that Maude was prosecuting Helen in one courtroom in Portsmouth Court, he was also defending a man in a murder trial in another courtroom with the assistance of junior counsel. He won both cases.

9   In fact, she made a pretty good living at times. She charged over £100 for a week of readings in Portsmouth.

performing an important service to the living. Malcolm thinks she may have turned to fraudulent methods simply because she was under a great deal of pressure to provide results.

"The standard line about Helen Duncan is that she was the greatest medium that ever lived," explained Malcolm. "However, that comes huge with pressure." It was almost as if Helen's followers were demanding so much from her, she couldn't possibly deliver.

Although it's been proven she sometimes faked results and messages and even the physical manifestations of her communication, Helen and her supporters saw such things as part of the process. Besides, it's very difficult to legally disprove Helen was speaking to the dead.

It's an accepted point of law, as Claire knows so well, that in criminal trials, the Crown must prove their case *beyond a reasonable doubt*. In contrast, the defense merely needs to raise a reasonable doubt—the accused doesn't have to prove their innocence, and it's impossible to prove a negative.

"In the Helen Duncan case," said Malcolm, "the crucial thing about using the Witchcraft Act was that you only had to prove that somebody had attempted to conjure spirits. So actually, they moved it away from fraud and moved it to attempting to conjure spirits, which of course was Helen Duncan's job. Charles Loseby KC got it completely wrong because he got forty-odd witnesses to prove that Helen Duncan had genuinely conjured the spirits. Therefore, she wasn't a fraud. But that's exactly what the Witchcraft Act of 1735 required. Every time one of his defense witnesses came up, the prosecution didn't really have to do anything."

The defense was seeking to prove there'd been no fraudulent behavior or deceit since Helen could, as a matter of fact, speak to the dead. But in the law, there was an underlying assumption that this was not possible. In essence, both the Vagrancy Act and the Witchcraft Act concerned crimes of deceit—of pretending someone could speak to the dead in séances or tell fortunes when they could not. So there was no way Helen could win her case with this argument.

Ultimately, the Witchcraft Act was repealed in 1951 and replaced with the Fraudulent Mediums Act. But that was too late for Helen; she was convicted in April 1944 and given nine months' imprisonment.

Helen's sentence illustrated perhaps the most important difference between the Witchcraft Act and the Vagrancy Act—an individual could not be jailed under the latter act, whereas a sentence of up to twelve months' imprisonment could be imposed under the Witchcraft Act. It was certainly preferable to the previous sentence of execution but still a devastating outcome for anyone who wasn't a hardened criminal.

The public response was mixed. Naturally, many were fascinated by the case. A great number of people felt sympathy toward Helen, and many wrote to the Home Office,[10] arguing that they were fighting Germany to ensure Great Britain kept her freedom, and this case was, in fact, state control.

After she was convicted, Helen appealed against both the conviction and the sentence on various grounds, most of which were dealt with in short order and rejected by the court, who found no merit in the legal arguments and didn't hear substantive argument on those issues. The ground of appeal that took the most time was the submission by Loseby that Helen couldn't have been guilty of the conspiracy to use conjuration because she didn't attempt to summon the Devil or evil spirits; rather, she summoned spirits of the dead. He relied on a definition of the law in a very early legal dictionary called *The Interpreter*, published in 1607 by John Cowell, which states, "It is especially used for such as have personal conference with the Devil or evil spirit."

---

10 The part of the British government responsible for domestic affairs, security, and law and order.

How to Accuse a Modern-Day Witch, Part 1: The Twentieth Century

The appeal court disagreed for two reasons. First, the Witchcraft Act says "any kind of...conjuration," which must mean there's more than one kind. In addition, the court's opinion was that the crime of witchcraft had been abolished because people no longer believed in it. The statute therefore doesn't that specify the crime of pretending to converse with spirits refers only to evil ones; it means any type of spirit, precisely because neither was believed in. The court explained: "Such a distinction would raise an issue of fact incapable of determination and based on no intelligible principle of law or religion."

In relation to sentence, the appeal court's opinion was stark: "On the footing of the verdict of the jury, nine months' imprisonment was, in our opinion, in no way excessive."

Ultimately, the case and conviction achieved what the authorities had set out to do: silence Helen and remove her from the public eye. We now know preparations were underway for D-Day, and it's undeniable the authorities did have a responsibility to prevent people from talking about shipping.

But knowing someone was sentenced under the Witchcraft Act in 1944 is mind-boggling. Helen said she wouldn't conduct séances after her time in jail, but some years after her release, police raided a house in Nottingham where she was performing again. She fell seriously ill shortly thereafter, and it was said by Spiritualist supporters that the police barging into the séance had forced the ectoplasm to snap back into Helen's body—like an otherworldly elastic band—and caused this illness. This time around, she evaded the earthly reach of the law, but she died shortly afterward on December 6, 1956.

While on the face of it, Helen Duncan's story is very different from the witch trials of the sixteenth to eighteenth centuries, we can draw some comparisons. Helen's case was about the Crown asserting dominance over a person who was, despite her fame, in poor health with many children and a husband with a disability and therefore vulnerable. She, like many of the accused during the witch trials period, was used as a figure to control the populace at a time of social anxiety and fear. And finally, as was true of many of the original accused, Helen was a woman.

15

How to Accuse a Modern-Day Witch, Part 2: The Twenty-First Century

Resolution Adopted by the Human Rights Council on 12 July 2021

Elimination of harmful practices related to accusations of witchcraft and ritual attacks [extract]

Expressing its concern that harmful practices related to witchcraft accusations and ritual attacks have resulted in various forms of violence, including killings, mutilation, burning, coercion in trafficking of persons, torture and other cruel, inhuman or degrading treatment and stigmatization, particularly for persons in vulnerable situations, including women, children, persons with disabilities, older persons and persons with albinism, and that these forms of violence are often committed with impunity,

- Urges States to condemn harmful practices related to accusations of witchcraft and ritual attacks that result in human rights violations;

- Also urges States to take all measures necessary to ensure the elimination of harmful practices amounting to human rights violations related to accusations of witchcraft and ritual attacks, and to ensure accountability and the effective protection of all persons, particularly persons in vulnerable situations;
- Calls upon States to ensure that no one within their jurisdiction is deprived of the right to life, liberty or security of person because of religion or belief, and that no one is subjected to torture or other cruel, inhuman or degrading treatment or punishment, or arbitrary arrest or detention on that account, and to bring to justice all perpetrators of violations and abuses of these rights in compliance with applicable international law;
- Invites States, in collaboration with relevant regional and international organizations, to promote bilateral, regional and international initiatives to support the protection of all persons vulnerable to harmful practices amounting to human rights violations related to accusations of witchcraft and ritual attacks, while noting that, in providing protection, attention to local context is critical.

Quite aside from the horrors of thousands of people being persecuted as witches between the sixteenth and eighteenth centuries in Scotland, we push on with our campaign because, quite unbelievably, it's still an ongoing issue.

Accusations of witchcraft and their attendant human rights abuses are so endemic in some parts of the world that some governments have been debating adding laws against practicing witchcraft back to their statutes. In response, the United Nations made a resolution against people being accused of witchcraft. The extract above is taken from

How to Accuse a Modern-Day Witch, Part 2: The Twenty-First Century

it. Some people[1] say to us, "Leave the past behind. We've moved on," or words to that effect, but we know from fellow campaigners who are kept incredibly busy in their own countries that sadly, this is absolutely not true.

As of 2025, there are several countries where witchcraft accusations are still rife. These include but are not limited to Nigeria, Malawi, Ghana, China, Papua New Guinea, and India. Figures are imprecise due to stigma and secrecy, but researchers are confident that accusations are in the hundreds. As with the Scottish experience, the accused are often (though not always) older, isolated women, and consequences can range from banishments (such as the witch camps of Ghana[2]) to physical punishments to—and we cannot believe we are writing this in the twenty-first century—executions.

Leo Igwe heads up an organization called Advocacy for Alleged Witches (AfAW), which works across various African countries but largely in Nigeria and Malawi. Coming from a humanist background, Leo is primarily interested in developing critical thinking in communities and is a good-humored and very engaging speaker. Although based in Nigeria, Leo travels a lot to educate and advocate.

Leo told us his work is focused on two main fronts. First, his team are on the ground intervening in as many cases of accusation as they can—fifteen last year, though they were called to more cases than their resources could provide for. Second, they target schools to assist in developing resources that encourage critical thinking skills. The aim is to help young people question socially held beliefs, making them less vulnerable to indoctrination and radicalization.

---

1 It has to be said, almost exclusively white, middle-aged men.

2 These camps are set up for women who've been excluded from their communities due to witchcraft accusations and are places they can live without fear of further attacks.

Billboard advertising a Nigerian "anti-witch" event, 2024

Why has the belief in witchcraft continued to hold sway in certain parts of Africa?

The reason is largely due to what Leo terms "gaps": "Gaps in law enforcement, political gaps, legislative gaps, humanitarian and social welfare gaps, human rights gaps," he said. "What we are trying to do is to draw attention to these gaps because over the years, they have been ignored, and witch accusations have been taken as cultural to Africans, which is a misrepresentation of the situation."

As was the case in Scotland, two big drivers of the accusations are poverty and prevailing philosophies. But what complicates the matter in African countries is a misconception that witchcraft accusations are just part and parcel of African culture. Leo is very clear that the European concept of "witchcraft" (i.e., one that involves communion with the Devil) is not African but rather an idea that Western anthropologists forced on a culture they did not understand. In many parts

How to Accuse a Modern-Day Witch, Part 2: The Twenty-First Century

of Africa, there's a long-established belief in supernatural causes for misfortune, meaning if something goes wrong, like someone dies in an accident or has a disappointment in business, people may assume an occult cause is to blame. Leo shook his head. "The Western anthropologists came and subsumed that into the level of witchcraft."

Within many African societies, said Leo, so-called witch doctors were originally viewed simply as healers. These were the people you would go to if you had a problem you thought had a supernatural source. It wasn't until Europeans came along that the connotations of the words changed.

"Back when this happened, we didn't speak English," said Leo. "Some people who speak English and who tell us what English words mean came and told us, '*This* thing is healing, and *this* thing is witchcraft. This is a witch doctor.' Now, because of colonization, because of Englishization, because of Westernization, we have adopted those words."

Leo said there are many different types of healers in African society. "We use the word 'healers' here because I don't know what to call them. Some of them are healers, some of them are partially healing and partially doing occult practices, because many of them are not well trained."

Often people grow up saying they have inherited power, meaning their families taught them their practices. Not unlike charmers of the witch-hunt period in Scotland, they work with both the physical (herbs) and metaphysical (spells and charms). These days, there are also many pastors and imams who both preach and use spiritual healing as part of their services.

"Africa has become a spiritual supermarket. So if you call the traditional healer a witch doctor, then the Christian pastor is a witch doctor. The Muslim imam is also a witch doctor. So when they say a witch doctor, they always have this idea of an old African man, sitting with tattered clothes, half-naked, working with herbs. But it is a misrepresentation."

The year 2024 began badly in Malawi. Leo was contacted by an advocate there about a case of an elderly woman who'd been accused of being a witch and was in the process of being buried alive. The police arrived just as the woman's accusers were about to close the grave up, killing the woman. Thankfully, they showed up just in time, and the woman survived.

While this woman in Malawi survived, not all stories end so well. In other parts of Africa, Leo's organization has encountered serious situations in which people were killed. A similar case occurred recently in Benue State in central Nigeria, where another person was buried alive. By the time AfAW became involved, it was too late. Afterward, the family wouldn't speak of the death.

Leo often finds that a circle of silence surrounds such cases, either out of shame or fear. But he also knows that only by highlighting what's happening will his organization be able to put pressure on accusers or local law enforcement to stop events from developing further. Leo's team gets the story in the media, emails the government, and shares it on social media. All these pressure tactics often force accusers to step back.

In another case that Leo was involved in, a woman was accused of witchcraft by her own brothers. Initially, they'd planned to throw her in the river to drown her, but they decided instead to banish her from the community. The woman's sons also turned on her, literally chasing her away. Leo's team used publicity tactics to force the government to intervene, and a reconciliation was arranged between the community and the woman who was accused. Sadly though, the aftereffects of the accusation meant the woman wasn't allowed back where she'd been living, and her business as a caterer was ruined—no one would buy from her, either because they believed she was a witch or they didn't

How to Accuse a Modern-Day Witch, Part 2: The Twenty-First Century

want to be associated with someone who'd been accused. AfAW raised money to get her a flat and start again.

Leo's organization makes sure the accused are safe, helps fund them to escape if necessary, and, if the case makes it to court, arranges a lawyer and helps with police participation. Sometimes once the police are involved, the situation settles, but not always. In those cases, the organization tries to educate the communities and agencies at play. They also work with the community and local police to develop what Leo terms "early warning systems," such as notifying law enforcement if a local person's (possibly untimely) death may lead to an accusation of witchcraft, in an attempt to head off possible future problems.

Bringing cases into the open is key. In this, the organization is aided by growing access to the internet and social media, which means word gets out quicker, and it's harder to hide what's happening. Leo has been told that in one community, the killing of alleged witches had been occurring for years: the community had been killing accused people and throwing their bodies into the river or the bush. But once the word got out via social media, Leo's group was able to intervene.

Leo said that in Nigeria, the state doesn't offer much in the way of protection for the vulnerable. Because of this, those with children are less likely to be accused, as they have the strength and support of a family, while those without family are more likely to be attacked. Another problem for Leo is the often rural location of the accusations, as the phone and internet networks are less reliable.

While we were speaking to Leo via Zoom from Nigeria, he was walking around his garden. The evening had deepened into nighttime, and Leo pointed out to us that the electricity had gone off, and he was in almost complete darkness. This is common in Nigeria, making one of the main struggles for his group a lack of consistent power and communication.

"One woman told us that it took about twenty-four hours for her to know that they had killed her mother in the village because there was no phone network," he said. "Sometimes that is part of the challenge."

Overall, Leo feels there's still a long way to go. "Until we have a critical mass of advocates, I don't think I can say that things are really getting better. We have made some progress, but that progress is just a scratch on the surface."

Particularly in Nigeria, a lot of this is down to the worsening of poverty. The Nigerian currency has been devalued, which has caused economic and social issues. The country is experiencing a brain drain, where educated people such as doctors are leaving to find better prospects in places like the UK, the U.S., and Europe. This then leaves a gap in healthcare, particularly in rural areas, where healers and so-called prophets (or "charlatans" as Leo terms them) step in to offer their services. Unfortunately, as long as this health care vacuum continues, there will be a demand for healers, diviners, and prophets, and people will look for nonscientific explanations for their misfortunes. This is all frighteningly similar to the conditions in Scotland all those centuries ago. Times change, but people rarely do.

However, Leo remains optimistic. He said he constantly references what happened in Scotland to show that things can change. "I don't see any reason we can't beat this battle," he said. "The challenges are there, but I think that the world is more interconnected than it was three hundred years ago, and we can use that to end the vestiges of witch hunts and barbaric practices. As long as we're alive, somehow problems will lead to solutions."

Charlotte Baker, who is a professor of French and critical disability studies at Lancaster University, initially started off working on albinism in sub-Saharan Africa for her doctoral project in 2006. Albinism[3] is a rare genetic condition where people have little or no melanin, often resulting in the person having very pale hair, skin, and eyes. The condition often causes problems with the eyes, such as rapid eye movements and poor vision, and it increases the chance of skin cancer. Most recent studies suggest there are around one in eighteen thousand people in North America with the condition, but the rate is as high as one in three thousand in Southern Africa.

Alongside the physical issues associated with the condition, people with albinism can also face huge social issues. This is particularly prevalent in parts of Africa, where there's a complicated mythological narrative intertwined with the condition. In some areas, people with albinism are seen as lucky; they may be viewed as valuable members of the community and can even be chiefs. However, more commonly, people with albinism are seen as malevolent—neither black nor white, neither dead nor alive. There's also a prevalent (and rather contradictory) idea that their body parts are invaluable in spell making and traditional medicine, which has led to attacks and murders.

In the mid-2000s, when reports reached the media of people with albinism being attacked for their body parts, Charlotte decided she couldn't continue to solely concentrate on representation of people with albinism in academia. She therefore created a network of people who could work on the new issue, with a focus on educating and advocating.

The people in this network are experts on all aspects of albinism, including the beliefs and sociocultural realities. But there are also medical experts, such as ophthalmologists with expertise in visual impairments associated with albinism, oncologists who have experience with skin cancer, education professionals, and policymakers. The network grew and became more visible.

---

3   This is the preferred term over calling someone the old-fashioned "albino."

"We started to work in all sorts of different ways to try and address the issues and to challenge some of the more harmful beliefs," said Charlotte when we interviewed her. Charlotte is calm, knowledgeable, and clearly very determined to see justice done and make sure these horrendous situations are brought into the light internationally. She began working with Ikponwosa Ero, a world-renowned expert on protecting the human rights of people with albinism. Through Charlotte's collaboration with various advocates and nongovernmental organizations, she also started working with Gary Foxcroft, who led the Witchcraft and Human Rights Information Network.[4]

"One part of our work was to influence policy," explained Charlotte. "We wanted a change, not just a bottom-up change, which is very much needed, but a top-down change as well. We [Charlotte, Ikponwosa, and Gary] agreed in 2015 that the three of us would lead work with other stakeholders toward the UN resolution.[5] That resolution was passed in 2021."

The network is now making sure the resolution is implemented and that change happens. Recent efforts have been focused on raising public awareness.

People with albinism fall under the same umbrella as those accused of witchcraft, and the two areas are often bound together. People are targeted and accused because of their difference and vulnerability. With albinism, people are very visibly different, and some communities try to explain that difference within their belief system and in relation to the spirit world. Even when people have had an explanation

---

4   WHRIN is a collective that responds to worldwide human rights violations relating to accusations of witchcraft and spirit possessions. The groups involved in the collective share information and develop solutions to prevent any further violations.

5   This is the same resolution from which we have included an excerpt at the beginning of the chapter.

How to Accuse a Modern-Day Witch, Part 2: The Twenty-First Century

of the genes involved and the condition being passed down through generations, they cling to the idea that the person's family has done something wrong or they're suffering a curse. Sadly, this is still very much a current issue. In 2006 or 2007, stories started coming out of Tanzania of accusations and attacks. Initially it seemed as if Tanzania was an unusually active area, but in reality, these stories were appearing because people were actually *reporting* them. In other areas, cases were being hushed up and hidden, and the scope of the issue has only become clearer through the work of activists and advocates.

A Canadian NGO called Under the Same Sun has been working hard to discover and collate records of attacks since 2007. Currently, they have evidence of seven hundred attacks, including killings, mutilations, and incidents of grave robberies, and researchers fear there are many more that will never be documented.

The idea of grave robbing is particularly chilling. This is done to find body parts such as limbs, teeth, and even hair of people with albinism. These items, believed to be very powerful, are then sold to people who want to use them in occult practices.

"A figure was put on a whole set of body parts by Amnesty, and it was just horrendous," said Charlotte. "Thousands and thousands of pounds for a whole set of body parts…this was now an international trade."

As a recessive genetic condition, albinism doesn't occur in every successive generation of a family, something that causes problems when explaining it in communities: people don't remember it occurring in previous generations and thus assume it must be supernatural. Add to that its relative rareness, and a magical narrative is created to explain it.

"When a woman gives birth to a baby with albinism, it is a huge shock, which can lead to all sorts of accusations," said Charlotte. "She can be accused of having slept with a white man. She can be accused of having been cursed herself, of having brought evil into the family."

Superstition, hatred, and crime around albinism are live issues in twenty-seven countries across sub-Saharan Africa. Charlotte said their research suggests that in some parts of Africa and in a few other places in the world, some children with albinism are even being killed at birth.

"We would expect to see a certain number of people with albinism in any community based on the genetic data," she explained, "but in some countries, there just aren't the number of people with albinism that we'd expect to find. That suggests that something is going on, but it's incredibly difficult to provide any data or evidence."

What the UN resolution is trying to do is stop harm from occurring to people. Following the successful adoption of the resolution, Charlotte and several colleagues created the International Network Against Witchcraft Accusations and Ritual Attacks. The language used is a deliberate choice and reflects the resolution's wording. But Charlotte was quick to state that people are still entitled to their beliefs. "We've been really careful with the resolution and with the work we're doing on the back of it not to challenge people's beliefs, because everyone is entitled to believe what they may."

Charlotte and her colleagues continue to make the issue visible and ensure it's a conversation topic. It's important work, as the global statistics are quite shocking. Between 2010 and 2019, more than twenty thousand occurrences of witchcraft-related harm were reported in various countries, not just on the African continent but also in China and India, where the research is only just beginning.

And if you think that false accusations of witchcraft are no longer an issue in the UK, Europe, or the U.S., you'd be mistaken. Charlotte is working with an organization called the National Working Group Against Spiritual and Ritual Abuse, which began their efforts in 2011. The group was created by the UK government, initially looking at child abuse that occurred in relation to religion, as a way to draw together various resources to share knowledge and create more robust

How to Accuse a Modern-Day Witch, Part 2: The Twenty-First Century

safeguarding. Currently, the group collaborates with around seventy organizations from the UK and the global community, and it has a very practical focus to educate and raise awareness among different agencies, such as social workers and the police.

The tragic case of Victoria Climbié is probably the most well known example of faith-based child abuse. In 2000 in London, eight-year-old Victoria was tortured and murdered by family members who claimed to believe she was possessed. Several new child protection initiatives were introduced in response to her heartbreaking murder.

Charlotte said there are still "many, many children targeted" and that recent data shows the highest figures for faith-based child abuse in the United Kingdom are in the northwest of England, where she's based.

"There's so much we still need to understand about this issue," she said. "Certain churches perpetuate beliefs around witchcraft. They wouldn't necessarily term it 'witchcraft,' but perhaps they would call it 'ritual cleansing' because they consider people to be cursed."

These churches, much like in Scotland during the witch trials, think they are doing God's work, but we know their actions lead to harm when vulnerable people can't defend themselves.

And this final thought feels very circular to us. Although we're several hundred years from the Scottish witch trials, the same things are still happening all around the world. People are singled out and hurt or indeed killed. It's so important we understand what happened in our past here in Scotland to ensure it doesn't happen again. This is why the work of activists and academics like Leo and Charlotte and their colleagues is so vitally important.

If we don't learn from our past, we are doomed to repeat it.

PORTRAIT OF THE ACCUSED

Miss B

NIGERIA, 2023

In Benue State, Nigeria, on Saturday, April 15, 2023, a junior secondary school pupil, known only as Miss B, was dragged out of her father's house to face a group of family members, who had gathered to question her following allegations of her being part of a coven.

One of Miss B's relatives, Oga Job Okwori, demanded she attend a discussion with elders in the family. Having no choice in the matter, the girl and her father, Nathaniel Ijir Odege, arrived at the family house. Prior to their arrival, an elder relative called Abeni Oga told the others to build and light a big fire.

At the discussion, Miss B's elder brother, Stephen, stated that a maid who'd been staying with their relative Item Adaikwu had been accused by Adaikwu's children of chasing them in their sleep whenever she suffered any punishments from their mother. The maid had been interrogated and confessed she was part of a coven. During her interrogation, the maid had identified Miss B as also being a member of the group.

When Miss B was questioned that night, she maintained her innocence. Angered by her resistance, the elders forced her to sit very close to the fire, which burned her. The child was forced to remain in that position through the night, all the while experiencing intense pain. Horrifyingly, Miss B's father was forced to witness this torture; the crowd threatened to attack him too, due to him being accused of using witchcraft to murder a family member some months before. He was terrified they would kill him if he gave the slightest provocation.

Eventually, Miss B couldn't endure the pain anymore, and at 7 a.m. the next morning, she confessed to witchcraft to make the torture end. Miss B and her father were able to leave.

Since the attack, the family and community have remained silent, despite Miss B's father and brother both reporting the incident to the police. The police were provided a list of suspects, but no arrests were made.

Leo's group, Advocacy for Accused Witches, became involved when they heard the horrific story, and they moved quickly to pay Miss B's medical bills. Miss B and her father were encouraged to leave the area and move to the city of Makurdi in central Nigeria, where AfAW initiated the prosecution against Miss B's torturers. This can be a slow and difficult process because of police reluctance and a culture of bribery and corruption.

Eventually, due to AfAW's pressure and perseverance, on May 8, the police in Oju arrested Abeni Oga, an elder relative of Miss B and her father, who had told others to start the fire. Oga was eventually charged in court with attempted murder on May 15, but not before AfAW had to pay sums of money to move the matter along.

The case is ongoing, and AfAW continues to support the girl and her family.

AFTERWORD

How to Forget a Witch, Then Remember Her

Why do we only remember Lilias Adie as "Scotland's most famous witch"? The question that kept haunting us as we explored this subject was where are the graves of the others?

We saw that the townsfolk of Torryburn took great care to dispose of Lilias's body in a way she could not become a revenant—somewhat ironically providing the very best example of a revenant that has ever been documented.[1] Lilias was very much the solitary exception—at least as far as is known—for a woman who confessed to witchcraft having a grave. Everybody else was lost.

The fact is that with the burning of the accuseds' bodies and their deaths being recorded in the official documents in only the most basic of terms—in some cases not even noting the names of those executed and just recording that "sundry witches" were burned—history quickly

---

1 Not resurrection: that is a different matter, and Jesus is much more famous.

forgot them. Recordkeeping was often very poor, and there was no benefit to recording the details of a witch. They weren't so much written out of history as never properly written *into* it. Although we know thousands were accused, there are rarely full records of what happened.

In stark contrast to what we know of the fate of Scotland's accused witches is the fate of the accused witches in Salem. Their history is very different precisely because soon after their witches were killed, there was an acknowledgment that they'd suffered a terrible miscarriage of justice. Because of that acknowledgment, the history of those accused was written up, their property was preserved, and now many thousands of folk claim direct descendancy from them. Given that around thirty-eight hundred people were accused in Scotland across the sixteenth and seventeenth centuries, and at the time Scotland was a country of around nine hundred thousand, it's very likely that if you're Scottish or have Scottish ancestry, you're in some way related to an accused or, perhaps even more likely, an accuser. You could be reading this now, totally unaware you are descended from an individual involved in the witchcraft trials.

Seeing as there are no graves and few records, where are the memorials to all these women and men who were so cruelly and wrongly killed?

One of the things that started the whole Witches of Scotland campaign was Claire realizing there were virtually no named monuments to the women of Scotland. Pretty much any little village or town you go to in Scotland has, quite rightly, memorials to those who died in the world wars. Naturally, these list men's names. And in many small towns, you'll find at least a handful of statues or plaques celebrating various male achievements (or nonachievements, depending on your interpretation of history). However, you generally won't find Scotland's great and good women named and remembered in statue form. If you take a walk through Edinburgh, you will see various statues including David Livingstone and John Knox and a huge range of other gentlemen. Actually, that's not true; it's not a huge range.

They're always white, and they usually made money and secured power through subjugating other people. We know what we want from our heroes in Great Britain!

The one privately commissioned "memorial" in Edinburgh, which marks the spot where hundreds of women and men were executed as witches, sits unassumingly in the corner of Edinburgh Castle esplanade. Doubtless, many hundreds of thousands of people visit the castle every year without ever seeing it. The memorial was commissioned by Sir Patrick Geddes (1854–1932), a town planner[2] who asked his friend John Duncan, an artist who specialized in folklore and mythological subjects, to draw up the plans. He designed a drinking fountain made of bronze with two heads facing out in opposite directions. It's often wrongly thought that the plaque depicts a young woman and an old crone, but the characters are actually the Greek deities Hygieia, the Greek goddess of good health, and her father, Asclepius, the god of medicine. Around their faces is wrapped a snake, and foxgloves are also featured.

The inscription reads as follows:

> This fountain, designed by John Duncan, R.S.A. is near the site on which many witches were burned at the stake. The wicked head and serene head signify that some used their exceptional knowledge for evil purposes while others were misunderstood and wished their kind nothing but good. The serpent has the dual significance of evil and wisdom. The foxglove spray further emphasizes the dual purpose of many common objects.

While we shouldn't be too critical, given that Geddes did attempt to remember those killed as witches, the rather obvious problem with the

---

[2] This being only one of his many various skills and interests.

memorial is that it proceeds on the basis that those killed were indeed witches.

Otherwise, across Scotland, there are hundreds of statues, but only a handful of them are women.

As Dr. Alison McCall, one of the admins on the Mapping Memorials to Women in Scotland website,[3] said, "One of the reasons there are so many more statues of men is that the first statue of a woman appears to have been Queen Victoria in 1844. So the age of statues had waned before women got a look-in." Hmm...convenient. The patriarchy strikes again.

In fact, across the whole of Scotland, there are only twenty-three named female statues—seven Queen Victorias (two in Aberdeen: one young, one old) and a small array of female worthies (several of whom aren't even Scottish, including Florence Nightingale and Linda McCartney). There are also six statues that represent groups of women, including the *Fisher Jessie* statue in Peterhead (2001) and the herring girls in Stornoway (2003).

"If you look at the dates, it's interesting to see that there has been a growing commitment to statues of women since 1997," said Alison. "And of course, a statue to Elsie Inglis[4] is in the pipeline."

How we remember people (for good or bad) is a growing conversation in the UK, not least the ongoing discussion about the statues of those who profited from the transatlantic slave trade and whether we should remove their monuments or keep them with supporting materials to teach the history. As Witches of Scotland, we're keen to

---

3   Mapping Memorials to Women in Scotland was started in 2011.

4   Elsie Inglis (1864–1917) was a doctor, surgeon, teacher, and suffragist who founded the Scottish Women's Hospitals. There's a current controversy surrounding the choice of sculptor. Following a call for artists to apply, the committee chose a male sculptor who hadn't entered the open call.

remember history accurately and commemorate ordinary people alongside the war heroes and inventors and artists. We believe statues help us connect with stories, as through them, we're able to see versions of ourselves in different times and places.

Memorialization is about connection. If we make the link between the past and ourselves, we're more likely not to repeat the more horrifying aspects of our history. Ultimately, we would like to see statues of women around Scotland that reflect what has made Scotland the country it is today. This, we feel, should incorporate the darker parts of our history, which necessarily means including the witch trials.

One place that understands this absolutely is Salem in the United States. You could argue they've forged the connection between past and present so successfully that the town, with its far lower numbers of accused, is now seen as the main location of witch trials in the world.

Salem is steeped in history, and there are many layers that make up its background and current status as a tourist attraction. The witch trials are only a small part of Salem's larger story. In among the accusations of witchcraft, there are also many tales of piracy and the Industrial Revolution, which had an enormous impact on the town.

Nonetheless, the witch trials themselves have been well commemorated. As well as the Salem Museum, there's also a memorial next to the cemetery, which was opened in 1992 (Arthur Miller, playwright of *The Crucible*, had attended the announcement of the plans the previous year). By virtue of Salem being a small town, the graves of some of the other people who were involved in the trials are there. In 2017, another memorial was placed at Proctor's Ledge, where some of the hangings took place. This memorial consists of a stone arc embedded with the names of each of the nineteen people who were hanged. A tree was planted there as well.

Another memorial can be found in downtown Salem. It has been designed as a space in which to sit and reflect quietly, taking the form of a peaceful, grassy square surrounded by the last words of some of the victims inscribed into stone paving slabs on the ground. The words are cut off on either side, representing how these people were silenced. Stone benches jut out on the perimeter with the names and the dates of death of the twenty people who were executed, including Giles Corey, who was pressed to death. There is also a further memorial at Hobart Street in the town of Danvers, which used to be a part of Salem. It features a granite Bible atop a box with metal shackles alongside as well as a three-panel granite wall with the names of each victim inscribed and is located just across the street from the site of the Salem Village meetinghouse, where many of the accuseds' examinations took place.

"The Salem witch trials were very important, but they're a tiny, tiny blip in the history of witchcraft," said Rachel Christ-Doane, the director of education for the Salem Witch Museum. "It's really surprising how there's a lack of historical interpretation of these events. There's a lack of memorialization, really, across Europe. There are some places, but it doesn't seem to be memorialized the way it should be, which is really fascinating, especially in an area like Scotland, where so many people were executed. It was so much more violent than Salem. There should be memorials all over the place. The names should be recognized. This is something that's so relevant today. It's very much important for us to learn about now."

In Vardø, Norway, the Steilneset Memorial is a stunning, provocative monument that marks the executions of ninety-one people for witchcraft in 1621. It opened in 2011 and was created by architect Peter Zumthor and artist Louise Bourgeois. This was Bourgeois's final work before her death in 2010, and we've always felt that because she is

How to Forget a Witch, Then Remember Her

one of the twentieth century's greatest artists—and one who fit the archetype of the witch-artist[5]—it was incredibly apt she took on this commission.

It's worth noting that as in Salem, the Vardø trials were a great deal smaller than the totality of the Scottish trials. Around one hundred people were accused, and seventy-seven women and fourteen men were sentenced to death by burning. Vardø is a town on an island off the northeastern tip of Norway, in the district of Finnmark. The area experienced the highest rate of witchcraft accusations in any part of Norway, with the trials peaking around 1662–3.

The memorial is made up of two parts: Zumthor's wooden area and Bourgeois's sculptures. Zumthor's installation is within a long wooden structure and consists of a narrow walkway with ninety-one small windows representing the people executed. There are accompanying texts based on original sources describing the victims and their trials at each window, and each opening contains a single light bulb. Bourgeois's work *The Damned, the Possessed and the Beloved* stands within a square room made of smoked glass where the walls don't quite reach the roof or floor. A metal chair has been placed in the center, and flames are projected through its seat. It's surrounded by seven oval mirrors mounted on poles, as if they're judges looking down on the condemned.

One of the issues we've faced in Scotland with creating memorials to the accused and executed is the question of money. In Norway, the money partly came from the Norwegian Public Roads Administration as a way of developing National Tourist Routes to encourage visitors to travel more widely around the country.

We spoke to Norwegian historian Liv Helene Willumsen about the part she played in the memorial (among other things, she wrote

---

5   We're using "witch-artist" here to mean someone whose work is often on the freakier side, on a larger scale, and involves feminist themes.

the exhibition text on display there), the similarities between what happened in Norway and Scotland, and the importance and relevance of memorials in the twenty-first century.

"The Steilneset Memorial is based on three components: art, architecture, and history," said Liv. "This place has a very painful history to tell, and the main idea was to lift this history into the public discourse and try to reflect on it and also try to understand better what happened during the seventeenth century."

Liv is keenly aware of the connection between the witch trials of the seventeenth century and the violence suffered by women today. She argues, and we would firmly agree, that the mechanisms that existed then to control and hurt women still exist. Then, they believed women were evil and weak and that they were likely to be seduced by the Devil. Today, we're much less likely in our secular, Western society to say that women are being seduced by the Devil, but we still see women persecuted, marginalized, and attacked.

The Damned, the Possessed and the Beloved, Louise Bourgeois, 2010; installed as part of the Steilneset Memorial in Vardø

How to Forget a Witch, Then Remember Her

The point Liv makes about the parallels between seventeenth-century witch trials and the experience of women today is striking. Women are still too often seen as potentially dangerous and so must be controlled.[6] When fearful men are running courts, states, and governments, then dangerous precedents and laws are created and enforced. Especially if religious men are in step with political and legal men. There are numerous examples of this today all over the world—see the battleground over women's reproductive rights in the U.S., Italy, and eastern Europe, for example. Other parts of the world face even graver problems: you need only look at the rolling back of women's and girls' ritghts in Afghanistan, where the Taliban, as a means of social control, have stopped girls from accessing education and have banned women from speaking out loud in public places (this includes laughing and singing) and holding conversations with other women. And before we get too comfortable about how superior we are in the "West," look at the resurgence of so-called trad wives,[7] who are endorsed by many politicians, religious leaders, and even some sporting icons. The fact that this "movement" is being promulgated by the TikTok algorithm is particularly sinister.

In the seventeenth century, women weren't seen as having the same worth or qualities as men. Women's weakness and susceptibility to

---

6 It amazes us almost daily that women haven't taken to the streets and burned the world to the ground.

7 This is an American movement where trad (traditional) wives are celebrated for being stay-at-home mothers presiding over big families. The concept centers on a notion of women in the days of America's expansion into the West. Picture lots of homeschooled blond kids drinking milk they've got from their own cow, presided over by a pretty, modest woman who does her husband's bidding. Mark our words, there will be an uprising of demented women in their late thirties in a few years' time. Or at least we fervently hope so.

falling into a pact with the Devil made them incredibly dangerous. This mindset was held by the male officials, and it shaped the laws and attitudes very clearly.

Liv believes this mechanism still exists in many countries today. It's all too clear that, generally speaking, women just don't hold the same worth as men.[8]

"I have been working in this area since the 1970s, and I think it is very sad to say that I see the pendulum now is going in the wrong direction," she said. "It is not better today than it was thirty, forty years ago. It is worse, and I think this is very serious."

This is the reason why Liv believes it's so important to discuss the witch trials in modern society: to understand the past and also to make the link between then and now.

The biggest con of the early twenty-first century is how many women believe we've reached parity. Yet the patriarchy is still trying to take away the rights we do have, and women are still being attacked and murdered on a daily basis. In 2021, at least 147 women were murdered in the UK alone. Around 53 percent of these women were killed by a current or ex-partner.[9] This may seem unrelated, but we need to be clear that the gendered aspect of the witch trials did not go away after the trials. The fear and hatred seen in our society over three hundred years later are a straight line drawn from those days and attitudes. We must find a way to break this inheritance and put it firmly in the past,

---

8 In so-called progressive societies, how many times have you, as a woman, been in a meeting and felt your view less valued than that of your male colleague? How many women have parity to men in the workplace in terms of the distribution of senior roles and equal pay?

9 These figures are taken from the horrendous but much-needed femicide census, which acts as "a unique source of comprehensive information about women who have been killed in the UK and the men who have killed them": Femicide Census, https://www.femicidecensus.org.

and we argue that understanding the drivers of the trials and the part that was played by embedded, often unconscious ideas about women, their worth, and their "danger" is an excellent method of confronting the past and changing the future.

This is another key aspect to Liv's work. "I think the Steilneset memorial has a very important part to play. As mature women, we must tell the younger generation that it is not okay. We have not reached the goals that we had in the 1970s, and you must not believe that we have come to the right solution and the right organizing of society and the right freedoms for women."

Because a memorial exists in the real world as a physical, tangible symbol, it's a very effective tool to reach people's attention, especially the young. Liv and her colleagues have deliberately involved schools, especially young people between the ages of twelve and fifteen, because that's the perfect point to engage with ideas about sexism and abuse of power. Pupils visit from schools and participate in a teaching package where each student focuses on the story of one individual in particular. Through that one person, the students can make a personal connection to what happened. If they can personalize it, they can see the humanity and the human cost.

"In Steilneset, what was important to me was that all these persons should have a name," Liv said. "We do not have any images from the sixteenth and seventeenth century, but they should have a name."

Visitors learn the individuals' names and stories and make the connection between their very ordinary lives and their extraordinary deaths. Hopefully, they then take that knowledge out into the world with them, engendering a change in attitudes that redirects society for the better.

The ambitious and striking Steilneset memorial shows the ambition and possibilities of a twenty-first-century memorial, one that provokes thought and action.

Of course, it's very difficult to remember things if you don't know about them in the first place. In Scotland, the best place to get a clear idea of who was accused and what happened to them is through the work of the Survey of Scottish Witchcraft—itself a staggering memorial of sorts and the place where almost all the names of the accused are gathered.[10]

In 1977, historian Christina Larner created *A Source-Book of Scottish Witchcraft*, which was later used as the foundation for the Survey of Scottish Witchcraft. The latter is an online database that features contemporary court documents covering the time period from 1563 to 1736. The database went live in 2003 after two years of work by Professor Julian Goodare and Dr. Louise Yeoman, working in conjunction with researchers Lauren Martin and Joyce Miller and the Department of Computing at the University of Edinburgh. We cannot overstate the importance of this work, as it's accessed by anyone and everyone who's researching in this field. If you live in Scotland, we'd strongly recommend looking up witches in your area.

When the project started in the 1990s, Julian Goodare and Louise Yeoman realized there was no use made of church records in the existing *Source-Book of Scottish Witchcraft* and that with the growing use of computers, they could create something much broader and—crucially—searchable. In the course of their research, they discovered there were a great deal more accused than initially thought. But many records have disappeared or been damaged over time, and much of the detail is lost to us. There might be a record of a name, a place, a date, a commission, and maybe some names of the co-accused, but then nothing about a

---

10 Thanks to the ongoing work of citizen detectives, independent scholars, and community campaigners, new names and stories are being uncovered all the time across Scotland.

trial or outcome. Julian suspects these people would've been executed, but we may never know.

There's been even more work done in recent years. We spoke to Ewan McAndrew, who is the Wikimedian in residence at the University of Edinburgh, facilitating Wikipedia entries related to the university's work and serving as a liaison between the university and the online encyclopedia. Wikipedia is incredibly useful in this research in many areas, including on witch trials, because it has been around since 2001 and is the largest open education resource in human history.

Ewan told us that six years ago, there were only three articles about Scottish witches. "Now we have forty-nine," he said. He went on to explain how the university got involved with the survey. "The university wants to teach students how to work with open data, so they wanted to see if there was something we could do with data science students working with the Survey of Scottish Witchcraft to make it more explorable."

Small, short-term projects were developed with students to look at machine-readable data about the accused witches, after which the team started to think about what else they could do using the survey.

"We noticed that there are lots of gaps in the database, obviously, because we're dealing with historical documents. One of the things we found was that there was often information about where the witches resided. For each of them but not all of them, there was the name of a place which we could try and hunt down. We could assign coordinate locations, put it on a map, and have the survey's information explorable in a completely different way."

Anne-Marie Scott, who was Ewan's line manager at the time, suggested hiring geography student Emma Carroll as an intern to hunt down eight hundred place-names using gazetteers, Gaelic resources, place-name books, and the Scottish archives. Heavy research was required because a lot of these places don't exist anymore.

"It was an enormous amount of detective work in six weeks," said Ewan. "Once they'd done all that, we could map the resource."

They built a website and entered all the map visualizations. They thought that was the end of it, but it turned out to be just the beginning. The public engaged massively, with huge interest from across the world. Another intern, Maggie Lin, discovered further trial details, which were then added to the website. In 2023, their third Witchfinder General intern,[11] Ruby Imrie, checked the data and made the site more searchable and interactive. Now residents of Scotland can check where they live, see who was accused there, and follow their story.

The Survey of Scottish Witchcraft is an evolving, highly useful, and compelling way of remembering the accused. Although it's different from, say, a statue or a plaque, perhaps in the twenty-first century, this is a fitting manner of remembering and exploring the past, being so democratic and accessible.

That said, we're still keen on having a physical memorial somewhere in Scotland. There are already several plaques dotted across the country commemorating the trials—sometimes for groups of women, sometimes individuals. It's very moving to know that people have researched and fundraised in their local areas to discover and remember those accused. But we're calling for a national monument, hopefully of the scale and drama of Steilneset—something provocative and engaging. What we definitely don't want to see is a pretty girl gazing forlornly into the middle distance, clutching her skirts against her legs.

We believe what's needed is something that connects the staggering barbarity of the trials with the fact these were real people, mostly real *women*, who were just like us and that bridges women's experiences today and hopefully helps make real, significant change.

---

11 Surely one of the best job titles ever.

How to Forget a Witch, Then Remember Her

When we started this journey five years ago, we were initially focused on a campaign for a memorial and justice for the people involved in these historical outrages. However, it immediately became obvious to us that we'd ignited a cultural conversation, because these issues are not actually in the past.

Just as in the days of the witch trials, as the global situation worsens, people become more and more fearful. The current febrile political environment often veers dangerously to the right. Many of us anxiously contemplate the present and future realities of the climate crisis, struggle with the financial and social pressures of modern life, watch on in impotent horror at the seemingly constant worldwide conflicts—all while actively participating in the emotionally heightening petri dish that is social media.

We must take great care to guard against a new iteration of the witch trials.

We'd like to believe we're too sophisticated for that to happen again, but with recent diatribes about witches being abroad, we're not convinced it's outwith the realms of possibility.

In summer 2018, U.S. Supreme Court Justice Ruth Bader Ginsburg spoke to Margaret Atwood, author of *The Handmaid's Tale*.[12] When

---

12 Atwood is on record as having said that in *The Handmaid's Tale*, she only wrote things that had already happened to women somewhere at some point in history. "I did not wish to be accused of dark, twisted inventions, or of misrepresenting the human potential for deplorable behavior. The group-activated hangings, the tearing apart of human beings, the clothing specific to castes and classes, the forced childbearing and the appropriation of the results, the children stolen by regimes and placed for upbringing with high-ranking officials, the forbidding of literacy, the denial of property rights—all had precedents, and many of these were to be found, not in other cultures and religions, but within Western society, and within the 'Christian' tradition itself."

Atwood suggested that the #MeToo movement would spark a backlash against women, RBG disagreed, also opining that the odds were not in favor of *Roe v. Wade* (the landmark abortion ruling in the States) being overturned. It's telling that Atwood's response at that time was to say, "I think there will be. We're already seeing it with Hillary Clinton… That's the first time we've seen this seventeenth-century talk of the female witch character."

It's 2025. *Roe v. Wade* was overturned, and the sniggered whispers of "witch" and witchcraft have turned to mainstream discussions about "demonic forces" in the U.S.[13] Red flags are waving like handmaid's gowns.

It's still the case that the weak and helpless are attacked to protect the rich and powerful. Social media is used constantly to bully, harass, and shut women down. Women are routinely sexually threatened if they stick their heads above the parapet. Domestic violence is just as prevalent now as it ever was. In the workplace, we still don't have parity. At home, we're still doing the lion's share of the domestic drudgery and childcare. Women were not safe then and are not safe now.

So what to make of all this? What's the point of us setting out in such detail why and how women were characterized as witches, blamed for things wholly beyond their control, and ultimately brutally executed by the state?

The answer is that humans don't change quickly enough. When

---

13 On September 28, 2024, then-U.S. vice-presidential candidate J. D. Vance spoke at an event hosted by an evangelical leader, Lance Wallnau, who had previously suggested Vice President Kamala Harris used witchcraft. He said, about a Kamala Harris debate, "She can look presidential. That's the seduction of what I would say is witchcraft. That's the manipulation of imagery that creates an impression contrary to the truth, but it seduces you into seeing it. So that spirit, that occult spirit, I believe is operating on her and through her."

times are bad, we still look for people to blame. We demonize those people until they are no longer human and then do unspeakably inhumane things to them.

Accusations against the vulnerable in society don't happen out of the blue. Could they happen again now? If you don't think they can, we'd suggest you've not been studying history or even given it the most casual of glances. Let's look at how that might come to pass in today's world:

+ First, when times are bad and people are scared, there are wild allegations of witchery, women who have devilish powers and are in league with Satan. This nonsense is believed by no one but the most tinfoil-hat-wearing of conspiracy theorists.

+ These witchcraft accusations are repeated until they become background noise in society. No one in power intervenes to deny such allegations. Then, in time, support is found for the allegations. In the old days, it would be a witness, a document. Now, it might be a video, a TikTok.

+ Are they real pieces of evidence or fraudulent? Made by AI? Few know. Few care.

+ Discussions take place on the basis that there's some proof of witchery. Now the accusations seem less crazy. You know someone who knows someone who was affected by a spell.

+ The witchcraft allegations become mainstream, talked about on daytime TV, the pros and cons debated. "Who are the witches? Join us after the break when we discuss who they are and how to spot them. Have you been affected? Call our viewer hotline at…"

+ A political party, realizing the popularity of witchcraft accusations, adopts what was once a wild allegation believed by no one as an issue that now must be addressed. It gains support; the party is voted in. Soon an issue is proposed in the legislature and voted for by the politicians. Then it becomes law.

+ And it's coming for you. But I'm not a witch! you say. Surely this is madness, and people can see that, right? Wrong. You're accused in a court of law. Evidence is gathered, the trial takes place, and after conviction, you're sentenced to execution.

So how do we stop this? How do we make sure our society doesn't normalize accusing women as witches again?

We say this. Whether you take the lead from someone like Helen Mirren, who wished she'd said "fuck off" more in her early career, or Julia Louis-Dreyfus, who recently said, "Listen to old women, motherfuckers," or indeed any number of nonfamous women who get up every day and against the odds keep pushing back against the tide of misogyny, we urge you: embrace the title of "quarrelsome dame" in your daily lives. Take up space, get involved in grassroots politics, educate people around you about what happened during the witch trials, and draw the parallel with today. When you are met with resistance, call it out.

Do not let the patriarchy silence you.

We need to be sure we elect those who will actively protect our safety, safeguard the rights we currently have, and promote real equality going forward. We need to hold our politicians and public bodies to account, and we need to join with women all over the world to stop modern witch trials and show our strength in numbers.

So we say, fuck "being nice" to keep the peace or to keep other people happy. Fuck having to keep quiet for fear of being labeled difficult (they'll do that anyway). Fuck living, laughing, loving. Try shouting, swearing, fighting.

Call out misogyny, challenge the norm, *be a quarrelsome dame.*

CLAIRE AND ZOE
WITCHES OF SCOTLAND

ACKNOWLEDGMENTS

Since we started the campaign in 2020, we have had the great fortune to speak to many wonderful experts in the field of witch trials, Scottish history, and human rights. Without these inspiring, illuminating, and horrifying discussions, we couldn't have written this book. It bears repeating that we are not historians and any (and all!) mistakes contained here are our entirely ours. We would strongly recommend that you dig further and read the tremendous books and research by Julian Goodare, Louise Yeoman, Malcolm Gaskill, Tabitha Stanmore, Marion Gibson, Martha McGill, Mary Craig, Mairi Kidd, and Liv Helene Willumsen. We thank Sara Sheridan whose book *Where are the Women?* inspired Claire to think about how we memorialize women in history.

We would encourage you to engage with and support the work done by Leo Igwe and Advocacy for Alleged Witches and Charlotte Baker and her colleagues at The International Network Against Witchcraft Accusations and Ritual Attacks. The issue of witch trials is not something of the past, but something that needs attention now in various locations around the world.

Acknowledgments

We would like to thank our skilled photographer Kathryn Rattray, Professor Niamh Nic Daeid, Douglas Spiers, the ever-fascinating Catherine MacPhee, and the indomitable Judith Langlands-Scott for her ongoing support and spirit, as well as Sarah Cook and Andy Walker for their friendship and enthusiasm.

Although the Witches of Scotland is a team of two, we couldn't do the podcasts without the sound engineering skills of David Mitchell (sorry we didn't stop at six episodes, David) and more recently, Lola-Ray Venditozzi. We'd like to also thank Yvonne Mitchell for her tireless, patient work with us on the Witches of Scotland tartan admin witchesofscotland.com.

Our agent, Jim Gill, is helping us navigate the world of publishing, for which we are truly thankful.

Thank you, too, to our American team at Sourcebooks, particularly Anna Michels, Sophia Ellinas, Emily Proano, Angela Corpus, and Hannah Kil for their support and guidance.

Claire would like to thank: 'my family—Pol, Redford, Crombie, Delia, Jim, Yvonne, David, and all the friends who put up with my eccentricities, for their love and support, especially my ride or dies: Mel, Shanti, Jackie, Rosemary, Nicola, Caroline, Aamer, and April who are always there for me, as are Kevin H, Kevin and Ross, Eddie J, Lesley H, Clare C, Stuart, David W, Sarah, Craig, Moira, Wendy, Kelly, Shelagh, Maggie, Gordon, Rosemary G, Garry S, Fred, Chris and Claire D, Catherine S and Mary M, I love you all.'

Zoe would like to thank: 'my children—Luca Tavita, Lola-Ray and Rocco; my family—Elspeth, Natalie, Martin, and auntie Sheena, and the OG McLanders Bet/Granny Mum; all my great friends who listened patiently when I was not working and I should have been. I'd especially like to thank Emily for her weekly therapeutic coffee sessions; Jennie and Leonie for their intervention; Jane for her decades long, steadfast friendship, Anna for getting me started in many ways;

Acknowledgments

also, Rachel, Paula, Susan, and Jill. Thanks too, to Sheldon for the very welcome distraction and ongoing support.'

Zoe and Claire would both like to thank Mel and Drew as it was Drew that helped Claire shape up the campaign in those very early days, and without you two getting married, Claire and Zoe may never have met!

Finally, we'd like to thank you Quarrelsome Dames and all our readers and listeners who have picked up this cause and are determined to right a historical wrong and improve the present to boot.

READING GROUP GUIDE

1. In what ways are the gossip and news of the 1500s similar to the social media landscape we have today? In what ways are they different?

2. Why was it easier to accuse and harm those seen as the outcasts of a village? What other groups of people throughout history have been deemed too "different" for society and were therefore stereotyped and demonized?

3. What was considered a woman's "role" in society during the witch hunts in Scotland? What happened if she chose not to follow that role? How has the role of women (and men) changed since that time?

4. There was a deep relationship between religion and witch accusations in Scotland, with much of the justification for the hunts stemming from religious beliefs. How did this make the case for witch accusations more believable to the common people? Why do you feel there was a need to justify the accusations?

5. How did men in general benefit from the accusations of women as witches? How did many men take advantage of the witch hunts?

6. Globally, why are the Salem witch trials so much more well known than the hunts in Scotland? What factors go into whether an event (or series of events) is remembered or forgotten?

7. Were you surprised to read about the "modern witches"? Why do you think witch hunts have persisted for so long?

8. How has sexism evolved since the 1500s? Where does it appear in modern society, compared to its position in history?

9. Why is it important to remember the stories of the women who died during these hunts and trials?

10. What kinds of issues do women still face today in terms of equality and prejudice? How do you see these examples of inequality arise in your daily life?

ABOUT THE WITCHES OF SCOTLAND TARTAN

The Witches of Scotland Tartan was created by designer Clare Campbell in collaboration with the Witches of Scotland. The tartan will be woven to make products and create a "living memorial" to those who suffered as a result of the Witchcraft Act 1563 to 1736 in Scotland.

The tartan's black and gray colors are intended to represent both the dark times of this period and the ashes of those burned. It also incorporates red and pink colors, symbolic of the legal tapes used to bind papers both during that time and now. The thread count of this design incorporates the years 1563 and 1736, represented as single entries, 1+5+6+3 = 15 and 1+7+3+6 = 17, shown in black and gray. These surround a white check of three threads that represent the core objectives of the organization: to ensure that a pardon, an apology and memorials are achieved. The large black section of 173 threads is intended to represent the 173 years of darkness, and the red and pink sections are repeated three times, for the three prime objectives of the Witches of Scotland organization.

About the Witches of Scotland Tartan

The Witches of Scotland Tartan has been used on the case of the *How to Kill a Witch* hardback edition and is available to view online at the Scottish Register of Tartans (www.tartanregister.gov.uk), reference: 14651.

GLOSSARY OF SCOTS WORDS

Scots[1] is one of the three officially recognized languages in Scotland, the others being English and Scottish Gaelic. Most folk speak English, only with Scots words peppering the vocabulary. Some would say[2] the best, most descriptive words are Scots, especially for types of rain and calling someone an eejit. The pronunciation of Scots words varies a lot due to the different accents in Scotland. The spelling varies even more—many of the words and phrases have been passed down through speech rather than in writing, so sometimes it's just phonetic guesswork. What follows is our attempt to demystify the language for non-Scottish readers.

---

1   Never "Scotch"—that's a drink, not a language.

2   Those some being Scottish folk.

Glossary of Scots Words

Ain: your own
Aw: all
Bairnes: children
Biding in: staying in
Braw: great
Canny: wise
Cantrip: spell
Couthy/couthie: a sound and friendly person or, if describing a place, a cozy, nice wee spot
Cummer: a trouble or disturbance, a close female friend, a godmother, or a female gossip
Dame: woman
Daur: dare
Deid: dead
Dreich: bleak, wet weather, a gloominess that pervades everything
Eejit: idiot
Folk: people
Haver: to babble, to speak foolishly
Heid: head
Hen: a kindly term for a woman you are friends with
Highheidyins: literally the "high-head ones" or senior people
Howff: graveyard
Ken: know
Lang: long
Mair: more
Muckle: a lot, a big amount
Noo: now
Oot: out
Outwith: outside of (it's a mystery to all Scots why this isn't used everywhere, but ironically it is not used outwith Scotland)
Scrieve: to write

Glossary of Scots Words

Smeddum: a fine ash, a medicinal powder
Smoored: to be choked or suffocated
Sneck: a latch
Sooked: sucked
Tak: take
Wan: one
Widdershins: to turn around counterclockwise
Willnae: will not
Wrang: wrong

SELECT RESOURCES

General

Julian Goodare, Lauren Martin, Joyce Miller, and Louise Yeoman, Survey of Scottish Witchcraft (website), 2003 (archived January 2023), https://witches.hca.ed.ac.uk/.
National Records of Scotland (website), https://www.nrscotland.gov.uk.
Scotland's People (website), https://www.scotlandspeople.gov.uk.
National Library of Scotland (website), https://digital.nls.uk.
Julian Goodare, ed., *The Scottish Witch-Hunt in Context* (Manchester University Press, 2002).
Lizanne Henderson, *Witchcraft and Folk Belief in the Age of Enlightenment: Scotland 1670–1740* (Palgrave Macmillan, 2016).
Christina Larner, *Enemies of God: The Witch-Hunt in Scotland* (Blackwell, 1983).
Stuart MacDonald, *The Witches of Fife: Witch-Hunting in a Scottish Shire, 1560–1710* (John Donald Publishers, 2014).

Introduction

"Pleadings in some remarkable cases before the Supreme Courts of Scotland since the year 1661 to which the decisions are subjoyn'd," University of Michigan Library Digital Collections, accessed March 18, 2025, https://name.umdl.umich.edu/A50746.0001.001.
Statistics of accused: "Witches of Scotland," Royal Society of Edinburgh, September 7, 2023, https://rse.org.uk/resource/witches-of-scotland/.
Sara Sheridan, *Where Are the Women? A Guide to an Imagined Scotland* (Historic Environment Scotland, 2021).
Robert Pitcairn, *Criminal Trials in Scotland* (Edinburgh: Ballantyne and Co., 1833).
Julian Goodare et al., "The Survey of Scottish Witchcraft," archived January 2023, https://witches.hca.ed.ac.uk/.

Select Resources

PART ONE: THE LAW OF THE LAND
Chapter 1: How to Believe in Magic
Diane Purkiss, "Sounds of Silence: Fairies and Incest in Scottish Witchcraft Stories," in *Languages of Witchcraft*, ed. Stuart Clark (Red Globe Press, 2000).
Diane Purkiss, *Troublesome Things: A History of Fairies and Fairy Stories* (Allen Lane, 2000).
"Any sufficiently advanced technology" quote: Arthur C. Clarke, "Hazards of Prophecy: The Failure of Imagination," *Profiles of the Future* (1962).
Tabitha Stanmore, *Cunning Folk: Life in the Era of Practical Magic* (Bodley Head, 2024).
Martha McGill and Julian Goodare, eds., *The Supernatural in Early Modern Scotland* (Manchester University Press, 2020).

Chapter 2: How to Start a Witch Hunt
Historical background: "The Scottish Reformation, c. 1525–1560," Scottish History Society, n.d., https://scottishhistorysociety.com/the-scottish-reformation-c-1525–1560/.
John Knox: *Encyclopaedia Britannica*, s.v. "John Knox," by James Stevenson McEwen, last modified January 1, 2025, https://www.britannica.com/biography/John-Knox.
James VI's sexuality: "Filled with 'a Number of Male Lovelies': The Surprising Court of King James VI and I," BBC Scotland, September 27, 2017, https://www.bbc.co.uk/programmes/articles/4qVDwb2kBfd2G4Pkz3P88kZ/filled-with-a-number-of-male-lovelies-the-surprising-court-of-king-james-vi-and-i.
Confession of Faith Ratification Act, 1560, c. 1, https://www.legislation.gov.uk/aosp/1560/1/contents.
Papal Jurisdiction Act, 1560, c. 2, https://www.legislation.gov.uk/aosp/1560/2.
1563 Witchcraft Act: Anentis Witchcraft, Mary c. 73, June 4, 1563, https://statutes.org.uk/site/the-statutes/scottish-laws/1563-mary-c-73-anentis-witchcraft/.

Portrait of the Accused: Euphame MacCalzean
Julian Goodare, ed., *The Scottish Witch-Hunt in Context* (Manchester University Press, 2002), 107–108.

Chapter 3: Know Your Enemy, Part 1: *Newes from Scotland*
Newes from Scotland, Declaring the Damnable Life and Death of Dr. Fian, a Notable Sorcerer (William Wright, 1591). Facsimile of text: https://www.johngraycentre.org/wp-content/uploads/2021/11/Newes-From-Scotland.pdf.
Confession of Agnes Sampson, January 29, 1590, Reference SP 52/47, National Archives, Kew.

Portrait of the Accused: Allison Balfour
"Orkney to Get Memorial for Island Witch Trial Victims," *Scotsman*, August 14, 2018,

https://www.scotsman.com/arts-and-culture/orkney-to-get-memorial-for-island-witch-trial-victims-266154.

Chapter 4: Know Your Enemy, Part 2: *Daemonologie*

King James VI, *Daemonologie, in Forme of a Dialogue, Divided into Three Books: By the High and Mightie Prince, James &c.* (Robert Waldegrave, 1597). Transcript of text: https://www.gutenberg.org/cache/epub/25929/pg25929-images.html.

1603 Witchcraft Act: Nicole Hartland, "Which Witch(craft Act) Is Which?," UK Parliament Blog, October 28, 2020, https://archives.blog.parliament.uk/2020/10/28/which-witchcraft-act-is-which/.

Portrait of the Accused: Janet Wishart

"Wishart Witches," The Wishart Society, October 31, 2016, https://wishart.org/index.php/wishart-witches/.

Chapter 5: How to Believe in a Witch

Author interview with Dr. Louise Yeoman, March 21, 2022.

Author interview with Professor Marion Gibson, January 7, 2022.

Scottish literacy rates: "The Rise of Literacy in Scotland," National Library of Scotland, n.d., https://www.nls.uk/collections/rise-of-literacy/.

Allan Kennedy, "The Trial of Isobel Duff for Witchcraft, Inverness, 1662," *Scottish Historical Review*, 101, no. 1 (April 2022): 109–122, https://doi.org/10.3366/shr.2022.0549.

Portrait of the Accused: Margaret Aitken

Louise Yeoman, "The Woman Who Stood Up to a Witch-Hunt," BBC News, November 9, 2019, https://www.bbc.com/news/uk-scotland-glasgow-west-50330147.

PART TWO: BUILDING A CASE

Portrait of the Accused: Agnes Finnie

Mary Craig, *Agnes Finnie: The "Witch" of the Potterrow Port* (Luath Press, 2023).

Chapter 6: How to Accuse a Witch

Author interview with Judith Langlands-Scott, July 14, 2024.

Brian P. Levack, "The Great Scottish Witch Hunt of 1661–2," *Journal of British Studies* 20, no. 1 (Autumn 1980): 90–108, http://www.jstor.org/stable/175544.

Quote from 1649 Scottish Witchcraft Act: J. R. Young, "The Covenanters and the Scottish Parliament, 1639–51," in *Enforcing Reformation in Ireland and Scotland, 1550–1700*, eds. E. Boran and C. Gribben (Ashgate, 2006).

English witchcraft laws and statistics: "Witchcraft," UK Parliament, n.d., https://www.parliament.uk/about/living-heritage/transformingsociety/private-lives/religion/overview/witchcraft.

Scottish economy in sixteenth century: C. A. Whatley, *Scottish Society, 1707–1830: Beyond Jacobitism, Towards Industrialisation* (Manchester University Press, 2000).

Chapter 7: How to Prick a Witch

Devil's mark origins: Richard M. Golden, *Encyclopedia of Witchcraft: The Western Tradition*, vol. 4 (Library of Congress, 2006).

"weaponized belief" quote: Adam Scovell, "The Terror of the Old Ways: 50 Years of *Witchfinder General*," British Film Institute, May 18, 2018, https://www.bfi.org.uk/features/witchfinder-general-michael-reeves-vincent-price.

Hopkins and Stearne: Malcolm Gaskill, *Witchfinders: A Seventeenth-Century English Tragedy* (Harvard University Press, 2007).

Hopkins's Stowmarket fees: A. G. Hollingsworth, *History of Stowmarket* (Ipswich, 1844).

Author interview with Mary Craig, October 21, 2022.

Bierricht explanation: Dolly Stolze, "The Bizarre Importance of Bleeding Bodies in Medieval Trials," Ancient Origins, February 11, 2016, https://www.ancient-origins.net/history-ancient-traditions/bizarre-importance-bleeding-bodies-medieval-trials-005337.

"John Kincaid, Witch Finder," Engole, August 12, 2018, https://engole.info/john-kincaid-witch-finder/.

Mary Craig, "John Kincaid the witch brodder," Mary W. Craig (blog), April 18, 2021, https://marywcraig.com/2021/04/18/john-kincaid-the-witch-brodder/.

"Christian Caddell: Scotland's Female Witch Pricker," Spooky Scotland, June 19, 2018, https://spookyscotland.net/christian-caddell/.

Louise Yeoman, "The Woman Who Became a Witch Pricker," BBC Scotland, November 18, 2012, https://www.bbc.com/news/uk-scotland-20315106.

James Fraser, *Chronicles of the Frasers: The Wardlaw Manuscript* (Forgotten Books, 2012).

"There came then to Inverness" quote: "The Patersons," Douglas Archives, August 11, 2021, https://www.douglashistory.co.uk/history/Septs/paterson.htm.

"…by waking, hanging them up by the thombes" quote: L. Henderson, "Witch-hunting and Witch Belief in the *Gàidhealtachd*" in *Witchcraft and Belief in Early Modern Scotland*, eds. J. Goodare, L. Martin, and J. Miller (Palgrave Macmillan, 2008).

Brian P. Levack, *Witch-Hunting in Scotland: Law, Politics and Religion* (Routledge, 2007).

Portrait of the Accused: Tituba

Stacy Schiff, "Unraveling the Many Mysteries of Tituba, the Star Witness of the Salem Witch Trials," *Smithsonian Magazine*, November 2015, https://www.smithsonianmag.com/history/unraveling-mysteries-tituba-salem-witch-trials-180956960/.

Select Resources

Chapter 8: How to Kill a Witch the American Way

Interview with Rachel Christ-Doane, July 19, 2024.

Gretchen Adams, *The Specter of Salem: Remembering the Witch Trials in Nineteenth-Century America* (University of Chicago Press, 2010).

Salem origins: "History and Origins of the Salem Witch Trials," Peabody Essex Museum, n.d., https://www.pem.org/the-salem-witch-trials-of-1692.

Diana DiZoglio quote: Maya Yang, "Last Salem 'Witch' Pardoned 329 Years After She Was Wrongly Convicted," *Guardian*, May 27, 2022, https://www.theguardian.com/us-news/2022/may/27/last-salem-witch-pardoned-elizabeth-johnson-jr-massachusetts.

American elections: "Witches Cast 'Mass Spell' Against Donald Trump," BBC News, February 25, 2017, https://www.bbc.com/news/world-us-canada-39090334.

La Brujineta: Fernando Romero Nuñez, "How 30,000 Witches Helped Argentina Win the World Cup," *Buenos Aires Herald*, December 25, 2023, https://buenosairesherald.com/sports/stars/world-cup-champions-2022/how-30000-witches-helped-argentina-win-the-world-cup.

Chapter 9: How to Gather Evidence Against a Witch

Robert Pitcairn, *Ancient Criminal Trials in Scotland*, vol. 3, part 2 (Bannatyne Club, 1833). Facsimile: www.google.co.uk/books/edition/_/9tdLAAAAYAAJ?hl=en&gbpv=1.

David Hume, *Commentaries on the Law of Scotland*, vol. 1 and 2 (Bell & Bradfute, 1797; reprinted Gale ECCO, 2018).

"Hattock" definition: Dictionaries of the Scots Language, s.v. "hattock," https://dsl.ac.uk/entry/snd/hattock.

Portrait of the Accused: The Paisley Witches

"She would become as stiff as a corpse" quote: Brian P. Levack, *New Perspectives on Witchcraft*, vol. 3 (Routledge, 2001).

Chapter 10: How to Try a Witch

"Criminal Appeal (Scotland) Act 1926," legislation.gov.uk, accessed February 24, 2025, https://www.legislation.gov.uk/ukpga/Geo5/16–17/15/enacted.

Portrait of the Accused: Janet Horne

W. N. Neill, "The Last Execution for Witchcraft in Scotland, 1722," *Scottish Historical Review* 20, no. 79 (April 1923): 218–21, https://www.jstor.org/stable/25519547.

1735 Witchcraft Act: Nicole Hartland, "Which Witch(craft Act) Is Which?," UK Parliament Blog, archives.blog.parliament.uk, October 28, 2020, https://archives.blog.parliament.uk/2020/10/28/which-witchcraft-act-is-which/.

"Witchcraft," UK Parliament, n.d., https://www.parliament.uk/about/living-heritage/transformingsociety/private-lives/religion/overview/witchcraft/.

Chapter 11: How to Burn a Witch

Author interview with Professor Niamh Nic Daeid, April 22, 2024.

"The Witches of Dundee," The Dundee City Archives Blog, May 14, 2020, https://dundeecityarchives.wordpress.com/2020/05/14/witch/.

Portrait of the Accused: Katherine MacKinnon

"Dress Act 1746," Scottish History, November 1, 2023, https://www.scottishhistory.org/resources/dress-act-1746/.

Alison Campsie, "Skye Woman 'Murdered' for Being a Witch 12 Years after Persecution Outlawed," The Scotsman, February 19, 2021, https://www.scotsman.com/heritage-and-retro/heritage/skye-woman-murdered-for-being-a-witch-12-years-after-persecution-outlawed-3140258.

Chapter 12: How to Bury a Witch

Author interview with Doug Speirs, January 9, 2021.

A Collection of Rare and Curious Tracts on Witchcraft and the Second Sight; with an Original Essay on Witchcraft (Edinburgh, 1820; Project Gutenberg), 129–146, https://www.gutenberg.org/files/41928/41928-h/41928-h.htm.

PART THREE: A THING OF THE PAST?

Chapter 13: How to Lose a Witch

Encyclopaedia Britannica, s.v. "Paton, Sir Joseph Noel," 1911 ed., https://en.wikisource.org/wiki/1911_Encyclop%C3%A6dia_Britannica/Paton,_Sir_Joseph_Noel.

Paton's religious beliefs: Alfred Thomas Story, *Sir Noel Paton, His Life and Work* (Art Journal, 1895).

"Scotland Has Long Held Claim to the Most Brutal of Witch Hunts throughout the Late 1500s and 1600s," Fife Coast & Countryside Trust, accessed February 2, 2025, https://fifecoastandcountrysidetrust.co.uk/witches-trail/.

"Forensic Artist Dr. Christopher Rynn Reconstructs Face of Scottish 'Witch,'" University of Dundee, October 31, 2017, https://www.dundee.ac.uk/stories/forensic-artist-dr-christopher-rynn-reconstructs-face-scottish-witch.

Portrait of the Accused: Helen Duncan

Harry Price: Paul G. Adams, "Harry Price: A Brief Survey of his Career in Psychical Research," Harry Price (website), n.d., http://www.harrypricewebsite.co.uk/Biography/price-psychic-career01.htm.

Paul Tabori, *The Art of Folly* (London: Prentice Hall, 1961).

"Britain's 'Last Witch': Campaign to Pardon Helen Duncan," BBC, June 15, 2012, https://www.bbc.co.uk/news/uk-england-18456106.

Select Resources

Chapter 14: How to Accuse a Modern-Day Witch, Part 1: The Twentieth Century

Malcolm Gaskill, *Hellish Nell: Last of Britain's Witches* (London: Fourth Estate, 2001).

Author interviews with Malcolm Gaskill, March 25, 2022, and April 8, 2024.

"About Us," The Spiritualists' National Union, accessed February 24, 2025, https://www.snu.org.uk/about-us.

Paul G. Adams, "Helen Duncan: Harry Price and the Regurgitating Medium," Harry Price (website), n.d., http://www.harrypricewebsite.co.uk/Seance/Duncan/duncan-intro.

Charles Loseby, "Papers on the Trial of Helen Duncan 1944–1945," Society for Psychical Research archive, Cambridge University Library, https://archivesearch.lib.cam.ac.uk/repositories/2/archival_objects/632155.

C. E. Bechhofer Roberts, ed., *The Trial of Mrs. Duncan* (Jarrolds, 1945). Full text: https://archive.org/stream/trialofmrsduncan00duncuoft/trialofmrsduncan00duncuoft_djvu.txt.

Witchcraft Act 1735, 9 George 2 c. 5, Statutes Project, https://statutes.org.uk/site/the-statutes/eighteenth-century/1735-9-george-2-c-5-the-witchcraft-act/.

John Cowell, *The Interpreter* (1607; 1658 edition), Oxford Text Archive, Bodleian Libraries, University of Oxford, https://ota.bodleian.ox.ac.uk/repository/xmlui/handle/20.500.12024/A34797.

Chapter 15: How to Accuse a Modern-Day Witch, Part 2: The Twenty-First Century

"Resolution adopted by the Human Rights Council on 12 July 2021: Elimination of harmful practices related to accusations of witchcraft and ritual attacks," UN Human Rights Council, July 16, 2021, https://digitallibrary.un.org/record/3936009?ln=en&v=pdf.

Author interview with Leo Igwe, February 28, 2024.

Author interview with Charlotte Baker, May 1, 2024.

Portrait of the Accused: Miss B

Dooyum Ingye, "Policing Child Witch Hunts in Benue State," Modern Ghana, October 14, 2023, https://www.modernghana.com/news/1265998/policing-child-witch-hunts-in-benue-state.html.

Afterword: How to Forget a Witch, Then Remember Her

Author interview with Dr. Alison McCall, April 1, 2024.

Rebecca Beatrice Brooks, "Salem Witch Trials: Historical Sites & Locations," History of Massachusetts Blog, October 26, 2015, https://historyofmassachusetts.org/where-did-salem-witch-trials-take-place/.

Author interview with Liv Helene Willumsen, April 16, 2024.

Liv Helene Willumsen, *Witches of the North: Scotland and Finnmark* (Brill, 2013).

Select Resources

Author interview with Ewan McAndrew, December 19, 2023.

Female murder figures in UK: Femicide Census, www.femicidecensus.org.

Margaret Atwood and Ruth Bader Ginsburg: Jeffrey Rosin, "'They Will Not Allow Progress to Be Reversed': Ruth Bader Ginsburg and Margaret Atwood Discuss #MeToo," *Vanity Fair*, November 1, 2019, https://www.vanityfair.com/news/2019/10/ruth-bader-ginsburg-margaret-atwood-debate-metoo?srsltid=AfmBOopwekFXloQvOUOk8sU3j9ygD7O_RifoH-pv7M5qZeq0utCCa1zs.

Margaret Atwood on *The Handmaid's Tale*: "Margaret Atwood on How She Came to Write *The Handmaid's Tale*," Literary Hub, April 25, 2018, https://lithub.com/margaret-atwood-on-how-she-came-to-write-the-handmaids-tale/.

Lance Wallnau quote: Mike Hixenbaugh and Alexandra Marquez, "Vance to Attend Event with Evangelist Who Said Harris Used 'Witchcraft,'" NBC News, September 27, 2024, https://www.nbcnews.com/politics/2024-election/jd-vance-event-evangelist-kamala-harris-witchcraft-rcna173020.

IMAGE CREDITS

Alamy Stock Photo
- *Chronicle 41, 59*
- *Science History Images 179*
- *The Picture Art Collection 211*
- *Trinity Mirror Mirrorpix 223*

Courtesy Dr. Christopher Rynn 215

Leo Igwe 233

Metropolitan Museum of Art: The Elisha Whittelsey Collection, The Elisha Whittelsey Fund, 1967 27

Rosie Andrew, www.rosieandrew.myportfolio.com / @r_o_s_i_eka 255

Shutterstock Creative: Maurizio Fabbroni. © The Easton Foundation/VAGA at ARS, NY and DACS, London 2025 253

TopFoto: Fortean 115

Wellcome Collection: The history of witches and wizards: giving a true account of all their tryals in England, Scotland, Swedeland, France, and New England; with their confession and condemnation/ Collected from Bishop Hall, Bishop Morton, Sir Matthew Hale, etc. By W.P. 15

Worldhistory.org/public domain 133

ABOUT THE AUTHORS

Photo © Mitchell / Venditozzi

Leading human rights lawyer Claire Mitchell KC and writer, Zoe Venditozzi formed the Witches of Scotland campaign with the aim of shining a light on the historic injustice of the Witch Trials. As a result, on International Women's Day, 2022, the First Minister of Scotland issued a formal state apology—the first time in 300 years there had been any formal recognition of those who were most wrongly accused.

Through their tireless campaigning, regular public appearances, and highly entertaining podcast, also called *The Witches of Scotland*, this pair of "quarrelsome dames" are currently working to build a lasting memorial to the murdered women, and campaign to draw

About the Authors

attention to the continued persecution of women as witches around the world today.

In 2022, Claire and Zoe were made Doctors of Laws by the University of Dundee in recognition of their work. Claire lives in Montrose and Edinburgh and Zoe lives in Fife.